History and Social Theory,
second edition

History
and
Social Theory,
second edition

Peter Burke

Cornell University Press
Ithaca, New York

First edition (cloth and paper) published in the United States in 1993 by Cornell University Press. Second edition (cloth and paper) published in the United States in 2005 by Cornell University Press.

International Standard Book Number 0-8014-4453-5 (cloth)
International Standard Book Number 978-0-8014-4453-1 (cloth)
International Standard Book Number 0-8014-7285-7 (paper)
International Standard Book Number 978-0-8014-7285-5 (paper)

Printed in Great Britain

Librarians: A CIP catalog record for this book is available from the Library of Congress.

Cloth printing   10   9   8   7   6   5   4   3   2   1

Paperback printing   10   9   8   7   6   5   4   3   2   1

Contents

Preface

At the beginning of my academic career, at the University of Sussex in the early 1960s, I volunteered to teach a course on 'Social Structure and Social Change' on the grounds that it was a good idea to know what 'Society' was before writing its history and that the best way to learn a subject is to teach it. Involvement with the course led to an invitation from Tom Bottomore to write a book on 'Sociology and History', published by Allen and Unwin in 1980, attempting to introduce students of each discipline to what they might find most valuable in the other. Over a decade later, Polity Press has given me the opportunity to revise, enlarge and rewrite that book.

This second version appears under a new title which represents more accurately what the book is about. The original preface explained that social anthropology 'plays a more important role in this essay than the title suggests', while there was also some discussion of economics and politics. In the 1990s, however, a discussion of social theory might reasonably be expected to include much more, including such disciplines or sub-disciplines as communications, geography, international relations, law, linguistics (especially sociolinguistics), psychology (especially social psychology) and religious studies. It is also virtually impossible to exclude interdisciplinary enterprises such as critical, cultural and feminist theory, or indeed philosophy (which might be defined as the theory of theory).

Broadening the scope of the essay in this way raises a number of problems. The field is too large for a single individual to master. Although I have been reading reasonably widely in social theory for the past thirty years, and thinking about its possible uses in the writing of history, my own historical experience is obviously limited. I have always worked on the cultural and social history of Europe in the sixteenth and seventeenth centuries, and have at best a patchy knowledge of other continents, other periods and other disciplines. Hence I have tended to choose concrete examples which are familiar to me from research and teaching, even at the price of a certain lack of balance.

To view what is going on in all these areas, the writer cannot avoid a personal standpoint. The perspective from which this essay is written is that of what the late Fernand Braudel used to call 'total history' – not an account of the past including every detail, but one which emphasizes the connections between different fields of human endeavour.

There is also a linguistic problem. What term should replace 'sociology' now that the discussion has widened? To write 'sociology, anthropology, etc.' is cumbrous. To speak of the 'social sciences', as used to be customary, is also awkward for anyone who does not believe that the model of the physical sciences (if there is such a unified model) is one to be followed by students of society. 'History and Theory' is an appealing title, but is likely to arouse false expectations of a rather more philosophical book than this one happens to be.

I have therefore decided to use the term 'social theory' (which should be understood as including 'cultural theory'). As the reader will soon discover, this choice does not imply the assumption that general theories are all that historians are likely to find interesting in sociology and other disciplines. Some of the concepts, models and methods employed in these disciplines have their uses in the study of the past, while case-studies of contemporary societies may suggest fruitful comparisons and contrasts with earlier centuries.

The decision to extend the book in this way was rather like the decision to enlarge a house. It has involved a great deal of reconstruction. Indeed, it might be more exact to say that a few fragments of the first edition have been incorporated into what is essentially a new structure. There are many references to studies published in the 1980s. All the same, I have done my best not to be too up-to-date. I continue to believe that Marx and Durkheim, Weber and Malinowski – to name no more – still have much to teach us.

The first version of the book was written in the interdisciplinary atmosphere of the University of Sussex. The new version is the fruit of more than a decade at Cambridge, and it too owes much to colleagues. Ernest Gellner, Alan Macfarlane, Gwyn Prins and the Historical Geography group which meets in Emmanuel College will all recognize what I have learned from their stimulus, their criticisms and their suggestions for further reading. So will a number of colleagues outside Britain, among them Antonio Augusto Arantes, Anton Blok, Ulf Hannerz, Tamás Hofer, Vittorio Lanternari, and Orvar Löfgren. The rewriting was begun at the Wissenschaftskolleg at Berlin, and the book owes much to the historians and anthropologists there, especially to André Béteille for his constructive comments on the draft. John Thompson, who has been responsible for my continuing education in sociology over the last few years, and my wife Maria Lúcia both read the penultimate version with care. Without their help I might still have meant what I said, but I would not always have been able to say what I meant.

Berlin – São Paulo – Cambridge, 1990–1

Preface to Second Edition

The first version of this essay, which appeared under the title *Sociology and History*, goes back a quarter of a century. Even the second version, *History and Social Theory*, is now thirteen years old. In that time, historians have gradually become more interested in social theory. It is no longer exceptional for them to cite sociologists, anthropologists or psychologists in their footnotes. As a result, an essay which was originally written as a manifesto for a certain approach to history is turning into something like a textbook.

Social theory has also changed in the last twenty-five years. Some sociologists and anthropologists, like a number of historians, have made a 'cultural turn'. As a result, culture is more prominent than before in these pages. Bakhtin and Gombrich, for instance, are discussed at greater length than before, and Thomas Kuhn has joined them. On the other hand, the rise of 'rational choice theory' in recent years led me to add a new section to the 'problems' chapter on the conflict between theorists who stress rationality and those who emphasize cultural relativism.

The bibliography has been updated to include a number of books and articles published between 1992 and 2004. New sections have been added, dealing for instance with social capital and postcolonialism, topics on which there was an outpouring of books and articles in the 1990s. In other sections new examples have been included. To make space for these additions, a few cuts have been made. A number of older items have disappeared from the bibliography, and the occasional older example from the text.

Cambridge, 2004

1

Theorists and Historians

This book is an attempt to answer two deceptively simple questions. What is the use of social theory to historians, and what is the use of history to social theorists? I call these questions 'deceptively simple' because the formulation hides certain important distinctions. Different historians or kinds of historian have found different theories useful in different ways, some as an over-arching framework and others as a means to crack a particular problem. Others have shown and still show a strong resistance to theory. It may also be useful to distinguish theories from models and concepts. Relatively few historians utilize theory in the strict sense of the term, but larger numbers employ models, while concepts are virtually indispensable.

The distinction between practice and theory is not identical with the distinction between history and sociology – or other disciplines such as social anthropology, geography, politics or economics. Some students of these disciplines produce case-studies in which theory plays only a small role. On the other side some historians, notably the Marxists, discuss theoretical issues with vigour, even when they complain, as Edward Thompson did in a famous polemical essay, of what he called 'the poverty of theory' (E. P. Thompson 1978). After all, two concepts which have been extremely influential in sociology, anthropology and political studies in the last few years were originally launched by British Marxist historians; Edward Thompson's own 'moral economy' and Eric Hobsbawm's 'invention of tradition' (E. P. Thompson 1991: 185–258 (orig. pub. 1971); Hobsbawm and Ranger 1983).

Generally speaking, however, workers in these other disciplines use concepts and theories more often, more explicitly, more seriously and more proudly than historians do. It is this difference in attitudes to theory which accounts for most of the conflicts and misunderstandings between historians and the rest.

A Dialogue of the Deaf

Historians and sociologists (in particular) have not always been the best of neighbours. Intellectual neighbours they certainly are, in the sense that practitioners of both disciplines are concerned (like social anthropologists) with society viewed as a whole and with the whole range of human behaviour. In these respects they differ from economists, geographers or specialists in political or religious studies.

Sociology may be defined as the study of human society, with an emphasis on generalizations about its structure and development. History is better defined as the study of human societies (or cultures) in the plural, placing the emphasis on the differences between them and also on the changes which have taken place in each one over time. The two approaches have sometimes been viewed as contradictory, but it is more useful to treat them as complementary. It is only by comparing it with others that we can discover in what respects a given society is unique. Change is structured, and structures change. Indeed, the process of 'structuration', as some sociologists call it, has become a focus of attention in recent years (Giddens 1979, 1984) (below, p. 140).

Historians and social theorists have the opportunity to free each other from different kinds of parochialism. Historians run the risk of parochialism in an almost literal sense of the term. Specializing as they usually do in a particular region, they may come to regard their 'parish' as completely unique, rather than as a unique combination of elements each one of which has parallels elsewhere. Social theorists display parochialism in a more metaphorical sense, a parochialism of time rather than place, whenever they generalize about 'society' on the basis of contemporary experience alone, or discuss social change without taking long-term processes into account.

Sociologists and historians each see the mote in their neighbour's eye. Unfortunately, each group tends to perceive the other in terms of a rather crude stereotype. Even today, some historians still regard sociologists as people who state the obvious in a barbarous and abstract jargon, lack any sense of place and time, squeeze individuals without mercy into rigid categories, and, to cap it all, describe these activities as 'scientific'. Sociologists, for their part, have traditionally viewed historians as amateurish, myopic fact-collectors without system, method or theory, the imprecision of their 'data base' matched only by their incapacity to analyse it. In short, despite the existence of an increasing number of bilinguals, whose work will be discussed in the pages which follow, sociologists and historians still do not speak the same language. Their conversation, as the French historian Fernand Braudel (1958) once put it, has often been 'a dialogue of the deaf'.

To understand this situation, it may be helpful to view the different disciplines as distinct professions and even subcultures, with their own languages, values and mentalities or styles of thought, reinforced by their respective processes of training or 'socialization'. Sociologists, for example, are trained to notice or formulate general rules and often screen out the exceptions, while historians learn to attend to concrete detail at the expense of general patterns (B. Cohn 1962; K. T. Erikson 1970).

From a historical point of view, it is clear that both parties are guilty of anachronism. Until relatively recently, many social theorists regarded historians as if they were still concerned with little more than the narrative of political events, as if the approach associated with the great nineteenth-century historian Leopold von Ranke were still dominant. In similar fashion, a few historians still speak of sociology as if it were stuck in the age of Auguste Comte, in the mid-nineteenth-century phase of grand generalizations without systematic empirical research. How and why did the opposition between history and sociology – or, more generally, between history and theory – develop? How, why and to what extent has this opposition been overcome? These questions are historical ones, and I shall try to give them historical answers in the next section, focusing on three moments in the history of Western thought about society: the mid-eighteenth century, the mid-nineteenth century and the 1920s or thereabouts.

The Differentiation of History and Theory

In the eighteenth century there were no disputes between sociologists and historians for a simple and obvious reason. Sociology did not exist as a separate discipline. The French legal theorist Charles de Montesquieu, the Scottish philosopher-historian Adam Ferguson and the lawyer-historian John Millar have since been claimed by sociologists and anthropologists (Aron 1965: 17–62; Hawthorn 1976). Indeed, they are sometimes described as 'founding fathers' of sociology. However, such a label gives the misleading impression that these men set out to found a new discipline, an intention they never expressed. A similar point might be made about the so-called founder of economics, Adam Smith, who moved in the same circles as Ferguson and Millar.

It might be better to describe all four men as social theorists, discussing what was called 'civil society' in the systematic way in which earlier thinkers, from Plato to Locke, had discussed the state. Montesquieu's *Spirit of the Laws* (1748), Ferguson's *Essay on the History of Civil Society* (1767), Millar's *Observations on the Distinction of Ranks* (1771) and Smith's *Wealth of Nations* (1776) were all concerned with general theory, with 'the philosophy of society', as Millar called it.

The authors discussed economic and social systems, such as the 'feudal system' in medieval Europe (a 'species of government' characterized by decentralization) or the 'mercantile system' (contrasted with the 'system of agriculture') in the work of Smith. They commonly distinguished four main types of society, on the criterion of their principal mode of subsistence: hunting, the raising of animals, agriculture and commerce. The *Essay on the Principle of Population* (1798) by Thomas Malthus, with its famous proposition that population tends to increase up to the limits of the means of subsistence, employed the same key concept.

One might equally well describe these social theorists as analytical or, to use the eighteenth-century term, as 'philosophical' historians. The third book of Smith's *Wealth of Nations*, which deals with the 'progress of opulence', is in effect a brief economic history of Europe. Montesquieu wrote a historical monograph on the greatness and decline of Rome; Ferguson wrote on the 'progress and termination of the Roman Republic'; and Millar on the relation between government and society from the age of the Anglo-Saxons to the reign of Queen Elizabeth. Malthus, like Montesquieu and the Scottish philosopher David Hume before him, was concerned with the history of world population.

At this time, scholars less concerned with theory were also turning from the traditional subject-matter of history, politics and war, to the study of social history in the sense of developments in commerce, the arts, law, customs and 'manners'. For example, Voltaire's *Essay on Manners* (1756) dealt with social life in Europe from the time of Charlemagne. The essay was not based directly on the sources, but it was a bold and original synthesis, and a contribution to what

Voltaire was the first to call the 'philosophy of history'. The German official Justus Möser's *History of Osnabrück* (1768), on the other hand, was a local history written from the original documents, but it was also an early example of the contribution of social theory to historical analysis. Möser had surely read his Montesquieu, and his reading encouraged him to discuss the relation between Westphalian institutions and their environment (Contrast Knudsen 1988; 94–111).

Again, Gibbon's famous *Decline and Fall of the Roman Empire* (1776–88) was a social as well as a political history. His chapters on the Huns and other barbarian invaders, emphasizing general features of the manners of 'pastoral nations', reveal the author's debt to the ideas of Ferguson and Smith (Pocock 1981). The capacity to see the general in the particular was for Gibbon a characteristic of the work of what he called the 'philosophical' historian.

A hundred years later, the relation between history and social theory was rather less symmetrical than it had been during the Enlightenment. Historians were moving away not only from social theory but from social history as well. In the later nineteenth century, the historian most revered in the West was Leopold von Ranke. Ranke did not reject social history outright, but his books were generally focused on the state. In his time and that of his followers, who were more extreme than their leader – as followers often are – political history recovered its old position of dominance (Burke 1988).

This retreat from the social may be explained in various ways. In the first place, it was in this period that European governments were coming to view history as a means of promoting national unity, as a means of education for citizenship, or, as a less sympathetic observer might have put it, a means of nationalist propaganda. At a time when the new states of Germany and Italy, and older states such as France and Spain, were still divided by their regional traditions, the teaching of national history in schools and universities encouraged political integration. The kind of history for which governments were prepared to pay was, naturally enough, the history of the state. The links between historians and the government were particularly strong in Germany.

A second explanation for the return to politics is an intellectual one. The historical revolution associated with Ranke was above all a revolution in sources and methods, a shift away from the use of earlier histories, or 'chronicles', to the use of the official records of governments. Historians began to work regularly in archives, and they elaborated a set of increasingly sophisticated techniques for assessing the reliability of the documents that they found there. They argued that their own histories were therefore more objective and more 'scientific' than those of their predecessors. The spread of the new intellectual ideals was associated with the professionalization of the discipline in the nineteenth century, when the first research institutes, specialist journals and university departments were founded (Higham, Krieger and Gilbert 1965: 320–58; Boer 1996).

The work of social historians looked unprofessional when compared with that of Rankean historians of the state. 'Social history' is really too precise a term for what was still treated in practice as a residual category. G. M. Trevelyan's notorious definition of social history as 'the history of a people with the politics left out' did no more than turn an implicit assumption into an explicit statement. The famous chapter on society in the late seventeenth century in Thomas Macaulay's *History of England* (1848) was described by a contemporary reviewer, cruelly but not altogether unjustly, as an 'old curiosity shop', because the different topics – roads, marriage, newspapers and so on – followed one another in no apparent order.

In any case, political history was regarded (at least within the profession) as more real, or more serious, than the study of society or culture. When J. R. Green published his *Short History of the English People* (1874), a book which concentrated on everyday life at the expense of battles and treaties, his former tutor E. A. Freeman is said to have remarked that if only Green had left out all that 'social stuff' he might have written a good history of England (cf. Burrow 1981: 179–80).

These prejudices were not peculiarly British. In the German-speaking world, Jacob Burckhardt's essay on *The Civilization of the Renaissance in Italy* (1860), later recognized as a classic, was not a success at the time of publication, probably because it was based on literary sources rather than official records. The French historian Numa-Denis Fustel de Coulanges, whose masterpiece *The Ancient City* (1860) was largely concerned with the family in ancient Greece and Rome, was relatively exceptional in being taken seriously by his professional colleagues while at the same time insisting that history was the science of social facts, the true sociology.

In short, Ranke's historical revolution had an unintended but extremely important consequence. Since the new 'documents' approach worked best for traditional political history, its adoption made nineteenth-century historians narrower and even in a sense more old-fashioned in their choice of subject than their eighteenth-century predecessors. Some of them rejected social history because it could not be studied 'scientifically'. Other historians rejected sociology for the opposite reason, because it was too scientific, in the sense that it was abstract and general and failed to allow for the uniqueness of individuals and events.

This rejection of sociology was made most articulate in the work of some late nineteenth-century philosophers, notably Wilhelm Dilthey. Dilthey, who wrote cultural history (*Geistesgeschichte*) as well as philosophy, argued that the sociology of Auguste Comte and Herbert Spencer (like the experimental psychology of Hermann Ebbinghaus) was pseudo-scientific because it offered causal explanations. He drew a famous distinction between the sciences, in which the aim is to explain from outside (*erklären*), and the humanities, including history, in which the aim is to understand from within (*verstehen*). Students of the natural sciences (*Naturwissenschaften*) employ the vocabulary of causality, but students of the humanities (*Geisteswissenschaften*) should speak the language of 'experience'. A similar position was taken by Benedetto Croce, who is best known as a philosopher but was also one of the outstanding Italian historians of his time. In 1906 he refused a request to support the foundation of a chair of sociology at the University of Naples, believing that sociology was only a pseudo-science.

For their part, social theorists became increasingly critical of historians, although they continued to study the past. Alexis de Tocqueville's *The Old Regime and the French Revolution* (1856) was a seminal work of history, based on original documents, as well as a milestone in social and political theory. Karl Marx's *Capital* (1867) – like Smith's *Wealth of Nations* – was a path-breaking contribution to economic history as well as economic theory, discussing labour legislation, the shift from handicrafts to manufactures, the expropriation of the peasantry and so on (G. Cohen 1978). Although it attracted relatively little attention from historians at the time, Marx's work came to exercise a powerful influence on the practice of history, especially in the period 1945–89. As for Gustav Schmoller, a leading figure in the so-called historical school of political economy, he is better known as a historian than as an economist.

Tocqueville, Marx and Schmoller were relatively unusual in combining theory with an interest in the details of concrete historical situations. What was much more common in the later nineteenth century, in a number of emerging academic disciplines, was a concern with long-term trends, and in particular with what contemporaries called social 'evolution'. For example, Comte believed that social history, or, as he called it, 'history without the names of individuals or even the names of peoples', was indispensable to the work of social theory, which he was the first to call 'sociology'. His life work might be described as 'philosophy of history' in the sense that it was fundamentally a division of the past into three ages: the age of religion, the age of metaphysics and the age of science. The 'comparative method' – another slogan of the time – was historical in the sense that it involved placing every society (indeed, every custom or artifact) on an evolutionary ladder (Aron 1965: 63–110; Burrow 1965; Nisbet 1969: ch. 6).

The model of laws of evolution linked the different disciplines. Economists described the development from a 'natural economy' to a money economy. Lawyers discussed the evolution from 'status' to 'contract'. Ethnologists presented social change as an evolution from 'savagery' (otherwise known as the 'wild' or 'natural' state of mankind) to 'civilization'. Sociologists such as Spencer used historical examples, from ancient Egypt to the Russia of Peter the Great, to illustrate the development from 'military' to 'industrial' societies, as Spencer called them (Peel 1971).

Again, the geographer Friedrich Ratzel and the psychologist Wilhelm Wundt produced remarkably similar studies of the so-called 'people of nature' (*Naturvölker*), the first concentrating on their adaptation to the physical environment, the second on their collective mentalities. The evolution of thought from magic to religion, and from 'primitive' to civilized, was the major theme in James Frazer's *Golden Bough* (1890), as it was in Lucien Lévy-Bruhl's *Primitive Mentality* (1922). Despite his emphasis on the 'primitive' elements surviving in the psyche of civilized men (and women), Sigmund Freud is a late example of this evolutionary tradition, as is apparent from such essays as *Totem and Taboo* (1913) and *The Future of an Illusion* (1927), in which the ideas of Frazer (for example) play a significant role.

Evolution was generally – but not always – viewed as change for the better. The famous book by the German sociologist Ferdinand Tönnies, *Community and Society* (1887), in which he described with nostalgia the transition from the traditional face-to-face community (*Gemeinschaft*) to a modern anonymous society (*Gesellschaft*), is only the most explicit of a number of studies expressing nostalgia for the old order as well as analysing the reasons for its disappearance (Nisbet 1966; cf. Hawthorn 1976).

Although the theorists took the past seriously, they often showed little respect for historians. Comte, for instance, referred with contempt to what he called the 'insignificant details so childishly collected by the irrational curiosity of the blind compilers of sterile anecdotes'. Spencer declared that sociology stood to history 'much as a vast building stands related to the heaps of stones and bricks around it', and that 'The highest office which the historian can discharge is that of so narrating the lives of nations, as to furnish materials for a Comparative Sociology'. At best, then, the historians were collectors of raw material for sociologists. At worst, they were totally irrelevant, because they did not even provide the right kind of material for the master builders. To quote Spencer once more, 'The biographies of monarchs (and our children learn little else) throw scarcely any light upon the science of society' (Peel 1971: 158–63).

A few historians were exempted from the general condemnation, notably Fustel de Coulanges, whose study of the ancient city has already been mentioned, and F. W. Maitland, the historian of English law, whose view of social structure as a set of relations between individuals and between groups, regulated by rights and obligations, had considerable influence on British social anthropology. However, the combination of an interest in history with a dismissal of what most historians were writing was characteristic of the majority of social theorists in the early twentieth century. A number of them – the French geographer Paul Vidal de la Blache, the German sociologist Tönnies and the Scottish anthropologist Frazer, for instance – had begun their careers as historians, especially as historians of the ancient world.

Others tried to combine the study of the past and the present of a particular culture. The anthropologist Franz Boas did this for the Kwakiutl Indians in the Vancouver area, while the geographer André Siegfried did something similar in his famous 'political picture' (*tableau politique*) of western France, in which he studied the relation between the local environment and the religious and political opinions of its inhabitants, arguing that 'there are political regions just as there are geological or economic ones' and comparing voting patterns with religious affiliation and the ownership of land.

The three most famous sociologists of this period – Pareto, Durkheim and Weber – were all well read in history. Vilfredo Pareto's *Treatise on General Sociology* (1916) discussed classical Athens, Sparta and Rome at considerable length, and also took examples from the history of Italy in the Middle Ages. Emile Durkheim, who was bent on carving out a territory for the new discipline of sociology by distinguishing it from history, philosophy and psychology, had himself studied history under Fustel de Coulanges and dedicated one of his books to Fustel. He wrote a monograph on the history of education in France. Durkheim also made it the policy of his journal, the *Année Sociologique*, to review books on history, provided they were concerned with something less 'superficial' than the history of events (Lukes 1973).

As for Max Weber, both the breadth and the depth of his histori-cal knowledge were truly phenomenal. He wrote books on the trading companies of the Middle Ages and the agrarian history of ancient Rome before making his famous study of *The Protestant Ethic and the Spirit of Capitalism* (1904–5). The great classical scholar Theodor Mommsen considered Weber a worthy successor. When he came to concentrate his attention on social theory, Weber did not abandon the study of the past. As well as drawing on history for material, he drew on historians for concepts. His famous idea of 'charisma', for example (below, p. 93), was derived from a discus-sion of the 'charismatic organization' of the early church by an eccle-siastical historian, Rudolf Sohm. What Weber did was to secularize the concept, to give it a more general application.

It was appropriate that the most historically minded of the great twentieth-century sociologists should have come from what was then the most historically minded culture in Europe. Indeed, Weber scarcely thought of himself as a sociologist. At the end of his life, when he had accepted a chair in the subject at Munich, he made the dry comment, 'I now happen to be a sociologist according to my appointment papers'. He viewed himself as either a political econo-mist or a comparative historian (Roth 1976; Kocka 1986).

The Dismissal of the Past

Durkheim died in 1917, Weber in 1920. For various reasons, the next generation of social theorists turned away from the past.

The economists were pulled in two opposite directions. Some of them, such as François Simiand in France, Joseph Schumpeter in Austria, and Nikolai Kondratieff in Russia, collected statistical data about the past in order to study economic development, especially trade cycles. This interest in the past was sometimes combined with contempt for historians of the kind already noted in the case of Spencer. Simiand, for instance, published a famous polemical article against what he called the three 'idols' of the tribe of historians, the idol of politics, the idol of the individual and the idol of chronology, rejecting what he was one of the first to call 'event-centred history' (*histoire événementielle*) and deploring the tendency to try to fit studies of the economy into a political framework, as in the case of a study of French industry during the reign of Henri IV. His own framework for economic history included the alternation of phases of expansion and contraction, or as he called them, A-phases and B-phases (Simiand 1903).

Other economists were increasingly drawn away from the past and towards a 'pure' economic theory on the model of pure mathematics. The theorists of marginal utility and economic equilibrium had less and less time for the historical approach of Gustav Schmoller and his school. A celebrated 'conflict over method' (*Methodenstreit*) polarized the profession into historicists and theorists.

Again, psychologists as diverse as Jean Piaget, author of *The Language and Thought of the Child* (1923), and Wolfgang Köhler, author of *Gestalt Psychology* (1929), were turning towards experimental methods which could not be applied to the past. They abandoned the library for the laboratory.

In similar fashion, social anthropologists discovered the value of 'fieldwork' in other cultures, as opposed to reading accounts of them by travellers, missionaries and historians. Franz Boas, for example, made protracted visits to the Kwakiutl (Boas 1966). A. R. Radcliffe-Brown lived in the Andaman Islands (in the Bay of Bengal) from 1906 to 1908 in order to study the local social structure, while Bronisław Malinowski spent most of the years 1915–18 in the Trobriand Islands (near New Guinea).

It was Malinowski who insisted most vigorously that fieldwork was the anthropological method *par excellence*. 'The anthropologist', he declared, 'must relinquish his comfortable position in the long chair on the verandah of the missionary compound, Government station or Planter's bungalow.' Only by going out into the villages, the 'field', would he be able 'to grasp the native's point of view'. Following Malinowski's example, fieldwork became a necessary stage in the training of every anthropologist (Stocking 1983). Sociologists too abandoned the armchair in the study (rather than the long chair on the verandah) and began to take more and more of their data from contemporary society.

For a dramatic example of the shift towards the present – 'the retreat of sociology into the present', as the historical sociologist Norbert Elias called it – one might take the first sociology department in the United States, founded at the University of Chicago in 1892. Its first chairman, Albion Small, had studied in Germany with the economic historian Gustav Schmoller as well as the sociologist Georg Simmel. In the 1920s, however, under the leadership of Robert E. Park, the Chicago sociologists turned to the study of contemporary society, especially their own city, its slums, ghettos, immigrants, gangs, hobos and so on. 'The same patient methods of observation', wrote Park, 'which anthropologists like Boas and Lowie have expended on the study of the life and manners of the American Indian might be even more fruitfully employed in the investigation of the customs, beliefs, social practice and general conceptions of life prevalent in Little Italy or the Lower North Side in Chicago' (Park 1916: 15; cf. Matthews 1977; Platt 1996: esp. 261–9).

An alternative strategy was to base social analyses on responses to questionnaires, together with interviews of selected respondents. Survey research became the backbone of American sociology. Sociologists generated their own data and treated the past as 'largely irrelevant to an understanding of how people came to do what they did' (Hawthorn 1976: 209).

Several different explanations might be given for this shift to the study of the present at the expense of the past. The centre of gravity of sociology was itself shifting from Europe to the USA, and in the American case (more especially that of Chicago) the past was less important and also less visible in everyday life than it was in Europe. A sociologist might argue that the rejection of the past was related to the increasing independence and the increasing professionalization of economics, anthropology, geography, psychology and sociology. Like the historians, workers in these fields were founding their own professional associations and specialized journals at this time. Independence from history and historians was necessary to the formation of the new disciplinary identities.

A historian of ideas, on the other hand, might stress an intellectual trend, the rise of 'functionalism'. In the eighteenth and nineteenth centuries, explanations of customs or social institutions were generally given in historical terms, using concepts like 'diffusion', 'imitation' or 'evolution'. Much of the history was speculative or 'conjectural'. The new alternative, inspired by physics and biology, was to explain these customs and institutions by their social function in the present, by the contribution of each element to the maintenance of the whole structure. On the model of the physical universe, or the human body, society was perceived as a system in equilibrium (a favourite term of Pareto's). In anthropology, this functionalist position was adopted by Radcliffe-Brown and by Malinowski, who dismissed the past as 'dead and buried', irrelevant to the actual working of societies (Malinowski 1945: 31).

It is hard to say whether it was the spread of fieldwork which led to the rise of functionalism, or vice versa. Slipping into the idiom of the functionalists themselves, one might say that the new explanation and the new method of research 'fitted' each other. Unfortunately, they also reinforced the tendency of social theorists to lose interest in the past.

It is certainly not my intention to dismiss such formidable intellectual achievements as functionalist anthropology, experimental psychology or mathematical economics. These developments in the study of human behaviour may well have been necessary in their day. They were reactions against genuine weaknesses in earlier theories and methods. Fieldwork, for example, provided a far more reliable factual basis for the study of contemporary tribal societies than the speculative evolutionary history which had preceded it.

What I do want to suggest, however, is that all these developments – like the style of history associated with Ranke – had their price. Neo-Rankean historians and functionalist anthropologists were more rigorous in their methods than their predecessors, but they were also narrower. They omitted, or rather deliberately excluded from their enterprise, whatever they were not able to handle in a way compatible with the new professional standards. Sooner or later, however, there was bound to be what a psychoanalyst might call a 'return of the repressed'.

The Rise of Social History

Ironically enough, social anthropologists and sociologists were losing interest in the past at just the time that historians were beginning to produce something like an answer to Spencer's demand for a 'natural history of society'. At the end of the nineteenth century, some professional historians were becoming increasingly unhappy with neo-Rankean history.

One of the most vocal of the critics was Karl Lamprecht, who denounced the German historical establishment for its emphasis on political history and great men. He called instead for a 'collective history' which would draw on other disciplines for its concepts. The other disciplines included the social psychology of Wundt and the 'human geography' of Ratzel, both colleagues of Lamprecht's at the University of Leipzig. 'History', Lamprecht declared with characteristic boldness, 'is primarily a socio-psychological science'. He put this socio-psychological approach into practice in his multi-volume *History of Germany* (1891–1909), a study which was favourably reviewed in Durkheim's *Année Sociologique* but was not so much criticized as mocked by more orthodox German historians, not only for its inaccuracies (which were in fact numerous) but for its so-called materialism and reductionism (Chickering 1993).

However, the violence of the 'Lamprecht controversy', as it came to be called, suggests that his real sin was to have called Rankean or neo-Rankean orthodoxy into question. Otto Hintze, later a follower of Max Weber, was one of the few historians to treat the kind of history advocated by Lamprecht as 'progress beyond Ranke' and Ranke's concern with the mountain-peaks of history, the great men. 'We want', wrote Hintze, 'to know not only the ranges and the summits but also the base of the mountains, not merely the heights and the depths of the surface but the whole continental mass.'

Around 1900 most German historians did not think in terms of going beyond Ranke. When Max Weber was making his famous studies of the relationship between Protestantism and capitalism, he was able to draw on the work of a few colleagues who were interested in similar problems, but it may be significant that the most important of them, Werner Sombart and Ernst Troeltsch, occupied chairs in economics and theology respectively, not in history.

Lamprecht's attempt to break the monopoly of political history was a failure, but in the United States and France, in particular, the campaign for social history met with more favourable responses. In the 1890s, the American historian Frederick Jackson Turner launched an attack on traditional history which was similar to Lamprecht's. 'All the spheres of man's activity must be considered,' he wrote. 'No one department of social life can be understood in isolation from the others.'

Like Lamprecht, Turner was impressed by Ratzel's historical geography. His essay, 'The Significance of the Frontier in American History', was a controversial but epoch-making interpretation of American institutions as a response to a particular geographical and social environment. Elsewhere he discussed the importance in American history of what he called 'sections', in other words regions, like New England or the Middle West, which had their own economic interests and their own resources (F. J. Turner 1893). Turner's contemporary, James Harvey Robinson, was another eloquent preacher of what he called 'the new history', a history which would be concerned with all human activities and draw on ideas from anthropology, economics, psychology and sociology.

In France, the 1920s were the years of a movement for a 'new kind of history', led by two professors at the University of Strasbourg, Marc Bloch and Lucien Febvre. The journal they founded, *Annales d'histoire économique et sociale*, was relentless in its criticisms of traditional historians. Like Lamprecht, Turner and Robinson, Febvre and Bloch were opposed to the dominance of political history. Their ambition was to replace it with what they called a 'wider and more human history', a history which would include all human activities and which would be less concerned with the narrative of events than with the analysis of 'structures', a term which has since become a favourite with French historians of the so-called '*Annales* school' (Burke 1990).

Febvre and Bloch both wanted historians to learn from neighbouring disciplines, although they differed in their preferences. Both men took an interest in linguistics, and both of them read the studies of 'primitive mentality' by the philosopher-anthropologist Lucien Lévy-Bruhl. Febvre was particularly interested in geography and psychology. So far as psychological theory was concerned, he followed his friend Charles Blondel and rejected Freud. He studied the 'anthropogeography' of Ratzel, but rejected his determinism, preferring the 'possibilist' approach of Vidal de la Blache, which stressed what the environment enabled men to do rather than what it prevented them from doing. Bloch, on the other hand, was closer to the sociology of Emile Durkheim and his school (notably Maurice Halbwachs, the author of a famous study on the social framework of memory). He shared Durkheim's interest in social cohesion and collective representations, and also his commitment to the comparative method.

Bloch was shot by a German firing-squad in 1944, but Febvre survived the Second World War to take over the French historical establishment. Indeed, as president of the reconstructed École des Hautes Études en Sciences Sociales, he was able both to encourage interdisciplinary co-operation and to give history a position of hegemony among the social sciences. Febvre's policies were continued by his successor, Fernand Braudel. Besides being the author of a book with a good claim to be regarded as the most important historical work of the century, Braudel was well read in economics and geography and a firm believer in a common market of the social sciences. He believed that history and sociology should be particularly close, because the practitioners of both disciplines try – or ought to try – to see human experience as a whole (Braudel 1958).

In other countries too it was possible to find social historians oriented by theory in the first half of the twentieth century. The Brazilian Gilberto Freyre, for example, who studied in the United States with the anthropologist Franz Boas, might equally well be described as a sociologist or a social historian. He is best known for his trilogy on the social history of Brazil, *The Masters and the Slaves* (1933), *The Mansions and the Shanties* (1936), and *Order and Progress* (1959). Freyre's work is controversial, and he has often been criticized for his tendency to identify the history of his own region, Pernambuco, with the history of the whole country, for viewing the whole society from the point of view of the 'great house' (especially, though not exclusively, the males in the great house), and for underestimating the degree of conflict in race relations in Brazil.

On the other hand, Freyre's originality of approach puts him in the same class as Braudel (who discovered Freyre's work when he was teaching at the University of São Paulo in the late 1930s). He was one of the first to discuss such topics as the history of language, the history of food, the history of the body, the history of childhood and the history of housing as part of an integrated account of a past society. He was also a pioneer in his use of sources, using newspapers to write social history and adapting the social survey to historical purposes. For his third volume on the history of Brazil, concerned with the nineteenth and twentieth centuries, he sent questionnaires to several hundred individuals born between 1850 and 1900 who were supposed to represent the main social groups within the nation (Freyre 1959).

The Convergence of Theory and History

There was no period when historians and social theorists lost touch with one another completely, as a few examples will show. In 1919 the great Dutch historian Johan Huizinga published his *Waning of the Middle Ages*, a study of fourteenth- and fifteenth-century culture which draws on the ideas of social anthropologists (Bulhof 1975). In 1929 the new journal *Annales d'histoire économique et sociale* included the political geographer André Siegfried and the sociologist Maurice Halbwachs on its editorial board. In 1939 the economist Joseph Schumpeter published his historically informed study of business cycles, and the sociologist Norbert Elias his book on *The Process of Civilization*, now recognized as a classic. In 1949 the anthropologist Edward Evans-Pritchard, a lifelong advocate of close relations between anthropology and history, published a history of the Sanusi of Cyrenaica.

In the 1960s, however, the trickle of examples became a stream. Such books as Shmuel N. Eisenstadt's *The Political Systems of Empires* (1963), Seymour M. Lipset's *The First New Nation* (1963), Charles Tilly's *The Vendée* (1964), Barrington Moore's *Social Origins of Dictatorship and Democracy* (1966) and Eric Wolf's *Peasant Wars* (1969) – to quote only a few of the best-known examples – all expressed and encouraged a sense of common purpose among social theorists and social historians (Skocpol 1984: 85–128; D. Smith 1991: 22–5, 59–61).

Since those days the trend has continued. An increasing number of social anthropologists, notably Clifford Geertz (1980) and

Marshall Sahlins (1985), have given their studies of Bali, Hawaii and other places a historical dimension. A group of British sociologists, notably Ernest Gellner, John Hall and Michael Mann, have revived the eighteenth-century project for a 'philosophical history', in the sense of a study of world history in the tradition of Adam Smith, Karl Marx and Max Weber, aimed at 'distinguishing different types of society and explaining the transitions from one type to another' (J. A. Hall 1985: 3; cf. Abrams 1982). On a similar scale was the anthropologist Eric Wolf's *Europe and the Peoples without History* (1982), a study of the relationship between Europe and the rest of the world since 1500.

The terms 'historical sociology', 'historical anthropology', 'historical geography' and (rather less frequently), 'historical economics' have come into use to describe both the incorporation of history into these disciplines and their incorporation into historical studies (Kindleberger 1990). Convergence on the same intellectual territory occasionally leads to border disputes (where does historical geography end, for instance, and social history begin?) and even to the coining of different terms to describe the same phenomena, but it also allows different skills and points of view to be exploited in a common enterprise.

There are obvious reasons for the increasingly close relation between history and social theory. By the 1960s, accelerating social change had virtually forced itself on the attention of sociologists and anthropologists, some of whom returned to the areas of their original fieldwork to find them transformed by their incorporation into a world economic system. Demographers studying the population explosion and economists or sociologists analysing conditions for the development of the agriculture and industry of Third World countries found themselves studying change over time – in other words, history – and some of them were tempted to extend their investigations to the more remote past.

Meanwhile there has been a massive shift of interest on the part of historians all over the world away from traditional political history (the narrative of the actions and policies of rulers) and towards social history. As one critic of the trend puts it, 'What was at the centre of the profession is now at the periphery' (Himmelfarb 1987: 4). Why? A sociological explanation may be in order. In order to orient themselves in a period of rapid social change, many people find it increasingly necessary to find their roots and to renew their links with the past, particularly the past of their own community – their family, their town or village, their occupation, their ethnic or religious group.

The preface to this book suggested that both the 'theoretical turn' on the part of some social historians and the 'historical turn' of some theorists are very much to be welcomed. In a famous passage, the seventeenth-century philosopher Francis Bacon formulated equally pungent criticisms of the antlike empiricists, who simply collected data, and of the pure theorists, spiders whose webs originated within themselves. Bacon recommended the example of the bee, which searches for raw material but also transforms it. His parable is as applicable to the history of historical and social research as it is to the history of the natural sciences. Without the combination of history and theory we are unlikely to understand either the past or the present.

There is of course more than one way in which history and theory can be combined. Some historians have accepted a particular theory and attempted to follow it in their work, as in the case of many Marxists. For an example of the – sometimes fruitful – tensions inherent in such an enterprise, one might examine the intellectual itinerary of Edward Thompson, who sometimes described himself as a 'Marxist empiricist' (Kaye and McClelland 1990).

Other historians are interested in theories, rather than committed to them. They use them to become aware of problems, in other words to find questions rather than answers. Reading Malthus, for example, encouraged some historians who do not accept his views to examine the changing relation between population and the means of subsistence. This kind of interest in theory has enriched the practice of history, especially in the course of the last generation.

All the same, it is only fair to add that we are not living in an intellectual golden age. As often happens in the history of intellectual endeavour, new problems have been generated by the attempts to solve old ones. Indeed, it has been argued that 'convergence' is the wrong word to use about the changing relationship between history and sociology, that it is 'too simple and too bland to do justice to a tangled, difficult relationship' (Abrams 1982: 4). To this objection one might reply that convergence is actually a rather modest term, which suggests only that the two parties are approaching each other. It says nothing about meeting, let alone agreement.

At times, indeed, rapprochement has led to conflict. When the American sociologist Neil Smelser published his *Social Change in the Industrial Revolution* (1959), analysing the family structure and working conditions of Lancashire weavers in the early nineteenth century – and in the process offering a veiled critique of Marxism – he provoked the wrath of Edward Thompson, who denounced the inability of 'sociology' to comprehend that 'class' is a term referring to process rather than structure (E. P. Thompson 1963: 10; cf. D. Smith 1991: 14–16, 162).

There have also been moments in the last few years when historians and anthropologists, rather than converging, appear to have been rushing past one another, like two trains on parallel lines. For example, historians discovered functional explanations at about the same time that anthropologists were becoming dissatisfied with them (Thomas 1971 and the review by H. Geertz 1975). Conversely, anthropologists were discovering the importance of events at a time when many historians were abandoning *histoire événementielle* for the study of underlying structures (M. Sahlins 1985: 72).

To complicate the situation still further, more kinds of theory are competing for attention than ever before. Social historians, for example, cannot afford to confine their attention to sociology and social anthropology. They need at the very least to consider the possibility that other forms of theory are relevant to their work. From geography, an old ally but also a discipline which has been changing rapidly in the last few years, historians may learn to take space or 'the power of place' more seriously, whether they are studying cities, frontiers or social and cultural 'flows' (Agnew and Duncan 1989; Amin and Thrift 2002). Again, literary theory now impinges upon historians as it does upon sociologists and social anthropologists, all of whom are increasingly aware of the existence of literary conventions in their own texts, rules which they have been following without realizing that they were doing so (White 1973; Clifford and Marcus 1986; Atkinson 1990).

We are living in an age of blurred lines and open intellectual frontiers, an age which is at once exciting and confusing. References to Mikhail Bakhtin, to Pierre Bourdieu, to Fernand Braudel, to Norbert Elias, to Michel Foucault, to Clifford Geertz, can be found in the work of archaeologists, geographers and literary critics, as well as in that of sociologists and historians. The rise of a discourse shared between some historians and sociologists, some archaeologists and anthropologists, and so on, coincides with a decline of shared discourse within the social sciences and humanities, and indeed within each discipline.

Even a sub-discipline such as social history is now in danger of fragmenting into two groups, one of them concerned with major trends, the other with case-studies on a small scale. In Germany in particular, the two groups are or were in conflict, with the so-called societal historians (*Gesellschaftshistoriker*) such as Hans-Ulrich Wehler, on one side, and the practitioners of 'micro-history', such as Hans Medick, on the other.

Despite this tendency to fragment, it remains striking how many of the fundamental debates about models and methods are common to more than one discipline. To discuss these debates is the aim of the following chapter.

2

Models and Methods

This chapter is concerned with four general approaches which are common to various disciplines, but highly controversial in some of them. It deals in turn with comparison, with the use of models, with quantitative methods and, finally, with the employment of the social 'microscope'.

Comparison

Comparison has always had a central place in social theory. Indeed, Durkheim declared that 'Comparative sociology is not a special branch of sociology; it is sociology itself'. He emphasized the value of the study of 'concomitant variation' in particular as a kind of 'indirect experiment' which allowed the sociologist to move from the description of a society to an analysis of why it takes a particular form.

Durkheim distinguished two kinds of comparison, both of which he advocated. In the first place, comparisons between societies which are similar in structure, or, as he put it in a revealing biological metaphor, 'of the same species', and in the second place, comparisons between societies which are fundamentally different (Durkheim 1895: ch. 6; cf. Béteille 1991). The influence of Durkheim on comparative linguistics and comparative literature, especially in France, is obvious enough.

Historians, on the other hand, often reject comparison, on the grounds that they are concerned with the particular, the unique, the unrepeatable. To this classic objection there is, however, an equally classic answer, given by Max Weber in 1914 to the historian Georg von Below in the course of a debate on urban history. 'We are absolutely in accord that history should establish what is specific, say, to the medieval city; but this is possible only if we first find what is missing in other cities (ancient, Chinese, Islamic)' (quoted in Roth 1976: 307).

What the American sociologist Reinhard Bendix (1967) calls 'contrast-conceptions' are fundamental to the comparative approach. It is only thanks to comparison that we are able to see what isn't there: in other words, to understand the significance of a particular absence, such as the notion of sin in Chinese culture. This was the point of Werner Sombart's famous essay, *Why is there no Socialism in the United States?* (as of later studies of the absence of feudalism in Africa, Marxism in Britain, and soccer in the USA) (Goody 1969; McKibbin 1984). This was also the strategy underlying Weber's own essay on the city, which argued that the truly autonomous city could only be found in the West (Sombart 1906; Weber 1920: iii. 1212–1374; cf. Milo 1990).

The implication of these examples is that the two approaches, particularizing and generalizing (or historical and theoretical), complement each other, and that both of them depend on comparison, whether explicit or implicit. The American historian Jack Hexter once divided intellectuals into 'lumpers' and 'splitters', arguing that the discriminating splitters are superior to those who regard diverse phenomena as a single lump (1979: 242). Of course no one wants to be a coarse lumper, incapable of making fine distinctions, but to see what apparently diverse phenomena have in common is surely as valuable an intellectual quality as to see how apparently similar phenomena differ. In any case, without comparison it is impossible to know where to split.

Among the first historians to follow the lead of Durkheim and Weber were Marc Bloch and Otto Hintze. Hintze learned the comparative method from Weber, though he confined his analysis to Europe. He concentrated on the development in different European states of what Weber called 'legal-rational' or 'bureaucratic' forms of government, noting, for example, the significance of the rise of the *commissarius*, an official who had not bought his office (as was customary in early modern Europe) and was therefore removable at the king's will (Hintze 1975: 267–301).

For his part, Marc Bloch learned the comparative method from Durkheim and his followers, notably the linguist Antoine Meillet (Sewell 1967; Rhodes 1978; Atsma and Burguière 1990: 255–334).

He defined the method in a similar way to them, distinguishing comparisons between 'neighbours' from those between societies remote from each other in place and time. He advocated comparison on similar grounds, because it allowed the historian 'to take a real step forward in the exciting search for causes' (Bloch 1928; cf. Détienne 1999).

Two of Bloch's comparative studies are particularly famous. *The Royal Touch* (1924) was a comparison between neighbours, England and France, the two countries whose rulers were believed to possess the power to cure the disease of scrofula by touching the sufferer. *Feudal Society* (1939–40) surveyed medieval Europe, but also included a section on Japan. Bloch noted the similarities in the position of knights and samurai, but also emphasized the difference between the unilateral obligation which bound the samurai to his master and the bilateral obligation between lord and vassal in Europe, where the junior partner had the right of rebellion if the senior partner did not keep his share of the bargain (cf. P. Anderson 1974: 435–61).

After the Second World War, comparative studies gained momentum, especially in the United States, with the rise of sub-disciplines such as development economics, comparative literature and comparative politics. The foundation of the journal *Comparative Studies in Society and History* in 1958 was part of the same trend (Atsma and Burguière 1990: 323–34). Although many professional historians remain suspicious of comparison, it is possible to point to a few areas where the method has proved to be extremely fruitful.

In economic history, for example, the process of industrialization is often viewed in a comparative perspective. Following the sociologist Thorstein Veblen, who published an essay on Germany and the Industrial Revolution, historians have asked whether other industrializing nations followed or diverged from the English model, and whether latecomers, like Germany and Japan, enjoyed advantages over their predecessors (Veblen 1915; Rostow 1958; Gershenkron 1962).

In the case of political history, it is the comparative study of revolutions which has attracted most interest. Among the best-known works in this genre are Barrington Moore's analysis of the 'social origins of dictatorship and democracy' (1966), which ranges from seventeenth-century England to nineteenth-century Japan; Theda Skocpol's study of France in 1789, Russia in 1917 and China in 1911 (1979), as three cases which 'reveal similar causal patterns'; and, more recently, Jack Goldstone's (1991) book on revolution and rebellion in early modern Europe, the Ottoman Empire and China.

Moore makes particularly effective use of comparison as a means of testing general explanations (he is interested in what doesn't fit, just as Weber was interested in what isn't there). In his own words,

> Comparisons can serve as a rough negative check on accepted historical explanations . . . after learning about the disastrous consequences for democracy of a coalition between agrarian and industrial elites in nineteenth- and early twentieth-century Germany, the much discussed marriage of iron and rye – one wonders why a similar marriage between iron and cotton did not prevent the coming of the Civil War in the United States. (Moore 1966: pp. xiii–xiv)

In intellectual history, the comparative approach has been used relatively often in the history of science. Joseph Needham, for instance, a biochemist turned sinologist, was concerned to explain why China failed to make a scientific revolution, while the ancient historian Geoffrey Lloyd has compared and contrasted modes of understanding the world in Greece and China (J. Needham 1963; cf. Huff 1993; G. E. R. Lloyd 2002).

In social history, the comparative study of feudalism, inspired by Marc Bloch, has continued to flourish, including discussions of India and Africa as well as Europe and Japan. The suggestion of the British anthropologist Jack Goody (1969) that it was the tsetse fly which – by attacking horses – prevented the development of anything like feudalism in West Africa is one of the most fascinating studies of 'what is missing', as Weber called it.

Comparative marriage patterns are the subject of a famous study by the demographer John Hajnal contrasting the West European system of late marriage, linked to the establishment of an independent household for the newly-weds, with practices prevalent in the rest of the world. In his turn Hajnal (1965) has stimulated other comparative studies, notably an essay by Goody (1983) arguing that the West European system was the creation of the medieval Church, which discouraged marriages between relatives in order to increase its chances of inheriting from the unmarried. Again, using a strategy much like Weber's, the historical anthropologist Alan Macfarlane has published a series of studies which attempt to define the Englishness of English society (individualism, a low propensity to violence, a culture particularly compatible with capitalism and so on), by means of comparisons and contrasts with other parts of Europe, from Poland to Sicily (Macfarlane 1979, 1986, 1987).

It would not be difficult to add to this brief list of examples, but they are perhaps sufficient to show that comparative history has a number of substantial achievements to its credit. It also has its dangers, two in particular.

In the first place, there is the danger of accepting too easily the assumption that societies 'evolve' through an inevitable sequence of stages. The comparative method of Marx, Comte, Spencer, Durkheim and other nineteenth-century scholars consisted essentially in identifying the stage which a particular society had reached, in placing it on the ladder of social evolution. To many scholars today, this assumption no longer seems tenable (below, p. 144). The problem, then, is to make comparative analyses which are neither evolutionist nor static – as Weber's tended to be – but take account of the different paths along which societies may travel, their 'trajectories', as the English Marxist historian Perry Anderson calls them (1974: 417).

In the second place, there is the danger of ethnocentrism. It may well seem odd to point out such a danger, since comparative analysis has long been associated with the increasing awareness of non-Western cultures on the part of Western scholars. All the same, these scholars have often treated the West as a norm from which other cultures diverge.

The case of 'feudalism' in the Indian kingdom of Rajasthan, for example, is a cautionary tale which would-be comparative historians might do well to bear in mind. In 1829, James Tod, an official in the service of the East India Company, presented to the public what he called a 'Sketch of a Feudal System in Rajasthan'. Relying on the historian Henry Hallam's recent *View of the State of Europe during the Middle Ages* (1818), Tod emphasized relatively superficial analogies between the two societies. With Hallam in his head, he failed to notice the greater importance of family relationships between 'lords' and 'vassals' in the Indian case (Thorner 1956; cf. Mukhia 1980–1; Peabody 1996).

Another problem is that of deciding what exactly to compare with what. The comparatists of the nineteenth century, such as the anthropologist James Frazer, concentrated attention on similarities between specific cultural traits or customs, ignoring the social context of those customs, which was often quite different. For this their analyses have been criticized, like Tod's, as superficial (Leach 1965).

What is the alternative? The functionalists (below, p. 128) would say that the true objects of study are the 'functional equivalents' in different societies. The American sociologist Robert Bellah, for example, noting the discrepancy between the Japanese economic achievement (as early as the seventeenth century) and Weber's hypothesis about the connection between capitalism and Protestantism, suggested that a certain type of Japanese Buddhism was functionally analogous in the sense of encouraging an ethos of hard work and thrift similar to the 'Protestant ethic' (Bellah 1959).

In the course of solving one problem, however, we find ourselves faced with others. The concept of a 'functional equivalent' forms part of an intellectual package, 'functionalism', which has been strongly criticized (below, p. 130). In any case, examples of functional equivalents are not always as clear as Bellah's. How do we decide what counts as an analogue? Critics of the approach like to say that 'you can't compare apples with oranges'. But who decides what counts as an orange and what as an apple in the study of society?

Comparatists face a dilemma. If we compare specific cultural traits, we have fixed on something precise, and can note its presence or absence, but we risk superficiality. The search for analogues, on the other hand, leads towards comparisons between whole societies. Yet how can one usefully compare or contrast societies which differ from each other in so many different ways?

The problems of comparison on the grand scale become apparent if we look at a famous example, Arnold Toynbee's massive *Study of History* (1935–61; McIntire and Perry 1989; McNeill 1989). Toynbee's unit of comparison was a whole 'civilization', and he distinguished some twenty such civilizations in world history. He had of course to reduce each civilization to a small bundle of traits in order to make comparison possible. As his critics were quick to point out, he also had to create artificial barriers between civilizations.

To make matters still more difficult, Toynbee lacked an adequate conceptual apparatus for such an ambitious work. Like Pascal discovering geometry for himself as a child, Toynbee created his own concepts, such as 'challenge and response', 'withdrawal and return', or 'external proletariat' – an ingenious adaptation of Marx in order to explain the incursions of 'barbarians' into empires – but they were not sufficient for his enormous task. It is difficult to resist the conclusion that a wider acquaintance with the social theory of his day would have assisted Toynbee with his analysis. Durkheim might have introduced him to the problems of comparison, for example, Norbert Elias to the idea of civilization as process, and Weber to the use of models and types.

Models and Types

A preliminary definition of a 'model' might be an intellectual construct which simplifies reality in order to understand it. Like a map, its usefulness depends on omitting some elements of reality altogether. It also makes its limited elements or 'variables' into an internally consistent system of interdependent parts. So far, 'model' has been described in such a way that it would be true to say that even historians, with their commitment to the particular, use models all the time. A narrative account of the French Revolution, for example, is a model in the sense that it is bound to simplify events and also to stress their coherence in order to tell an intelligible story.

However, it is probably more useful to use the term 'model' more strictly. Let us add one more element to this model of a model and say that it is an intellectual construct which simplifies reality in order to emphasize the recurrent, the general and the typical, which it presents in the form of clusters of traits or attributes. Models and 'types' then become synonyms – which is perhaps appropriate, since *typos* is Greek for mould or 'model', and Max Weber wrote of 'Ideal Types' (*Idealtypen*) where modern sociologists would write 'models' (Weber 1920: i. 212–301). Not 'French Revolution' but 'revolution' makes an example of a model in the sense in which the term will be used from now on.

An example which will recur in these pages is that of two contrasting models of society, the 'consensual' and the 'conflictual'. The 'consensual model', associated with Emile Durkheim, emphasizes the importance of social bonding, social solidarity, social cohesion. The 'conflictual model', associated with Karl Marx, emphasizes the ubiquity of social 'contradiction' and 'social conflict'. Both models are obviously simplifications. It seems equally obvious, at least to the present writer, that both models contain important insights. It is impossible to find a society from which conflict is absent, while without solidarities there would be no society at all. All the same, as I shall try to show in later sections, it is not difficult to find sociologists and historians who work with one of these models and apparently forget about the other.

Some historians deny having anything to do with models and assert, as we have seen, that it is their job to study the particular, especially the unique event, not to generalize. In practice, however, most of them use models as Molière's Monsieur Jourdain used prose, without realizing that they do so. For example, they commonly make general statements about particular societies. Burckhardt's famous essay on *The Civilization of the Renaissance in Italy* (1860) was explicitly concerned with what the author called 'the recurrent, the constant, the typical'. In his *Structure of Politics at the Accession of George III* (1928), Lewis Namier studied 'why men went into

Parliament' in eighteenth-century England. For the last century or so, historians have found it difficult to avoid such general terms as 'feudalism' and 'capitalism', 'Renaissance' or 'Enlightenment'. Avoiding the word 'model', they often allow themselves to speak about a 'system' – the phrase 'the feudal system' goes back to the eighteenth century – or about the 'classic' or 'textbook' form of a phenomenon such as the medieval manor.

In a famous polemical essay, the German economic historian Werner Sombart (1929) told economic historians that they needed to be aware of economic theory, on the grounds that this was the way in which they could move from the study of isolated facts to the study of systems (cf. Hicks 1969: ch. 1). These systems are generally discussed in the form of simplified models. Thus economic historians use the term 'mercantilism', although, as the Swedish scholar Eli Heckscher put it, 'Mercantilism never existed in the sense that Colbert or Cromwell existed'. It is a model, actually one of the two models used by Adam Smith in *The Wealth of Nations* (1776) in his famous contrasts between the 'system of agriculture' and the 'mercantile system' (Heckscher 1931: 1).

'Capitalism' is another model which it is extremely difficult for economic historians to do without. So is the 'peasant economy', analysed in a classic study by the Russian economist Alexander Chayanov (1925: cf. Kerblay 1970). The city-state is yet another type of economic organization which has been helpfully described in the form of a model emphasizing recurrent features. For example, the political dominance of the city over the countryside around it is often combined with the exaction of a quota of food at a low price, because the city government is more afraid of urban food riots than of peasant revolt (Hicks 1969: 42ff; cf. Burke 1986: 140–52).

Cultural history is at first sight the least promising terrain for the employment of models, and yet . . . what are terms such as 'Renaissance' or 'Baroque' or 'Romantic' if they are not the names of clusters of traits? Or take the case of 'Puritanism'. Paraphrasing Heckscher, one might say that Puritanism never existed in the sense that the Protestant preachers Richard Sibbes or John Bunyan existed, but that it might be useful to use the term to refer to a constellation of traits such as a stress on original sin, an arbitrary God, predestination, an ascetic morality and a fundamentalist reading of the Bible. In the case of early modern England, this precise definition is extremely useful. On the other hand, anyone interested in cross-cultural comparison (between Christianity and Islam, for instance) would be well advised to follow the example of Ernest Gellner and operate with a broader concept of 'generic puritanism' which might include asceticism and fundamentalism but not, for instance, original sin (1981: 149–73).

Turning to politics, we find that many historians and historical sociologists have found the model of 'revolution' indispensable, often contrasting it with the notion of 'revolt' (defined as a protest against individuals or abuses, rather than an attempt to change a whole system). They have offered similar explanations for revolutions extremely distant in space and time. Some of them make use of the famous sociological hypothesis of 'relative deprivation', according to which revolutions occur not so much when times are bad as when they get worse, or more precisely, when there is a discrepancy between the expectations of a particular group and their perception of reality.

The sociologist Theda Skocpol has argued that what is common to the French, Russian and Chinese revolutions (but distinguishes them from less successful revolts) is the combination of two factors: 'intensified pressures' on the state from 'more developed countries abroad' and agrarian structures which 'facilitated widespread peasant revolts against landlords'. These states were caught between 'cross-pressures', with increasing international competition for power on one side and on the other the constraints imposed on the government's response by the economic and political structure of the society. On the other hand, in a study of Europe and Asia in the Early Modern period, Jack Goldstone concluded that ecological changes were fundamental, leading to demographic changes and so to 'state breakdown' (Skocpol 1979, criticized in Aya 1990: 73–5, 90–2; Goldstone 1991).

To return to neighbourly comparisons: historians have often tried to generalize about institutional changes in neighbouring countries in a particular period, coining such phrases as 'the new monarchies', 'the Tudor revolution in government', 'the rise of absolutism', 'the nineteenth-century revolution in government' and so on. From a comparative point of view, all these changes look rather like local examples of stages of transition from the type of government Max Weber called 'patrimonial' to the kind he called 'bureaucratic' (1920: iii. 956–1005).

This distinction of Weber's has inspired a considerable amount of historical research on different regions, from Latin America to Russia. (Samples of research in Pintner and Rowney 1980; Litchfield 1986. A comparative approach in Mann 1986–93: ii. 444–78.) It may be formulated in terms of six contrasted attributes, as follows:

patrimonial system	bureaucratic system
1. undefined areas of jurisdiction	fixed areas
2. informal hierarchy	formal hierarchy
3. informal training and testing	formal training and testing
4. part-time officials	full-time officials
5. oral commands	written orders
6. partiality	impartiality

The contrast is not one between good and bad systems, or even between efficient and inefficient ones (although the concept of 'efficiency' may only arise in a bureaucracy). The important thing is that the two systems 'fit' different kinds of society more or less well. They have their benefits, but also their costs. The impartiality of the bureaucratic system means fairness in the sense of equality, but also standardization, an institutionalized unconcern for differences between individuals. Following rules may increase effectiveness, but it may also reduce it, entangling people in 'red tape'. Bureaucracy is associated with what James Scott (1998) calls 'seeing like a state', a rationalization and standardization of information in the service of ambitious plans for changing society that is combined with a contempt for local knowledge and not infrequently leads to disaster.

One reason for suspicion of models on the part of historians is the belief that using them leads to indifference to change over time. This has sometimes been the case. Weber, for example, was justly criticized for ignoring change when he wrote about 'puritanism' as if this system of values had remained uniform from Jean Calvin in the sixteenth century to Benjamin Franklin in the eighteenth.

However, models can incorporate change. For example, it is possible to focus not on bureaucracy but on the process of bureaucratization. Antithetical models may be a useful way of characterizing complex processes of change, from feudalism (say) to capitalism, or from pre-industrial to industrial society. These labels are of course descriptive and do not say how change occurs, but attempts have been made to identify typical sequences of change, as in the case of the model or theory of 'modernization' to be discussed in detail below (p. 142).

Using models without admitting that they are doing so or without being aware of their logical status has sometimes landed historians in needless difficulties. Some well-known controversies have turned on one historian's misunderstanding of another historian's model, as two case-studies may suggest: in the first place, the once celebrated controversy about the medieval manor between Sir Paul Vinogradoff and F. W. Maitland. Vinogradoff suggested that

> The structure of the ordinary manor is always the same. Under the headship of the lord we find two layers of population – the villeins and the freeholders, and the territory occupied divides itself accordingly into demesne land [the produce of which went directly to the lord] and 'tributary land'. The entire population is grouped into a village community which centres round the manorial court or halimote, which is both council and tribunal. My investigation will necessarily conform to this typical arrangement. (1892: 223–4)

This is the 'classic' medieval manor as it has been drawn on innumerable blackboards. However, Maitland (1897) argued – in an equally classic critique – that 'to describe a typical *manerium* is an impossible feat'. He showed that each of the traits in the cluster identified by Vinogradoff was lacking in some instances. Some manors had no villeins, others no freeholders, others no demesne, others no court.

Maitland was absolutely right in these respects. Vinogradoff seems to have been uncertain about the logical status of his generalizations (note the shift from 'always' in the first sentence of the quotation to 'typical' in the last). If he had been aware that he was using a model, however, he might have been able to make an effective reply to Maitland's criticisms.

The point is that two kinds of model may be distinguished according to the criteria for membership in the group of entities – in this case, manors – to which the model applies. Technical terms are unavoidable at this point, since we need to distinguish a 'monothetic' group of entities from a 'polythetic' group. A monothetic group is one 'so defined that the possession of a unique set of attributes is both sufficient and necessary for membership'. A polythetic group, on the other hand, is a group in which membership does not depend on a single attribute. The group is defined in terms of a set of attributes such that each entity possesses most of the attributes and each attribute is shared by most of the entities (R. Needham 1975). This is the situation described by the philosopher Ludwig Wittgenstein in terms of 'family resemblances'. Mothers and sons, brothers and sisters, resemble one another, yet these resemblances may not be reducible to any one essential feature.

It should be clear that Maitland's critique of Vinogradoff assumed that he was talking about all manors or defining the 'typical' manor with reference to a monothetic group. Vinogradoff could have answered this critique – had the concept been available – by saying that his model was polythetic. The onus would then have been on him to show that each of the attributes in his cluster was shared by most manors. When a Soviet historian made a statistical study of thirteenth-century manors in the Cambridge area, he did in fact discover that over 50 per cent of them were of Vinogradoff's type, with demesne, villein land and freeholds (Kosminsky 1935).

For a second example, we may turn to the model of 'class'. In most if not all societies there are inequalities in the distribution of wealth and other advantages such as status and power. To describe the principles governing this distribution, and the social relationships to which these inequalities give rise, it is difficult to do without a model. Social actors themselves frequently employ spatial metaphors, whether they speak of a social 'ladder' or 'pyramid', or of 'upper' or 'lower' classes, or describe individuals or groups as looking 'up to' or 'down on' others. Social theorists do the same. 'Social stratification' and 'social structure (base, superstructure)' are metaphors borrowed from geology and architecture.

The best-known model of the social structure is surely that of Karl Marx, despite the fact that his chapter on 'class' in *Capital* consists of no more than a few lines, followed by the tantalizing editorial note 'here the manuscript breaks off'. Attempts have been made to supply the missing chapter by fitting together fragments from Marx's other writings in the manner of a jigsaw (Dahrendorf 1957: 9–18). For Marx, a class is a social group with a particular function in the process of production. Landowners, capitalists and workers who own nothing but their hands are the three great social classes, corresponding to the three factors of production in classical economics: land, labour and capital. The different functions of these classes give them conflicting interests and make them likely to think and act in different ways. Hence history is the story of class conflict.

The criticism most frequently levelled against this model is also the most unfair: that it simplifies. It is the function of models to simplify in order to make the real world more intelligible. The social historian of nineteenth-century Britain, say, working from official documents such as the census, finds that the population is described by a bewildering number of occupational categories. To make general statements about British society, it is necessary to find a way of collapsing these categories into broader ones. Marx provided some broad categories together with an explanation of the criteria for his choice. He offered social history the 'backbone' it has sometimes been accused of lacking (Perkin 1953–4). It is true that he emphasized differences between his three classes at the expense of variations within each group, and that he omitted marginal cases, such as self-employed people, who do not easily fit into his categories; but such simplifications are only to be expected from a model.

It is more worrying that Marx's model is not quite as clear and simple as it looks. Commentators have noted that he used the term 'class' in several different senses (Ossowski 1957; Godelier 1984: 245–52). On some occasions he distinguished three classes: the owners of land, capital and labour. On other occasions, however, he distinguished only two classes, the opposite sides in the conflict between exploiters and exploited, oppressors and oppressed. Marx sometimes employs a broad definition of class, according to which Roman slaves and plebeians, medieval serfs and journeymen, were all part of the same class, opposed to the patricians, lords and masters. At other times he works with a narrow definition according to which the French peasants were not a class in 1850 because they lacked class consciousness – in other words, a sense of solidarity with one another across regional boundaries. They were, according to him, merely an aggregate of similar but distinct individuals or families, like 'a sack of potatoes'.

Class consciousness deserves a little more discussion. The phrase implies that a class is a community in an almost Durkheimian sense. We therefore have to ask the obvious question, whether or not there have been conflicts within classes as well as between them. For this reason the idea of an autonomous 'fraction' of a class was introduced into Marxist analyses. The term 'ascribed' or 'imputed' class consciousness was coined in order to speak of a 'working class' at a time when its members lacked the necessary sense of solidarity. I must confess that I do not find this idea of an unconscious consciousness to be helpful. The language of class 'interests' is surely more explicit and less misleading.

In the last twenty years or so, there has been a major change in the way in which historians use the term 'class'. They used to treat it as a social fact, but now they see it as essentially or primarily a linguistic phenomenon. The change is particularly visible in the case of historians of nineteenth-century Britain. A study of the 'language of class' goes back to 1960, but it was only in the 1980s and 1990s that the importance of language in the development of consciousness, and so in the construction of social classes, began to be emphasized (Briggs 1960; G. S. Jones 1983; Joyce 1991; Feldman 2002: esp. 201–6). This shift was of course part of a more general 'linguistic turn' in history and social theory, focusing on the 'discursive construction' not only of classes but also of tribes, castes and nations (below, p. 175).

Quantitative Methods

As we saw in the last section, the controversy between Vinogradoff and Maitland was settled, to some extent at least, by counting manors. However, the use of quantitative methods in history and sociology, in particular, has been a matter of some controversy over the last generation. In the 1960s and 1970s, the supporters of these methods were self-confident and aggressive, criticizing other approaches as 'merely impressionistic', using the language of science (a room used for the content analysis of texts might be described as a 'laboratory'), and claiming that historians had no choice but to learn to programme computers. In the 1980s and 1990s, there was a reaction against the trend, linked to the rise of 'micro-history' (below, p. 38). Today may be a good moment for a more balanced analysis.

Quantitative methods of research have a long history. Regular censuses of the empire were taken in ancient Rome, while grain prices in different cities were published in eighteenth-century France. Economists have long based their analyses on statistics dealing with prices, production and so on, and economic historians were already following their example in the nineteenth century.

What is relatively new, and remains controversial, is the idea that quantitative methods can be useful in the study of other forms of human behaviour and even attitudes. Sociologists, for example, conduct what they call 'survey analysis' by issuing questionnaires, or conducting interviews with a group of people large enough for the answers to be analysed statistically. Psychologists too make use of questionnaires and interviews. Students of politics study voting statistics – 'psephology', as this approach has been called – and public opinion polls, which are a kind of social survey. Demographers study variations in the rates of birth, marriage and death in different societies. More controversially, some students of communication practice what is called 'content analysis', which often takes the form of a quantitative study of newspapers, journals, books or television programmes, examining how much space is allotted to a particular topic, how often certain keywords occur, and so on.

A number of historians have followed these paths. When Gilberto Freyre (1959) was writing his history of late nineteenth-century Brazil, he sent a questionnaire to several hundred survivors of the period (including President Getulio Vargas, who failed to reply). The methods of content analysis, or 'lexicometry', have been applied to historical documents, such as the lists of grievances produced by towns and villages at the beginning of the French Revolution. Historical demographers have counted births, marriages and deaths in parish registers and similar sources. The rise of the personal computer encouraged historians to use quantitative methods, freeing them from the need to punch cards, consult programmers and so on, although a reaction against these methods, viewed as pseudo-scientific, was developing at much the same time (below, p. 38).

There is more than one quantitative method, however, and some are more suitable for historians than others. Tailor-made for the needs of historians is the statistical analysis of a series, showing changes over time in the price of grain, for example, the average age of women at their first marriage, the percentage of votes cast for the Communist Party in Italian elections, the number of Latin books offered for sale at the annual book fair in Leipzig, or the proportion of the population of Bordeaux going to communion on Easter Sunday. This is what the French describe as 'serial history' (*histoire sérielle*).

However, 'quanto-history', or 'cliometrics', as it is variously called, has taken a number of forms. In the case of historical survey analysis, there is an obvious distinction to be made between total and sample surveys. The Roman Senate and the English Parliament have been studied through the biographies of all their members, a method known as 'prosopography'. In these cases the whole group, the 'total population' as statisticians would say, has been studied. This method is appropriate for the study of relatively small elites or for societies in which information is sparse, so that historians in these fields are well advised to collect all the data they can find.

Historians of industrial societies, on the other hand, tend to have access to more information than they can handle, so they have to proceed by sampling. The technique of sampling was developed by statisticians from the late seventeenth century onwards in order to estimate the population of London, say, or France, without going to the trouble and expense of a complete survey. The problem is choosing a small group which 'represents' the total population.

Gilberto Freyre, for example, tried to find 1,000 Brazilians born between 1850 and 1900 who would represent the main regional and social groups within the nation, although he did not explain by what method this sample was selected. Paul Thompson picked 500 surviving Edwardians for interview on the basis of a 'quota sample' which provided a balance between men and women, town and country, north and south, and so on, similar to the balance prevailing in the whole country at the time (which can be calculated from the census) (Freyre 1959; P. Thompson 1975: 5–8).

Other quantitative methods are more complex. The so-called 'new economic history' of the 1960s, for example, differs from the old in its emphasis on the measurement of the performance of whole economies, the calculation of the Gross National Product in the past, especially for Western countries since 1800, when statistics become relatively plentiful and less unreliable than they had been (Temin 1972). The conclusions of these historians are often presented in the form of a 'model' of the economy.

For a simple example, one may return to Braudel, who described the Mediterranean economy of the later sixteenth century as follows. Population: 60 million. Urban population: 6 million, or 10 per cent. Gross product: 1,200 million ducats a year, or 20 ducats per head. Cereal consumption: 600 million ducats, half of the gross product. The poor (defined as those with an income below 20 ducats a year): 20–25 per cent of the population. Government taxes: 48 million ducats, in other words below 5 per cent of the average income (Braudel 1949: pt. 2, ch. 1, sect. 3).

This general description is a model in the sense that (as he admits) Braudel did not have statistics for the whole region, but had to extrapolate from partial data which did not form a sample in the strict sense of the term. Historians of industrial economies, working with relatively rich and precise data, construct mathematical models which can be expressed in the form of equations, models which are rather like recipes in the sense that it is possible to specify the amount of input (labour, capital and so on) for a given output. The models can be tested by means of computer simulation, a kind of experiment. Historical demographers have also made use of computer simulation.

Without quantitative methods, certain kinds of history would be impossible, most obviously the study of price and population movements. The use of these methods in some parts of the discipline encourages other historians to pause before using terms like 'more' or 'less', 'rise' and 'fall', and to ask themselves whether there is quantitative evidence for what are implicitly quantitative statements. This approach gives a sharper edge to comparison, making apparent the similarities and differences between two societies and also the possible correlations between (say) the degree of urbanization and literacy in each.

However, quantitative methods have certain limitations. In the first place, the sources are not as accurate or as objective as used to be assumed. It is not difficult to show that a particular census contains mistakes and omissions, and more generally that many of its basic categories ('servants', 'citizens', 'the poor' and so on), however useful at a particular moment, are imprecise (Burke 1987: 27–89). Social classes, for example, are not as objective as the various species of plants. They have much to do with the stereotyped ways in which groups see themselves or others (below, p. 112).

The great difficulty for the user of quantitative methods, however, is the well-known one of the difference between 'hard' data, which are measurable, and 'soft' data, which are not. 'All too often', as a veteran of social surveys, Barbara Wootton, sadly remarked, 'it is the soft data which are valuable, and the hard which are relatively easy to get.' Hence the problem is to find 'hard facts which can be relied upon to serve as good indices of soft ones'.

An index may be defined as something measurable which is related to or varies together with something which is not ('correlation' and 'co-variance' are the technical terms). Some scholars have shown themselves to be extremely ingenious in their search for indices. In the 1930s, for example, the American sociologist F. S. Chapin claimed that the furniture in the living room of a given family normally correlated well with income and occupation, so that it could be taken as an index of that family's social status. On the 'living-room scale', a telephone or a radio, for example, scored high (+8), while an alarm clock scored very low (−2).

There remains the problem whether income and occupation are exact indices (rather than vague indicators) of 'status', itself a somewhat imprecise concept (below, p. 62). Again, what looks at first sight like an index may turn out to have its own rules of variation. For some time, historians of literacy believed that a signature on a marriage register, for example, was a good index of the capacity to read, though not of the capacity to write anything else. More recently, doubts have been raised. It has been pointed out that some people who were able to read were unable to sign (because certain schools taught reading but not writing), and even that some people who were able to write may have made a cross in the marriage register rather than signing in order not to embarrass an illiterate spouse. These objections are not insuperable, but once again they do highlight the difficulties of moving from hard to soft data (Tóth 1996: 61–2).

Sociologists of religion have to deal with an even more acute problem, that of finding indices to measure the intensity or the orthodoxy of religious belief. In the Christian world they have tended to fasten on church or chapel attendance figures, or in Catholic countries such as France or Italy, on the number of Easter communicants. An ingenious French historian even tried to calculate the decline of devotion in eighteenth-century Provence from the falling weight of candles burned before images of the saints (Vovelle 1973).

There can be little doubt that statistics of this kind have a story to tell, since they vary so much between regions and change so much, sometimes quite suddenly, over time. Whether historians are able to decipher that story is another matter. If we are going to use the communion statistics to study the intensity of devotion in a particular region, then we need to know (among other things) what the practice of Easter communion meant to the people involved. It is difficult to be sure whether the peasants of the Orléans region in the nineteenth century, say, shared orthodox clerical views of the importance of making their 'Easter duties'. If they did not share these views, then absences from communion cannot be taken as an index of dechristianization. To take the religious temperature of a community, whether it is hot, cold or lukewarm, is no simple matter.

The problems of inferring political attitudes from voting figures are of the same order. Indeed, the very notion of a 'series' is problematic, since it depends on the assumption that the object of study (wills, grain prices, church attendance or whatever) does not change over time in form, meaning and so on. How could these documents or practices fail to change over the long term? But how can one measure change if the instrument of measurement is itself changing?

For this kind of reason, among others, there has been something of a reaction against quantitative methods in the study of human behaviour, and still more against the grand claims which used to be made for such methods. The intensity of this reaction should not be exaggerated. The use of prosopography by historians is probably more widespread than ever before. It is difficult to deny the value of family reconstitution or the attempt to compare the Gross National Product in different periods in the past. All the same, a search for alternative approaches is under way. It is partly for this reason that ethnography, in which the use of quantitative methods was always minimal, has become a model which some sociologists and historians aspire to follow. This ethnographic approach is associated with the study in depth of the small-scale.

The Social Microscope

Like sociologists, the social historians of the 1950s and 1960s generally employed quantitative methods, concerned themselves with the lives of millions of people and concentrated on the analysis of general trends, viewing social life 'from the twelfth floor', as the sociologist Kai Erikson put it. In the 1970s, however, some of them turned from the telescope to the microscope. Following the lead of social anthropologists, sociologists paid more attention to microsocial analysis and historians to what has come to be known as 'micro-history'.

Three famous studies did much to put micro-history on the map. The first was an essay on the cock-fight in Bali by the American anthropologist Clifford Geertz. Using Jeremy Bentham's concept of 'deep play' (in other words betting for high stakes), Geertz analysed the cock-fight as 'fundamentally a dramatization of status concerns'. In this way he moved from what he called a 'microscopic example' to the interpretation of a whole culture (C. Geertz 1978: 912–54, esp. 432, 437). This essay has been cited many times by historians and is fundamental to the understanding of the micro-history movement.

The other two studies are concerned with the past: *Montaillou*, by the French historian Emmanuel Le Roy Ladurie (1975) and *The Cheese and the Worms*, by the Italian historian Carlo Ginzburg (1976). Both studies are based essentially on registers describing the interrogation of suspected heretics by the Inquisition, documents which Ginzburg has compared to videotapes on the grounds that great care was taken to record not only the exact words of the accused but also their gestures and even their groans under torture. Another comparison which has sometimes been made is that between inquisitor and anthropologist, both of them outsiders of high status asking ordinary people questions the point of which they often find hard to grasp (Rosaldo 1986).

Ginzburg's book might be taken as an extreme case of the micro-historical method, since it is concerned to reconstruct the ideas, the vision of the cosmos of a single individual, a sixteenth-century miller from north-east Italy known as 'Menocchio'. Le Roy Ladurie, for his part, described a village in south-west France at the beginning of the fourteenth century. He noticed that no fewer than twenty-five suspect heretics summoned before the Inquisition came from the village of Montaillou, and decided to use their testimonies to write a study of the village itself, discussing the pastoral economy of the region, the structure of the family, the position of women, and the local conceptions of time, space, religion and so on.

Since these famous studies by Le Roy Ladurie and Ginzburg, a whole shelf of micro-histories have been produced. Some of the most interesting of them focus on a dramatic incident such as a trial or an act of violence. For example, the American historian Natalie Davis has written about a *cause célèbre* in sixteenth-century France, in which a peasant was accused of the impersonation of another man. Another American historian, Bertram Wyatt-Brown, inspired by Geertz, has described a lynching in Natchez, Mississippi, in 1834, analysing this act of 'popular justice' against a man who had murdered his wife as 'a moral scenario in which actions spoke a language that revealed inner passions and intensely felt social values', notably the local sense of honour (Wyatt-Brown 1982: 462–96, at 463).

Another well-known example of the approach is a study of the small town of Santena in Piedmont in the late seventeenth century by Giovanni Levi. Levi (1985) analyses the trial of the local parish priest, Giovan Battista Chiesa (charged with unorthodox methods of exorcism), as a social drama revealing the conflicts which divided the community, notably the struggle between two families and their followers. He stresses the importance of what he calls 'non-material inheritance', arguing that Chiesa's spiritual power was another form of the dominance exercised by his family.

The turn towards micro-history has been closely associated with the discovery by historians of the work of social anthropologists. Le Roy Ladurie, Ginzburg, Davis and Levi are all well read in anthropology. The micro-historical method has much in common with the community studies undertaken by anthropologists early in the twentieth century, or the 'extended case study' developed by the anthropologist Max Gluckman and others in the 1940s. The first historical community study of the Montaillou type was made by a Swedish ethnologist, Börje Hansen, in the 1950s, working on the village of Österlen. *Montaillou* itself consciously follows the model of community studies of Andalusia, Provence and East Anglia (Hansen 1952).

Although his own work was mainly concerned with trends on a grand scale, the social theorist Michel Foucault encouraged micro-studies by his discussion of power not only at the level of the state but also at the level of the factory, the school, the family and the prison – the 'micro-physics of power' as he sometimes called it. Foucault's image of this micro-physics was not of a simple top-down process but one of 'capillary' or branching forms as power 'reaches into the very grain of individuals, touches their bodies and inserts itself into their actions and attitudes, their discourses, learning processes and everyday lives' (Foucault 1980: 89; cf. Foucault 1975: *passim*). The study by Levi mentioned above offers a vivid historical illustration of this idea.

The shift from large-scale to small-scale studies raises certain fundamental problems which require discussion here. One might begin with the charge that the micro-historians trivialize history by studying the biographies of unimportant people or the difficulties of small communities. Some contributions to the genre have indeed done little more than tell what journalists call 'human interest stories' about the past. However, the aim of micro-historians is often more intellectually ambitious. They argue, like Sherlock Holmes, that 'the observation of trifles' can lead to important conclusions (Muir and Ruggiero

1991: pp. vii–viii). If they do not aspire to show the world in a grain of sand, these historians do claim to draw general conclusions from local data. According to Ginzburg, Menocchio the miller is a spokesman for traditional oral popular culture, while Le Roy Ladurie presents the world of the medieval village through his monograph on Montaillou, which he calls a drop in the ocean.

These claims are problematic. Of what larger group is the case-study supposed to be typical, and on what grounds is the claim supported? Is Montaillou typical of a Mediterranean village, a French village, or simply a village of the Ariège? Can a village containing so many suspect heretics be regarded as typical at all? As for Menocchio, he was very much his own man, and he seems to have been regarded as something of an eccentric in his own community. The problem is not of course one for these two historians alone. By what means do anthropologists transmute their field notes (often based on observations made in a single village) into descriptions of a whole culture? Geertz has famously claimed that anthropologists do not study villages, they study 'in villages'. On what grounds can they justify the claim that the people with whom they lived represent 'the Nuer' or 'the Balinese'?

All the same, the use of the social microscope can be justified on a number of grounds. The choice of an individual example to be studied in depth may be prompted by the fact that it represents in miniature a situation that the historian or anthropologist already knows (on other grounds) to be prevalent. Again, it has been powerfully argued that different kinds of explanation are in order when working on the large scale and the small scale, so that changes of scale illuminate social processes by allowing them to be viewed from different standpoints. Historians such as Braudel, who preferred the telescope, tend to stress determinism, while individual freedom is more visible under the microscope (Revel 1996: 87, 141).

Although the rise of micro-history formed part of a reaction against quantitative methods, an attempt to discern individual faces in the crowd, a number of its practitioners – the so-called 'social' school as opposed to 'cultural' micro-historians such as Ginzburg – analyse social networks (Cerutti 2004). The concept of network seems to have come into use independently in three areas: in research on communications, in urban studies and in social anthropology.

It is the third group, notably the so-called Manchester School of anthropology headed by Max Gluckman, which has inspired micro-historians such as Maurizio Gribaudi and Simone Cerutti. Dissatisfied with categories such as 'craft guild', 'social class' and 'popular culture', because these categories did not explain how

particular individuals acted, these historians have attempted to reconstruct ego-centred networks of social relations in order to discover
how people defined themselves and account for their social 'strategies' (Gribaudi 2004).

Not all micro-historians concern themselves with typicality. On the
contrary, a particular case may be selected for study precisely because
it is exceptional and shows social mechanisms failing to work. It was
to discuss this situation that the Italian historian Edoardo Grendi
coined the phrase 'the exceptional normal'. The tragic fate of the
loquacious Menocchio, who was executed for heresy, tells us something about the silent majority of his contemporaries. Open conflicts,
such as riots, may reveal social tensions which are present all the time
but visible only on occasion.

Alternatively, micro-historians may focus, like Giovanni Levi, on
an individual, an incident or a small community as a privileged place
from which to observe the incoherences of large social and cultural
systems, the loopholes, the crevices in the structure which allow an
individual a little free space, like a plant growing between two rocks
(Levi 1985, 1991). It should be pointed out, however, that inconsis-
tencies between social norms may not always work to the benefit of
the individual. The plant may be crushed between the rocks.

As an example of this problem, one might turn to a celebrated incident in Japanese history, a social drama which involved only a few
people at the time but has been remembered ever since, and represented many times in plays and films, on account of its exemplary or
symbolic value. The story is that of 'the forty-seven *ronin*'. At the
beginning of the eighteenth century, two nobles quarrelled at the
court of the *shogun*, the effective ruler of Japan. The first, Asano,
considered himself insulted, drew his sword and wounded the other,
Kira. As a punishment for drawing his sword in the *shogun*'s
presence, Asano was ordered to commit ritual suicide. The samurai
in his service therefore became masterless men, or *ronin*. These ex-
retainers decided to avenge their master. After waiting long enough
to lull suspicion, they attacked Kira's house one night and put him
to death. Having done so, they surrendered to the government. For
its part, the government faced a dilemma. The retainers had obviously broken the law. On the other hand, they had done just what
was required by the informal code of honour among samurai, according to which loyalty to one's lord was one of the highest virtues, and
this code was also supported by the government of the *shogun*. The
way out of the dilemma was to order them to commit ritual suicide
as their master had done, but also to respect their memory (Ikegami
1998: 223–40).

The appeal of this story to the Japanese, at the time and ever since, together with the debates to which it gave rise, is surely related to the way in which it makes manifest (indeed, dramatically so) a latent conflict between fundamental social norms. In other words, it tells us something important about Tokugawa culture. If the micro-historical movement is to escape the law of diminishing returns, its practitioners need to demonstrate the links between small communities and macro-historical trends. In an age in which we hear so much about the interaction between the local and the global (below, p. 186), historians and theorists alike have become increasingly aware of this need (Hannerz 1986; M. Sahlins 1988).

3

Central Concepts

The main purpose of this chapter is to consider the use which historians have made or might make of the conceptual apparatus created by social theorists, or at least – since it is clearly impossible to consider the whole body of concepts in a few pages – of a few of the most important ones. Some of these concepts, such as 'feudalism' or 'capitalism', are so much part of historical practice that they will not be discussed here. Others, like 'class' or 'social mobility' are familiar to historians, but the various controversies over their use may not be so well known. Yet others, like 'hegemony' or 'reception', are still unfamiliar enough to be commonly regarded as a kind of jargon.

Historians often accuse social theorists of speaking and writing an incomprehensible 'jargon'. British intellectuals are perhaps more prone than most to accuse one another of this sin, thanks to the survival of the tradition of the gentlemanly amateur. In these cases, 'jargon' means little more than the other person's concepts.

Let us assume that every divergence from ordinary language is in need of justification, because it makes communication with the general public more difficult. There remains a minimum of technical terms from social theory which historians would be well advised to adopt. Some of these terms have no equivalents in ordinary language – and lacking a word for it, we may fail to notice a particular aspect of social reality. Other terms are defined more precisely than their ordinary-language equivalents, and so enable finer distinctions and a more rigorous analysis.

Another objection to the technical terms of social theory is worth taking more seriously. A historian may well ask why it should be considered necessary to offer modern substitutes for the concepts used by contemporaries (by the 'actors', as the theorists say) to understand their society. After all, contemporaries knew their society from within. The inhabitants of a seventeenth-century French village doubtless understood that society better than we will ever be able to do. There is no substitute for local knowledge.

Some theorists at least have considerable sympathy with this point. Anthropologists in particular stress the need to study the ways in which ordinary people experience their society, and the categories or models (in a broad sense of the term 'model') which they employ to make sense of that world of experience. Indeed, it might be suggested that even historians, long concerned to reconstruct past attitudes, have something to learn from the thoroughness with which these scholars reconstruct what Malinowski called 'the native's point of view', the concepts and categories employed in the cultures or subcultures which they study. Unlike traditional historians, they pay as much attention to unofficial categories as to official ones. Their aim is to recover what they call the 'folk models' or 'blueprints' for action without which much of human behaviour would remain unintelligible. (Holy and Stuchlik 1981; C. Geertz 1983: 55–72).

The point, however, is not to replace but rather to supplement folk models with modern ones. Contemporaries do not understand their society perfectly. Later historians have at least the advantages of hindsight and a more global view. At the national level, at least, they may even be said to understand the problems of the seventeenth-century French peasantry (say) better than the peasants themselves. In fact, it would be difficult to understand French history, let alone European history, if we had to limit ourselves to local categories. As the last chapter pointed out, historians often make general statements about large areas (such as Europe) in particular periods. They also make comparisons. To do so, they have created their own concepts: 'absolute monarchy', 'feudalism', 'the Renaissance' and so on.

I should like to suggest that these concepts, although still useful, are not enough, and that historians might be well advised to learn the language – or rather, the languages – of social theory. This chapter offers what might be described as an introductory phrase-book or, to vary the metaphor, a basic tool-kit suitable for some of the most common breakdowns in historical analysis. The metaphor is in fact somewhat misleading, since concepts are not neutral 'tools'. They tend to come in packages of assumptions which need to be scrutinized with care – hence the concern in this chapter with the original meaning and context of the concepts examined. Since the proof of a concept's value lies in its application, each term will also be discussed with reference to concrete historical problems.

However, the chapter is addressed not to historians alone, but to social theorists as well. Historians are sometimes accused of stealing theory without paying for it, of a dependence on theorists which almost justifies Spencer's gibe (above, p. 8) about historians as carriers of bricks for sociologists to make into buildings. On the contrary (so I shall argue), they do have something of value to offer in return.

Given that the main concepts employed in social theory were created by students of nineteenth- and twentieth-century Western societies (or in the case of anthropology, by Western students of what they called 'primitive' or 'tribal' societies), it is extremely likely – to put it mildly – that these concepts are culture-bound. They are often associated with theories about social behaviour which are equally culture-bound. Hence they may require to be adapted, rather than simply 'applied', to other periods as well as to other parts of the world.

The so-called laws of classical economics, for instance, are not necessarily universal. Alexander Chayanov (1925) argued that the theory of marginal utility was irrelevant to the peasant family, which would go on working marginal land, despite decreasing returns, as long as its needs remained unsatisfied (Kerblay 1971). A similar argument can be found in a book by a distinguished Polish economic historian, the late Witold Kula.

Kula's *Economic Theory of the Feudal System*, published in 1962, studied some great estates owned by Polish nobles in the seventeenth century. In this book, an unusually explicit example of the construction and testing of a historical model, Kula pointed out that the laws of classical economics did not work in this case. When the price of rye rose, production fell; and when the price fell, production rose. To explain the anomaly, Kula (1962) emphasized two factors: the aristocratic mentality and the existence of serfdom. Seventeenth-century Polish aristocrats were not interested in making ever-increasing profits, but in receiving a steady income which would enable them to live in the manner to which they were accustomed. When the price of rye fell, they needed to sell more of it to maintain their standard of living, and they presumably asked the overseers to work the serfs harder. When the price of rye rose, everyone relaxed.

This reinterpretation of Polish economic history is of course extremely controversial, but it is an intellectual *tour de force* as well as a challenge to traditional assumptions. Einstein did not undermine the Newtonian system, but he showed that it applies only under certain conditions. In a similar manner, Kula showed that the laws of classical economics may not apply everywhere. He historicized them. Further examples of this kind of historicization will be discussed in the course of the chapter.

Roles and Performances

One of sociology's most central concepts is that of 'social role', defined in terms of the patterns or norms of behaviour expected from the occupant of a particular position in the social structure. The expectations are often, but not always, those of one's peers. 'Child', for example, is a role defined by the expectations of adults, expectations which have changed a good deal in Western Europe since the Middle Ages. The French historian Philippe Ariès went so far as to suggest that childhood is a modern invention, which, according to him, originated in seventeenth-century France. In the Middle Ages, he claimed, the seven-year-old, who had reached what the Church called the 'age of reason', was expected to behave as much like an adult as possible. He or she was regarded as a small, weak, inefficient, inexperienced and ignorant adult, but an adult all the same. Given these expectations, what we call 'childhood' must have been very different in the Middle Ages from anything Westerners experience today. The conclusions of Ariès (1960) are considered by many historians to be somewhat exaggerated, but the suggestion that 'child' is a social role remains a valuable one.

Historians have much to gain by making a greater, a more precise and a more systematic use of the concept of 'role' than they have done so far. Doing so would encourage them to take more seriously forms of behaviour which have generally been discussed in individual or moral rather than social terms and condemned too easily and ethnocentrically.

Royal favourites, for example, have often been regarded as if they were simply evil men who had a bad influence on weak kings such as Edward II of England and Henri III of France. It is more illuminating, however, to treat 'favourite' as a social role with precise functions in court society (it may be worth adding that the position survived into the twentieth century, as is shown by the career of Philipp Eulenburg at the court of Kaiser Wilhelm II) (Röhl 1982: 11). Rulers, like other people, need friends. Unlike other people, they need unofficial advisers, particularly in societies where the right to give official advice was a monopoly of the aristocracy. Rulers also need some means of bypassing the formal machinery of their own government, at least on occasion. They need someone they can trust, someone independent of the nobles or officials who surround them, someone who can be relied on to be loyal to them because his own position depends entirely on this loyalty, and, not least, someone to take the blame when things go wrong.

A favourite was all these things. Specific favourites, such as Piers Gaveston in the reign of Edward II or the Duke of Buckingham in the reigns of James I and Charles I, may well have been political disasters (Peck 1990: 48–53). They may have been chosen because the ruler was attracted to them – James I wrote to Buckingham as his 'sweet child and wife' – rather than for their ability. All the same, like the power of eunuchs in the Byzantine and Chinese empires, the power of favourites cannot be explained simply in terms of the weakness of the monarch (Coser 1974; K. Hopkins 1978: 172–96). There was a place in the court system which needed to be filled by the king's friend, and also a pattern of behaviour associated with this role.

One problem for favourites was that their role was not viewed in the same way by nobles and ministers as it was by the ruler. Different groups may have incompatible expectations of the individuals occupying a particular role, leading to what is known as 'role conflict' or 'role strain'. For example, it has been argued that the *oba*, the sacred ruler of the Yoruba, was surrounded by chiefs who expected him to assert himself but also to accept their decisions (P. C. Lloyd 1968).

A similar point might be made about the relationship between many European rulers and their nobility. Reverence for the role of king might inhibit open criticism of its holder, on the grounds that 'the king can do no wrong', but it did not prevent attacks on his policies by other means, notably the denunciation of his 'evil councillors'. This recurrent denunciation was at once an indirect way of criticizing the king and an expression of hatred for advisers who (like favourites) were not noble in origin but 'raised from the dust' by the royal favour. The continuity of such criticisms, from the England of Henry I and the twelfth-century chronicler Ordericus Vitalis to the France of Louis XIV and the Duc de Saint-Simon, suggests that the problem was indeed a structural one (Rosenthal 1967).

In many societies, from ancient Greece to Elizabethan England, contemporaries have been well aware of social roles. They have viewed the world as a stage on which 'each man in his life plays many parts'. All the same, social theorists have taken these ideas further. A notable figure in this respect was the late Erving Goffman (1958), who was fascinated by what he called the 'dramaturgy' of everyday life. Goffman linked the concept of 'role' to those of 'performance', 'face', 'front regions', 'back regions' and 'personal space', in order to analyse what he called 'the presentation of self' or 'impression management'.

It may seem odd for a historian to turn to Goffman, who based his work on observations of contemporary life, for the most part in the United States, and was not particularly concerned with differences between cultures or change over time. However, I would argue that his approach is even more important for the study of the Mediterranean world of the past than it is for American society in the present. Goffman's analysis is of obvious relevance to Renaissance Italy, for example. Machiavelli's *Prince* and Castiglione's *Courtier* are, among other things, instructions on making a good impression – *fare bella figura*, as the Italians say – when performing particular social roles. Machiavelli's treatise is very much concerned with 'name' or 'reputation'. Indeed, at one point he goes so far as to say that it is not necessary to possess the qualities of an ideal ruler, only to appear to do so. In this case there is a relatively good fit between the actor's models of social reality and more recent social theory.

Goffman's ideas have also attracted the interest of historians interested in the 'individualism' traditionally associated with the Renaissance man, or the presentation of self in the Renaissance portrait. Portraits, for example, reveal what the artist considered – or what he thought his client considered – the pose, gestures, expression and 'properties' appropriate to the sitter's role, including armour for nobles who never fought and books for bishops who never studied (Weissman 1985; Burke 1987: 150–67). In this case, reading Goffman has sensitized historians to certain features of Italian society. Unlike Goffman, however, they are concerned centrally with the question of variation. They want to know whether there was more concern with the presentation of self in certain places or periods or among certain groups, and whether the style of presentation changed or varied.

The concept of social role also has its uses for historians of the nineteenth and twentieth centuries. Hitler, for instance, has been described as a role-player, who 'always appeared more ruthless, more cold-blooded, more certain than he actually was' (Mason 1981: 85). It is not difficult to think of more examples, from Mussolini, who is supposed to have left the lights on in his study to give the impression of working into the night, to Churchill, who was well aware of the importance of 'props' such as his famous cigar. At the collective level, the long debate over the importance of deference in nineteenth-century Britain has been enriched by the suggestion that for at least some members of the working class, deference, and even respectability, was not a fundamental part of their social identity but simply a role to be played in front of a middle-class audience (P. Bailey 1978).

Going a little further in this direction, we move from social 'role' to social 'drama'. The term 'social drama' was coined by the British anthropologist Victor Turner to refer to a small-scale conflict which reveals latent tensions in the society at large and goes through a sequence of four phases – breach, crisis, redressive action and reintegration. This sequence has also been identified in some conflicts on a grander scale, for example the revolt of Naples against Spanish rule in 1647, a revolt that was led – to the surprise and indeed the scandal of some contemporary observers – by a fisherman, Masaniello (V. Turner 1974; Burke 1987: 191–206).

It has become relatively commonplace to speak of rioters and rebels as drawing on a cultural 'repertoire', dramatizing their grievances by hanging unpopular figures in effigy or complaining against the price of food by parading with loaves of bread on the end of sticks. The lynching described in the previous chapter (above, p. 39) also drew on a well-known repertoire. Some historians and social theorists would go so far as to say that rioters and lynch mobs follow cultural 'scripts'.

Others, however, reject the notion of 'script' as too rigid, not only in the case of riots but in that of rituals as well, arguing that the term 'performance' does more justice to the element of improvisation, to the fact that the 'same' ritual is a little different on every occasion that it is carried out. We may say that the 'theatre' model or metaphor has been good not to follow but to think with, encouraging distinctions to be drawn and different features of these events to see the light (Burke 2005).

Sex and Gender

In the first chapter it was suggested that the relationship between history and theory has generally been indirect. Historians have found theories more useful in suggesting questions than in suggesting answers. Feminist theory offers a vivid illustration of this generalization. If one examines studies of women's history – the work of Natalie Davis, for example, Elizabeth Fox-Genovese, Olwen Hufton, Joan Kelly or Joan Scott, or Caroline Bynum – one finds relatively few references to the work of theorists, from Hélène Cixous and Luce Irigaray (say), to Nancy Chodorow and Elaine Showalter (Moi 1987). On the other hand, feminism has made an enormous indirect contribution to the writing of history. Like 'history from below', women's history offers a new perspective on the past (J. W. Scott 1991; D. Smith 2001; Wiesner-Hanks 2001; Jordanova 2002; Miller 2003). For example, in an age in which God's gender has become a matter for debate, a medievalist has studied the image of Jesus as mother (Bynum 1982: 110–66).

One result of this new perspective, it has been argued, is 'to call into question accepted schemes of periodization' (J. Kelly 1984: 19; cf: J. W. Scott 1988). After all, many of these schemes – with the obvious exception of the periods of demographic history – were devised without thinking of women. Women have been described as virtually 'invisible' to professional historians (themselves over-whelmingly male, at least until quite recently) in the sense that the importance of their everyday work and their political influence has generally been overlooked, while social mobility has generally been discussed in terms of men alone (Bridenthal and Koonz 1977; J. W. Scott 1988; on female historians B. G. Smith 1998). In another strik-ing metaphor, women have been described as an example of a 'muted' group, only able (in many times and places) to express their ideas through the language of the dominant males (Ardener 1975).

However, the feminist movement and the theories associated with it encouraged female and male historians alike to ask new questions about the past – about male dominance, for example, in different times and places. Was patriarchy reality or myth? Did it take differ-ent forms in different periods or different parts of the world? To what extent and by what means could it be resisted? In what regions and periods and in what domains – within the family, for example – did women exercise unofficial influence? (Rogers 1975; Segalen 1980: 158–72).

Another set of questions concerns women's work. What kinds of work were performed by women in particular places and times? Has the status of working women declined since the Industrial Revolu-tion, or even since the sixteenth century? Women's work has often been neglected by male historians, not least because – in a striking example of the problem of 'invisibility' – much of it went unrecorded in the official documents, surveys of workers ordered and carried out by male officials. In the city of São Paulo in the early nineteenth century, for example, the activities of many poor working women, black and white – activities such as selling food in the street, for example – can be recovered only by indirect means, notably the judicial records of crimes and disputes which occurred during work (Tilly and Scott 1978; Dias 1983).

It has already been suggested that this new perspective on the past is equivalent in importance to that of 'history from below'. One might also say that it runs a similar risk. In compensating for the omissions of traditional history, both new forms of history risk perpetuating a binary opposition, between elite and people in one case, male and female in the other. From the point of view adopted in this study, that of 'total history', it would be more useful to focus on changing relations between men and women, on gender boundaries and conceptions of what is properly masculine or feminine. That this change of focus has been taking place is suggested by the foundation of a journal in 1989 with the title *Gender and History*.

Feminist emphasis on the cultural construction of gender, like the emphasis on cultural construction in general, has made a considerable impact on historical practice (Butler 1990). If the differences between men and women are cultural rather than natural, if 'man' and 'woman' are social roles, defined and organized differently in different periods, then historians need to make explicit what was almost always left implicit at the time, the rules or conventions for being a woman or a man of a particular age-group or social group in a particular region and period. More precisely – since the rules were sometimes contested – they need to describe the 'dominant gender conventions' of dress, speech and so on (Fox-Genovese 1988; cf. J. W. Scott 1988: 28–50).

A paradoxical consequence of the former absence of women from written history was what has been called the 'suppression' of the gender of males (Ditz 2004). From the 1990s onwards, however, a substantial number of studies of masculinity in different places and times have appeared, including work on stereotypes and contrast-conceptions such as the 'Manly Englishman' and the 'Effeminate Bengali' (Sinha 1995). A number of monographs discuss the ways in which manhood is lost in a given culture (by showing cowardice, for instance, or by being insulted), the ways in which it is regained (by a duel, for instance), and they emphasize the continual need in some cultures to assert one's virility, often by violence or at least by what might be called a 'theatre of aggression' (Nye 1993; Mosse 1996; Hitchcock and Cohen 1999). The challenge is now to integrate the two series of studies, to show how ideas of masculinity and femininity in a particular culture are complementary opposites, and how changes in the conventions of behaviour for one gender express reactions to changes in conventions for the other.

More and more historical problems are being examined from the perspective of gender. The witch-trials of early modern Europe, given the well-known fact that in most countries the majority of the accused were female, are an obvious example (Thomas 1971: 568–9; Levack 1987: 124–30; Ankarloo and Henningsen 1990). Again, the history of institutions such as monasteries, regiments, guilds, fraternities, cafés and colleges is being illuminated by considering them as examples of 'male bonding', with relatively few female equivalents (nunneries, colleges for girls, Women's Institutes and so on). So is the history of politics, whether scholars focus on female voters or on the exclusion of women from the so-called public sphere in different cultures (Landes 1988; Wiesner 1993) (below, p. 81).

The process of the social or cultural construction of gender is also under historical scrutiny. A striking example is a study of 119 Dutch women who lived as men (notably in the army and navy) in early modern Europe, their motives for this change of life, and the alternative cultural tradition which made their decisions possible. Maria van Antwerpen, for example, was an orphan, taken in but mistreated by her aunt. She entered domestic service, but was dismissed, so she decided to enlist as a soldier. According to her autobiography, she did so because she had heard of other women who had done so and because she was afraid of being forced into prostitution (Dekker and van de Pol 1989: esp. 64–5).

Sex has been approached in a similar way, thanks in particular to the bold reconceptualizations of Michel Foucault, who went so far as to suggest that homosexuality (like sexuality itself) was a modern 'invention', a new form of discourse about human relationships (on 'discourse', below, p. 99). Foucault contrasted this discourse with 'the manner in which sexual activity was problematized by philosophers and doctors' in ancient Greece, ancient Rome and the early Christian centuries, noting for example that classical texts refer to homosexual acts rather than homosexual persons.

Foucault's approach has been widened and deepened in recent studies by anthropologists and classical scholars that attempt to reconstitute the rules and assumptions underlying sexual activity in different cultures. It has been argued, for instance, that for the ancient Greeks, pleasure was not mutual, but confined to the dominant partner. As a result, sex was 'symbolic of (or constructed as) zero-sum competition' between 'hard' winners and 'soft' losers. A sexual relationship between men was not shameful in itself, but to play the subordinate or 'female' role put honour at risk (Foucault 1976–84; Ortner and Whitehead 1981; Winkler 1990: esp. 11, 37, 52, 54).

Family and Kinship

The most obvious example of an institution composed of a set of mutually dependent and complementary roles is surely the family. From the 1950s to the 1980s the history of the family became one of the most rapidly growing fields of historical research, leading to a dialogue between historians, sociologists and social anthropologists in which each group has both learned from the others and forced the others to revise some of their assumptions.

In an early sociological classic, *L'Organisation de la famille* (1871), Frédéric Le Play distinguished three main types of family. There was the 'patriarchal', now better known as the 'joint' family, where the married sons remain under their father's roof; the 'unstable', now known as the 'nuclear' or 'conjugal' family, which all the children leave on marriage; and in between the two, the type most closely associated with Le Play, the 'stem family' (*famille souche*), in which only one married son remains with his parents (Laslett 1972: 17–23; Casey 1989: 11–14).

The next step was to arrange these three types in a chronological order, and to present the history of the European family as a story of gradual contraction, from the early medieval 'clan' (in the sense of a large group of kin), through the stem family in early modern times, to the nuclear family characteristic of industrial society. However, this theory of 'progressive nuclearization', which used to be sociological orthodoxy, was challenged by historians in the 1960s, notably by Peter Laslett and his colleagues in the Cambridge Group for the Study of Population and Social Structure, but also in other countries such as the Netherlands (1972: 299–302).

The Group offer a slightly different threefold classification to Le Play's, concentrating on the size and composition of the household and distinguishing 'simple', 'extended' and 'multiple' family households. Their best-known finding is that between the sixteenth and the nineteenth centuries, household size in England scarcely varied from a mean of 4.75. They also note that households of this size have long been characteristic of Western Europe and Japan (Laslett 1972).

The household approach is both precise and relatively easy to document, thanks to the survival of census records, but it does have its dangers. Two of these dangers in particular have been noted by sociologists and anthropologists, in fresh contributions to the dialogue between disciplines.

In the first place, the differences between the households described as 'multiple', 'extended' or 'simple' may – as Chayanov (1925) had already pointed out in the 1920s – be no more than phases in the developmental cycle of the same domestic group, which expands while the young couple are bringing up their children and contracts again as the children marry and move out (cf. Laslett 1972: 335–74).

A second objection to the treatment of household size and composition as an index of family structure brings us back to the problem of the hard and soft data (above, p. 37). What we want to discover is the way in which family relationships are structured in a given place and time, but this structure may not be revealed by the size of the household. The family is not only a residential unit but also – at least on occasion – an economic and a legal unit. Most important of all, it is a 'moral community', in the sense of a group with which the members identify and with which they are emotionally involved (Casey 1989: 14). This multiplicity of functions poses problems, because the economic, emotional, residential and other units may not coincide. Hence an index based on co-residence may not tell us what we most need to know about family structure.

For instance, a sociological study of the working class in East London in the 1950s pointed out that relatives who live in separate households may live near one another and see one another virtually every day. In this case a 'conjugal' household coexisted with an 'extended' mentality. Historical examples of this coexistence are not hard to find. In Renaissance Florence, for instance, noble kinsmen often lived in neighbouring palaces, met regularly in the family *loggia*, and collaborated closely in economic and political affairs. The history of the patrician family in Florence, or Venice, or Genoa (to go no further afield), cannot be written in terms of the household alone (Kent 1977; cf. Heers 1974).

A revised version of the nuclearization theory was launched by Lawrence Stone in a study concentrating on the upper classes in England between 1500 and 1800. Stone (1977) argued that what he calls the 'open lineage family' dominant at the beginning of the period was replaced first by the 'restricted patriarchal nuclear family' and then, in the eighteenth century, by the 'closed domesticated nuclear family'. However, even this revision has been questioned by Alan Macfarlane (1979), who suggests that the nuclear family was already in place in the thirteenth and fourteenth centuries.

The controversy over the dating of the nuclear family in England is not a matter of purely antiquarian interest, but reflects different views of social change. On one side, there is the thesis that economic changes, notably the rise of the market and the early Industrial Revolution, reshape social structures, including those of the family. On the other, we find the argument that social structures are highly resilient, and that the rise of Western Europe in general and of England in particular is to be explained by the 'fit' between pre-existing social structures and capitalism (Macfarlane 1986: 322–3).

Whatever their position on these general questions – to be discussed in more detail in chapter 5 – historians of the family now work with a more precise vocabulary than they previously did and are able to make finer distinctions than was possible before they concerned themselves with social theory. In return, they have persuaded sociologists to revise some of their original generalizations in this field.

Family structures have been one major focus of research. Another is what might be called family 'strategy', to use a term that Pierre Bourdieu borrowed from the art of war and adapted to the study of peasant marriages in Pau, in south-west France (the area and the social group from which Bourdieu himself came). The questions – who decides who marries whom, and on what grounds – receive very different answers in different cultures and periods.

For example, according to Lawrence Stone, there was a gradual shift in early modern England from parents choosing a bride or groom for their children (with the children having a veto), to children choosing for themselves (with the parents having a veto). As for the reasons for marrying, Stone emphasized what he called 'a pragmatic calculation of family interest' in the case of children as well as parents from the propertied classes (the poor were freer to marry whom they chose) (Stone 1977: 180–91).

Some famous examples from the world of the nobility in other parts of Europe support Stone's claim. The Duke of Saint-Simon, for instance, tells us in his memoirs that when he was arranging his marriage in 1694 (his father being dead), he admitted to his prospective father-in-law that it was him he wished to marry. Again, the memoirs of a Polish gentleman of the seventeenth century, Jan Pasek, described his time as an eligible bachelor. 'Two gentlemen . . . each wished me to marry into their families . . . but my heart rather inclined to Sladowska, for I heard them say that out there on her estate not only wheat grew in every field but onions too.' In some ways the seventeenth century appears very remote indeed.

Problems remain. When we say that the 'parents' decided on a marriage partner, we are assuming a consensus that may not have existed. In theory, in a patriarchal society, the father decided, but in practice, things may have worked out differently. The delicate balance between emotions and interests differed from one individual to another. All that historians can say is that 'family interest' played a more important part in marriages in some places, times and social groups than in others.

Communities and Identities

In the last section, the family was described as essentially a 'moral community'. The concept of community has come to play an increasingly important part in historical writing. As we have seen, community studies were already well established in anthropology and sociology by the middle of the twentieth century. In the case of history, the tradition of monographs on villages is much older, but these studies were generally made for their own sake, or as an expression of local pride, rather than as a means of understanding the wider society. By contrast, Le Roy Ladurie's *Montaillou* (1975) adopts a more sociological or anthropological approach, like some older studies of France that emphasize political and religious differences between the *plaine* and the *bocage*, in other words between arable regions and the more wooded pastoral regions in north-west France.

Community studies of early modern England also reveal cultural contrasts between types of settlement in different environments. The difference between arable and pasture, for example, was associated with differences in the extent of literacy and even with religious attitudes or contrasting allegiances in the Civil War. For example, settlements in wooded areas were smaller in scale, more isolated, less literate and more conservative in their attitudes than corn-growing villages (Underdown 1985). Studies of this kind, emphasizing the relationship between the community and its environment, avoid the twin dangers of treating a village as if it were an island and ignoring the relation between analysis at the micro and the macro level.

There is also a case for pursuing this approach in a very different kind of environment, where the very existence of communities is problematic, in great cities. An older generation of urban sociologists, notably Georg Simmel, stressed the anonymity and isolation of individuals in the city. More recently, however, sociologists and anthropologists have come to view the city as a set of communities or 'urban villages' (Simmel 1903; Gans 1962; Suttles 1972). The challenge to urban historians is to study the construction, maintenance and destruction of such communities, bearing in mind that the term 'community' is almost as indefinable – as well as indispensable – as the term 'culture'.

Recent studies of ritual and symbol may help in the response to this challenge. For example, the anthropologist Victor Turner, developing an idea of Durkheim's about the importance of moments of 'creative effervescence' for social renewal, coined the term 'communitas' to refer to spontaneous, unstructured social solidarities (his examples ranged from the early Franciscans to the hippies of the 1960s) (Durkheim 1912: 469, 475; V. Turner 1969: 131). These solidarities are necessarily impermanent, because an informal group either fades away or congeals into a formal institution. All the same, *communitas* can be revived from time to time, within institutions, thanks to rituals and other means for what has been called 'the symbolic construction of community' (A. P. Cohen 1985).

In the early modern European city, for example, parishes, wards, guilds and religious fraternities all had their annual rituals. These rituals declined in importance – but did not disappear altogether – when cities grew larger and became more – though not completely – anonymous. Indeed, they still exist in some cities, from the St Patrick's Day parade in New York to the Notting Hill Carnival in London, though they now express and construct ethnic rather than occupational or religious identities.

Collective identity, like ethnicity, is a concept which has become increasingly prominent in the last generation, in the academic world as well as in politics. The formation of national identity in particular has stimulated a number of distinguished recent works. More and more scholars have been recruited to the study of such embodiments of identity as national anthems, national flags and national rituals (such as Bastille Day). The power of memory, of imagination and of symbols in the construction of communities is increasingly emphasized (Hobsbawm and Ranger 1983; Nora 1984–93).

On the other hand, the question of the conditions under which national identities were formed, especially in the nineteenth century, remains controversial. For Benedict Anderson (1983), for instance, the important factors in the creation of these 'imagined communities', as he famously called them, are the decline of religion and the rise of vernacular languages (encouraged by 'print capitalism'). For Ernest Gellner, on the other hand, the crucial factor is the rise of industrial society, which creates a cultural homogeneity which 'appears on the surface in the form of nationalism' (1983: 39). For his part, Eric Hobsbawm (1990) has been careful to distinguish the nationalism of governments from the nationalism of the people, arguing that what ordinary people felt about nationality became a matter of political importance only in the late nineteenth century.

Similar problems are posed by the revival or re-emergence on to the political scene of other collective identities: regional (in the north of Italy, for instance, or the south of France), religious (in India, Bosnia or Northern Ireland) and 'ethnic' (in Africa or the Americas). The definition of ethnicity is controversial, but Max Weber's characterization of ethnic groups remains useful: 'human groups (other than kinship groups) which cherish a belief in their common origins of such a kind that it provides a basis for the creation of a community'.

One important clue to the understanding of these revivals has been emphasized by three anthropologists: Pierre Bourdieu, Arjun Appadurai and Anton Blok. Bourdieu argued that 'social identity lies in difference, and difference is asserted against what is closest, which represents the greatest threat'. Appadurai links ethnic violence to 'uncertainty about categories'. For his part, Blok, using Freud's concept of 'the narcissism of minor differences' to analyse recent events in Northern Ireland, Bosnia, Rwanda and Sri Lanka, concludes that violence is often sparked by fear of 'the imminent loss of differences' (Bourdieu 1979: 479: Appadurai 1996: 154–5; Blok 2001: 115–3 at 131).

An earlier conflict that the Freud–Bourdieu–Blok theory illuminates took place in Russia. In 1667, the Orthodox Church split into two, when a church council, meeting in Moscow, supported recent innovations and excommunicated the supporters of local tradition, later known as the 'Old Believers'. The explicit issues in this debate appear to have been trivial. Should the gesture of blessing be made with two fingers or three? Should the name of Jesus be spelled with one i (Isus) or two (Iisus)? It is not difficult to guess how later rationalist historians described these debates, viewing them as typical of the religious or superstitious mind, remote from real life and unable to distinguish the significant from the insignificant. However, it is more illuminating to treat these minor differences as symbols of identity. On one side, there was the group who identified with Eastern Christendom as a whole; on the other, those for whom the Russian form of Orthodoxy was part of their identity. Both parties could claim tradition on their side – different traditions.

Again, in the history of the Catholic Church, more energy has sometimes been expended on attacking 'heretics' who differ from the orthodox on points of detail (consubstantiation rather than transubstantiation, for example) than on converting unbelievers. Indeed, even earlier than Freud, Georg Simmel noted how in the case of religion, 'the minutest divergence' could become the source of major conflicts (1908: 43). A similar point might be made about the Communist Party in Russia and elsewhere: it was often more dangerous to be an unorthodox Marxist (a Trotskyist, say, in Stalin's Russia) than to be a non-Marxist or even an anti-Marxist. It was the deviant Marxists who were most often imprisoned and even executed.

The way in which the identity of one group is defined against, or by contrast to, others – Protestants against Catholics, males against females, northerners against southerners, and so on – has been illuminated in a remarkable work of historical anthropology which studies the relationships between Africans and African Americans. In Brazil in the late nineteenth century, some freed slaves of West African descent decided to return to Africa, to Lagos for example, a decision which suggests that they considered themselves as Africans. On their arrival, however, they found themselves regarded by the local community as outsiders, as Brazilians (Carneiro da Cunha 1986). This example reminds us of the importance of studying both individual and collective identity from two angles, from inside and from outside. It cannot be assumed that others see us in the same way as we see ourselves.

The term 'community', then, is at once useful and problematic. It has to be freed from the intellectual package in which it forms part of the consensual, Durkheimian model of society (above, p. 27). It cannot be assumed that every group is permeated by solidarity; communities have to be constructed and reconstructed. It cannot be assumed that a community is homogeneous in attitudes or free from conflicts – class struggle, for example. The problems of 'class' are the subject of the following section.

Class and Status

Social stratification is an area where historians are especially prone to use technical terms such as 'caste', 'social mobility' and so on, without being aware of the problems associated with them or the distinctions which social theorists have discovered to be necessary (above, p. 32). It is not exactly surprising to find that the historians who have found the class model most useful are those concerned with industrial society, especially in Britain (the society in which Marx himself was writing and one in which the language of class was used by many contemporaries) (Briggs 1960; G. S. Jones 1983; Joyce 1990; Cannadine 1998; Feldman 2002). Class has even been regarded as the key to modern British history.

Even in this case, however, there have been major controversies about the uses of the concept, raising two questions in particular. In the first place, how widely is the term 'class' applicable? To how many parts of the world, and in how many periods? In the second place, is class an objective characteristic of certain societies, or simply an intellectual category imposed on them? The second question is relevant to other categories of analysis as well, and will therefore be discussed later (below, p. 175). It is the first question that demands attention here.

In the case of class, like some other categories employed by historians, we find an apparent fit between actors' models and scholars' models. However, the strengths and weaknesses of a model generally become clearer by stretching it – in other words by attempting to use it outside the area for which it was originally designed. For this reason it may be illuminating to discuss some attempts to analyse pre-industrial societies in class terms.

A well-known example of such an analysis is the one offered by the Soviet historian Boris Porshnev in his study of popular revolts in France in the early seventeenth century. There were a considerable number of such revolts in the towns and the countryside alike, from Normandy to Bordeaux, especially between 1623 and 1648. Porshnev emphasized the conflicts opposing landlords and tenants, masters and journeymen, rulers and ruled, and presented the rebels as men with a conscious aim, to overthrow the ruling class and end the 'feudal' regime which was oppressing them. The book was criticized for anachronism by French historians such as Roland Mousnier precisely because Porshnev insisted on using the term 'class' – in Marx's broad sense – to describe seventeenth-century conflicts. According to these historians, the revolts were protests against increases in taxation by the central government, and the conflict which they expressed was that between Paris and the provinces, not between the ruling class and the people. At the local level, what these protests revealed were links rather than conflicts between ordinary people and the nobility, urban and rural (Porshnev 1948; Mousnier 1967: pt 1; Bercé 1974; Pillorget 1975).

Supposing for the moment that the criticisms summarized above are well founded, and that the class model is not helpful in understanding social protest or indeed the social structure in seventeenth-century France. What should historians put in its place?

According to Mousnier, the right model to use for this particular analysis is that of the three estates, or three orders: the clergy, the nobility and the rest. This was a model which went back to the Middle Ages and was employed by contemporaries themselves – Mousnier makes considerable use of a treatise on 'Orders and Dignities' by a seventeenth-century French lawyer, Charles Loyseau. The division of society into three was consecrated by the law. In France before the Revolution of 1789, the clergy and the nobility were privileged estates, exempt from taxation, while the unprivileged formed the residual 'third estate' – hence Mousnier's claim that Porshnev was trying to impose on the old regime concepts which apply only to the period after the Revolution.

It is worth pointing out that Mousnier did not derive his social theory from seventeenth-century treatises alone. He also read some sociologists, such as the American Bernard Barber (Burke 1992b). These sociologists stand in a tradition of which the most distinguished representative is Max Weber. Weber distinguished 'classes', which he defined as groups of people whose opportunities in life (*Lebenschancen*) were determined by the market situation, from 'estates' or 'status groups' (*Stände*), whose fate was determined by the status or honour (*ständische Ehre*) accorded them by others. The position of the status groups was normally acquired at birth and defined legally, but it was revealed by their 'style of life' (*Lebenstil*) (Weber 1948: 180–94; cf. Bush 1992).

Whereas Marx defined his classes in terms of production, Weber came near to defining his estates in terms of consumption. In the long run, he suggested, property confers status, although in the short run, 'both propertied and propertyless people can belong to the same *Stand*' (Weber 1948: 186–7). It will be clear that Weber derived his concept of 'status group' from the traditional idea of the three estates, but also that he refined the concept and made it more analytical, so that to analyse the seventeenth century in Weberian terms is not quite the circular tour it appears to be.

Weber's model was put forward as an alternative to that of Marx, and Marxists have in their turn answered Weber, pointing out, for example, that values like 'status' are not so much the expression of a general social consensus as values which the dominant class attempts to impose – with greater or less success – on everyone else (Parkin 1971: 40–7). It might also be argued that some contemporary statements about the structure of a particular society should be taken not as neutral descriptions but as attempts by members of a particular group to justify their privileges.

For example, the well-known division of medieval society into the three estates or the three functions of 'those who pray, those who fight, and those who work' looks extremely like a justification of the position of those who do not work. In a brilliant study, the historian Georges Duby (1978), making discreet use of the philosopher Louis Althusser (1970: 121–73), examined the rise of this threefold division of society in France in the eleventh and twelfth centuries, explaining its success in terms of the social and political situation of the time.

In the case of the debate over seventeenth-century French society, it may be argued that Mousnier accepted the official view of the system rather too easily. Loyseau, the lawyer on whom Mousnier relied most heavily, was not a disinterested, dispassionate observer. He was not simply describing French society in his time but was articulating a view of it from the standpoint of an occupant of a particular position within that society, that of an ennobled magistrate. His view needs to be compared and contrasted with that of the traditional nobles, who rejected the magistrate's claim to high status, and also, if possible, with views of the same society from below.

The debate between Marx and Weber is complicated by the fact that the two men were trying to answer different questions about inequality. Marx was especially concerned with power and with conflict, while Weber was interested in values and life-styles. The class model has become associated with a view of society as essentially conflictual, minimizing solidarities, while the model of orders has become associated with a view of society as essentially harmonious, minimizing conflict. There are important insights embodied in both models, but the danger of oversimplification is obvious.

It may therefore be useful to treat the rival models as complementary rather than contradictory ways of viewing society, each of them throwing some features of the social structure into high relief at the price of obscuring others (Ossowski 1957: 172–93; Burke 1992b). The orders model seems most relevant to pre-industrial societies and the class model to industrial ones, but insights may also be gained by using both models against the grain.

Historians of non-European societies are forced to do this in any case, since the rival concepts originated, as we have seen, in a European context. Were Chinese mandarins, for example, a status group or a social class? Is it useful to redefine Indian castes as a kind of status group, or is it better to regard Indian society as a unique form of social structure? The most vigorous supporter of the latter view was the French anthropologist Louis Dumont, who argued that the principles underlying inequalities in Indian society, notably purity, are different from their equivalents in the West. Unfortunately, Dumont went on to identify the contrast between hierarchical and egalitarian societies with that between India and the West, as if the privileged orders of clergy and nobility had never existed in Europe (Dumont 1966, 1977; a critique in Dirks 2001: 54–9).

In fact, the concept of purity was sometimes used in Europe too in order to justify the position of certain social groups. In Spain in particular, 'purity of blood' (*limpieza de sangre*) was officially essential for high status, and elsewhere, in France for example, the nobility often described their social inferiors as unclean. Such concepts were used – without success – to prevent social mobility.

Social Mobility and Social Distinction

Like 'class', 'social mobility' is a term familiar enough to historians, and monographs, conferences and special issues of journals have been devoted to this theme. Less familiar, perhaps, are some of the distinctions drawn by sociologists, at least three of which have their uses in historical practice. The first is between movement up and down the social ladder, since the study of downward mobility has been relatively neglected. The second distinction is that between mobility within an individual lifetime ('intragenerational', as the sociologists say) and mobility spread over several generations ('intergenerational'). The third distinction is that between individual and group mobility. British university professors, for example, enjoyed a higher status a century ago than they do today. On the other hand, certain Indian castes can be shown to have risen socially over the same period (Srinivas 1966).

There are two major problems in the history of social mobility: changes in the rate of mobility and changes in its modes. It has been remarked that historians of all periods seem to resent the imputation that 'their' society is closed or immobile. Although a Byzantine emperor once decreed that all sons should follow the occupation of their fathers, it is unlikely that any stratified society has ever existed in a state of complete immobility, which would mean that all children, male or female, enjoyed (or suffered from) the same status as their parents. There is, incidentally, an important distinction to be drawn between what one might call the 'visible' mobility of men in patrilineal societies and the 'invisible' mobility of women through marriages in which they change their names.

The crucial questions to ask about social mobility in a given society are surely relative ones. For example: was the rate of social mobility (upward or downward) in seventeenth-century England higher or lower than that in seventeenth-century France, seventeenth-century Japan or England in an earlier or later period? A comparative, quantitative approach virtually imposes itself, despite possible pitfalls.

One example of these pitfalls is provided by a study of China in the Ming and Qing periods, in other words from 1368 to 1911, which argued that Chinese society was much more open than European society in the same period. The evidence for the unusually high rate of social mobility in China was provided by the lists of successful candidates in the civil service examinations, lists which provided information about the social origins of candidates. However, as a critic was quick to point out, 'data on the social origins of a ruling class do not constitute data on overall amounts of mobility or on the life chances of lower-class persons'. Why not? Because it is necessary to take account of the relative size of the elite. As elites go, Chinese mandarins formed only a small percentage of the population. Even if access to this elite had been relatively open – and even this is controversial – the life-chances of the sons of merchants, craftsmen, peasants and so on would have remained low (Ho 1958–9; Dibble 1960–1).

A second major question to ask about social mobility is one about its modes, in other words about the various paths to the summit and the different obstacles in the way of potential climbers (downward mobility probably shows less variation). If the desire to rise in the world is a constant, the mode of rising varies from place to place and changes over time.

To return to China, we find that over a long period (from the end of the sixth century to the beginning of the twentieth), the royal road or, better, the imperial road to the top was provided by the examination system. As Max Weber once remarked, in Western society a stranger would be asked who his father was, but in China he would be asked how many examinations he had passed. Success in examinations was the principal means of entry to the Chinese bureaucracy, and posts in the bureaucracy conferred status, wealth and power.

In practice, the system was less meritocratic than in theory, since the children of the poor did not have access to the schools teaching the skills required for success in the examinations. All the same, the Chinese system of recruiting mandarins – which inspired the reform of the British civil service in the mid-nineteenth century – was one of the most sophisticated and also, in all probability, one of the most successful attempts at recruitment by merit ever developed by a pre-industrial state (Weber 1964: Ch. 5; Miyazaki 1963; Chaffee 1985; Elman 2000).

The main rival of imperial China in this respect was the Ottoman Empire, where the so-called tribute of children (*devşirme*) was levied by the Sultan, especially in the fifteenth and sixteenth centuries. In this system the administrative and military elites were both recruited from the Christian subject population. The children were apparently selected on the basis of their abilities and given a thorough education. The A-stream, including the brightest boys, joined the 'Inside Service' in the Sultan's household, which might lead to important positions such as Grand Vizier, while the B-stream entered the 'Outside Service' in the armed forces. All the recruits were required to turn Muslim. Their conversion to the dominant religion of the empire had the effect – indeed, the function – of cutting them off from their cultural roots, thus making them more dependent on the Sultan. Since Muslims were obliged to bring up their children as Muslim, conversion ensured that the sons of elite members were ineligible for office (Parry 1969; Inalcik 1973).

In pre-industrial Europe, one of the main avenues of social mobility was the Church. To follow Stendhal's famous typology, careers were more open to talent in 'black', in the Church, than they were in 'scarlet', in the army. The son of a peasant might even end his ecclesiastical career as pope, as Sixtus V did in the later sixteenth century. Leading churchmen might also be employed in high positions in the state. In seventeenth-century Europe, for example, the leading ministers of state included cardinals Richelieu and Mazarin, both of them in the service of the kings of France, Cardinal Khlesl, in the service of the emperor, and Archbishop Laud, in the service of Charles I. Richelieu came from the lesser nobility, but Khlesl was the son of a baker, and Laud the son of a clothier. For European rulers, one of the advantages of the appointment of Catholic clergy, in particular, as ministers was their inability to produce legitimate children who might claim to succeed them in their posts. In this sense the use of the clergy in Western Europe parallels the Ottoman reliance on the *devşirme* and the employment of eunuchs in high positions in the Roman and Chinese empires. They are all examples of what has been called 'gelding' (Gellner 1981: 14–15).

Another means of rising socially in early modern Europe was to imitate the style of life of a group higher in the social scale, and to engage in what is often called 'conspicuous consumption'.

Consumption and Exchange

Earlier in this chapter, I discussed Kula's criticism of the laws of classical economics on the ground that they did not account for the actual economic behaviour of some groups, such as the Polish magnates of the seventeenth and eighteenth centuries. These nobles did not fit the conventional model of 'economic man'. They were not interested in profit or thrift, but in a steady income to spend on imported luxuries such as French wine, a form of 'conspicuous consumption'. This phrase goes back to the American sociologist Thorstein Veblen at the end of the nineteenth century.

The phrase formed part of a theory. Veblen – a passionate egalitarian and a man with a conspicuously simple life-style – argued that the economic behaviour of the elite, the 'leisure class' as he called it, was irrational and wasteful, motivated only by 'emulation'. He applied to pre-industrial and industrial societies alike the conclusions reached by the anthropologist Franz Boas in his studies of the Kwakiutl. The most famous Kwakiutl institution was the 'potlatch', the destruction of goods (notably blankets and copper plates) by the chiefs.

However, the apparent wastefulness of the potlatch had what might be called a 'latent rationality' (below, p. 89). It formed part of a strategy of domination. The destruction of goods was a way of demonstrating that the chief who organized the potlatch had more wealth than his rivals, and so of humiliating them. It was a way of 'fighting with property'. The chiefs were interested not in accumulating wealth, but in using it to gain status and power (Veblen 1899; Boas 1966; cf. Codere 1950).

In the 1970s, the French sociologist Pierre Bourdieu pursued a similar approach to consumption as part of a more general study of the strategies by which people – especially upper- and middle-class French people – distinguish themselves from others. Like Boas and Veblen, he argued that 'economic power is first and foremost the power to distance oneself from economic necessity; that is why it is always marked by the destruction of wealth, conspicuous consumption, waste and all forms of gratuitous luxury' (Bourdieu 1979).

Since the publication of Bourdieu's book, more and more historians have adopted the concept of conspicuous consumption (Brewer and Porter 1993). These studies not only illustrate the theory but elaborate it and qualify it in a number of respects. For example, historians have noted that some contemporaries at least understood what was going on and indeed analysed it in terms not unlike Veblen's. In the early modern period, a key concept was 'magnificence', a term which sums up very neatly the conversion of wealth into status and power. Writers of fiction were well aware of the importance of status symbols, especially clothes. The Spanish 'literature of the picaresque' of the sixteenth and seventeenth centuries centres on the attempts of the hero (actually a rogue, or *picaro*) to pass himself off as a noble by precisely these means.

Awareness of the use of symbols in the struggle for high status was not confined to writers of fiction. A seventeenth-century burgomaster of Gdańsk even had the motto 'in order to be envied' (*pro invidia*) inscribed on the facade of his house. At much the same time a Florentine writer referred to 'the attempt by the rich to distinguish themselves from others', while a Genoese described the patricians of his city as spending more than they needed 'in order to give pain to those who were unable to do the same and to make them sick at heart' (Burke 1987: 134–5).

These last comments are obviously moralizing and satirical. They remind us of the need to distinguish different attitudes to conspicuous consumption within the same society. It has been shown that in early modern Europe, the view of 'magnificence' as an obligation of the great coexisted with the theory that it exemplified spiritual pride. In practice, conspicuous consumption seems to have varied from region to region (high in Italy, low in the Dutch Republic, for example), as well as from one social group to another. There was also a change over the long term, with competitive consumption reaching an apparent peak in the seventeenth century.

Refining the concepts further, we may say that strategies of distinction took different forms, including that of conspicuously refraining from consuming, a 'Protestant ethic' (as Weber called it) which was not in fact confined to Protestants. This option seems to have been increasingly popular in the eighteenth century, the age of a debate over the harmful consequences of 'luxury'. A strategy of this kind provided a possible escape from the self-destructive consequences of competitive consumption.

Consumption needs to be analysed not only by social class but also by gender. In Europe it has been dominated by women, at least in the domains of clothing and furnishings, since the so-called birth of consumer society in eighteenth-century England or even earlier (Brewer and Porter 1993: esp. 119–20, 274–301). In France in the later seventeenth century, for instance, a journal called the *Mercure galant* – perhaps the first women's magazine – offered information every month on the latest trends in fashion.

Conspicuous consumption is only one strategy for a social group to show itself superior to another. On the other hand, this form of behaviour is much more than a strategy. One of the dangers of theorizing is the propensity to see the world as nothing but illustrations of the theory. In this case, the assumption that consumers simply want to display their wealth and status has been attacked by a British sociologist, Colin Campbell (1987), who suggests that the reason why people buy many luxury objects is to sustain their image of themselves. What they are really buying is identity, individual or collective (cf. Clammer 1997).

The simplest means to correct the propensity to reductionism is to turn to a rival theory. It may therefore be useful to look at conspicuous consumption from another angle, that of exchange or reciprocity, studied in the 1940s by the Hungarian economist Karl Polanyi. Like Kula twenty years later, Polanyi criticized economists for assuming that their generalizations were universally valid, and distinguished three basic systems of economic organization. Only one of them, the market system, is subject to the laws of classical economics. Polanyi (1944) called the other two modes of organization the 'reciprocity' and 'redistribution' systems (cf. Skocpol 1984: 47–8).

The system of reciprocity is based on the gift. In a study of the islands of the western Pacific, the Polish anthropologist Bronisław Malinowski had pointed to the existence of a circular system of exchange. Shell armlets travelled in one direction, shell bracelets in the other. The exchange had no economic value, but it maintained social solidarities. In his famous essay on the gift, the French sociologist Marcel Mauss generalized from examples of this kind, arguing that this 'archaic form of exchange' had great social and religious significance, and that it was based on three unwritten laws: the obligation to give, the obligation to receive, and the obligation to repay. There is no such thing as a 'free' gift (Malinowski 1922; Mauss 1925; Douglas 1990). Polanyi carried generalization one stage further by making the gift the central feature of the first of his three models of economic systems.

Polanyi's second system is based on redistribution. Where gifts are exchanged between equals, redistribution depends on a social hierarchy. Tribute flows in to the metropolis of an empire and flows out again to the provinces. Leaders distribute to their followers the goods they have taken from outsiders. The followers give their leaders loyalty and perform services for them.

These ideas have had considerable influence on historians concerned with economic life in pre-industrial societies, although they have tended to ignore Polanyi's distinction between reciprocity and redistribution and to contrast two systems, the archaic and the modern. Georges Duby (1973) emphasized the functions of gift exchange in the rise of the early medieval economy, while Fernand Braudel's ambitious study of material life and capitalism in early modern times also owes a considerable debt to the ideas of Polanyi, who is quoted a number of times in the text (Braudel 1979: 2, 26, 225, 623).

Whether or not it was derived from a reading of Polanyi, E. P. Thompson's influential idea of a 'moral economy' may be located in this tradition. As was suggested earlier, the idea of a moral economy is one of the relatively few examples of a concept coined by a historian and later taken up by colleagues in other disciplines. To be exact, Thompson found the phrase 'The Moral Economy of the Factory System' in Andrew Ure's *Philosophy of Manufactures* (1835), which discussed religion in economic terms as part of the 'moral machinery' of the system. However, Thompson turned Ure on his head by using the phrase to refer to a moralized economics built on the idea of the just price and enforced in times of dearth by eighteenth-century crowds (E. P. Thompson 1963: 389ff, 1991: 188–258; a critique in Stevenson 1985). Whether these crowds looked back to a golden age in the past, as Thompson suggests, is a matter for debate. What is clear is that studies of other societies, some of them as remote from England as south-east Asia, have found the concept of a 'moral economy' to be a fertile one (J. C. Scott 1976; cf. E. P. Thompson 1991: 341–9).

Cultural and political historians have also written about the importance of gifts, looking at who (superiors, equals, inferiors) gives what (swords, rings, cups, clothes, books, wine, pheasants), to whom ('friends' in a wide sense of the term), when (at New Year or at weddings), according to what rituals and so on. Like the anthropologists, they suggest that gifts are material objects with a message ('Say it with pheasants'), making friends and maintaining a social network. They do not always present the exchanges as smoothing social relations, as they are intended to do, but also note the importance of 'gifts gone wrong', of accusations of ingratitude and of conflicts of interest. Gifts are difficult to refuse, but in the seventeenth century gifts to judges, for instance, might lead to accusations of bribery, as in the case of Lord Chancellor Francis Bacon (Gurevich 1968; Bestor 1999; N. Z. Davis 2000; Groebner 2000).

Many studies of gift exchange assumed that it was a feature of traditional or, as Mauss put it, 'archaic' societies alone, but some recent work emphasizes its continuing importance after the Industrial Revolution and even in our own time. Different kinds of exchange are distinguished, including gifts by and to women and men, and the exchange repertoires of different cultures are compared (Strathern 1988; J. Davis 1992; Godbout 1992). A major area of debate concerns the rationality of giving, whether it is better seen as altruism or investment, the creation of social or cultural 'capital'.

Cultural and Social Capital

According to Bourdieu, for instance, apparent waste, such as lavish gifts or entertainment, is actually a means for converting economic capital into political, social, cultural or 'symbolic' capital. Spending now in order to acquire less tangible benefits later may be regarded as a form of investment. His favourite example was the French education system. Noting the difference in academic achievement between the sons and daughters of the bourgeoisie and those of the working class, Bourdieu explained the higher achievement of the former in terms of the 'cultural investment strategies' followed by their parents, strategies such as giving them classic novels to read or taking them to concerts and museums. The acquisition of good degrees by bourgeois students, thus assisting their later careers, was described as the conversion of inherited capital into acquired capital (Bourdieu 1979: 80–3).

This conversion is a means of what Bourdieu calls 'cultural reproduction'. This phrase refers to the tendency of society in general, and the educational system in particular, to reproduce itself by inculcating in the rising generation the values of the past (Bourdieu and Passeron 1970; cf. Althusser 1970). Traditions do not persist automatically, out of 'inertia', as historians sometimes put it (Mosse 1996: 485–7). They are transmitted as the result of a good deal of hard work by parents, teachers, priests, employers and other agents of socialization.

The concept 'cultural reproduction' is useful in drawing attention to the effort involved in running on the spot – in other words, keeping a society more or less as it is. The qualification 'more or less' has to be added because, as the anthropologist Marshall Sahlins argues, 'every reproduction of culture is an alteration, insofar as in action, the categories by which a present world is orchestrated pick up some new empirical content' (1985: 144). If each generation reinterprets the norms only slightly in the process of receiving and retransmitting them, appreciable social changes will take place over the long term.

The metaphor of capital and investment seems to be increasingly attractive. A recent study of politics is built around the idea of 'moral capital' – in other words, the investment of the reputation of a political leader (Charles De Gaulle, for example, or Nelson Mandela) in order to achieve a difficult task, such as a peaceful exit from Algeria in the case of France or a peaceful transition to democracy in the case of South Africa (Kane 2001).

As for social capital, the concept became a focus of interest in the 1990s, thanks in particular to the publication of two studies by the American political scientist Robert Putnam. In the first study, he argued that institutions worked better in northern Italy than in the south of the country, that there was more co-operation and less mistrust. He explained this contrast in terms of the civic traditions of the north. Thanks to these traditions the north possessed more 'social capital'. Social capital is the equivalent of what used to be called 'public spirit', defined more precisely in terms of 'trust, norms and networks', informal social links that may be mobilized to get something done. In a second study, Putnam turned to the United States, arguing that its stock of social capital, measured by participation in voluntary associations, had steadily declined over the last half century (Putnam 1992, 2000; cf. Portes 1998; Field 2003).

In both the Italian and the American cases, Putnam was making claims about the past as well as the present. These claims naturally attracted the attention of historians, and in 1999 the *Journal of Interdisciplinary History* devoted two special issues to his notion of social capital. Two historians of Italy commented on the argument that the civic spirit of the north Italians went back to the age of the independent city-states of the Middle Ages and the Renaissance. One of these historians noted that the social capital of these regimes included 'civic religion' – in other words the strong link between religion and the city, symbolized by the patron saint (St Mark in Venice, St John the Baptist in Florence, and so on), whose feast-day would be one of the major events of the year, not only a religious occasion but a celebration of the city itself. Religion therefore contributed to what the Italians of the time called the *vita civile*, the politically active life of a citizen. However, the other historian emphasized the weakness and the limitations of these urban regimes, implying that Putnam had viewed them through rose-coloured spectacles. Another historian has raised a more general issue, that of 'network closure', concerning the harm that associations and networks do to the people they exclude, taking the example of the exclusion of women from guilds in early modern Germany (Brucker 1999; Muir 1999; Ogilvie 2004).

Another possible criticism of Putnam's thesis goes still deeper. The concept of 'social capital' appears to be neutral and descriptive, but it is actually normative, implying that Western-style democracy is the best form of government. Putnam slips silently from 'making democracy work' to making institutions work, claiming that institutional performance is 'higher' in the north and its regional governments more 'successful', thanks to the 'norms of reciprocity' and 'networks of civic engagement' in that part of Italy.

However, using the concept of social capital in a neutral manner, it might reasonably be argued that north and south have different forms of it (both norms and networks) which are mobilized for different purposes but with equal effectiveness. There are two main forms of social capital in southern Italy (and indeed many other societies) (on Africa, see Chabal and Daloz 1999). The first form is the family. One American student of southern Italy notoriously described its social system in terms of 'amoral familism', but attachment to one's family might be better characterized as 'moral'. The second form of social capital in the south is patronage.

Patrons, Clients and Corruption

When he discusses social capital, Putnam seems to be thinking primarily of voluntary associations, including his famous example of bowling clubs, and so of 'horizontal' links between equals. He sees these associations as schools of citizenship. However, his suggestion that informal networks facilitate effective political action might also illuminate the workings of patronage in the past.

Patronage may be defined as a political system based on 'vertical' links – in other words, personal relationships between unequals, between leaders (or patrons) and their followers (or clients). The two parties often use the idiom of friendship, including 'friends of friends', or the idiom of kinship, like the now notorious 'godfather'. However, it is more realistic to view their relationship as a form of exchange. Each party has something to offer the other. Clients offer patrons their political support and also their deference, expressed in a variety of symbolic forms (gestures of submission, language of respect, gifts and so on). For their part, patrons offer clients hospitality, jobs and protection. This is how they are able to convert wealth into power.

Some degree of patronage exists in every society, however 'modern'. In some cultures, however, where 'bureaucratic' norms are weak (above, p. 29), and 'vertical solidarity' is particularly strong, society may be described as based on the patronage system. Problems remain, however. The assumption that the links between patron and client are fundamental, like the idea of an 'estate society' (above, p. 61) encourages the observer or historian to overlook both horizontal solidarities and conflicts between rulers and ruled (Gellner and Waterbury 1977: 7–19, 167–83).

Anthropologists and sociologists have made many analyses of the working of patronage, in the Mediterranean world in particular. Their conclusions have undermined, or relativized, what might be called 'classical' political theory as effectively as Polanyi and others relativized classical economic theory. They have shown that – like the market in economics – parliamentary democracy and bureaucracy cannot be treated as a universal political model, and that alternative systems have their own logic. Such systems cannot be treated as mere 'corruption' or as 'pre-political' forms of organization. They too draw on social capital in the form of networks, norms and trust.

Let us take the example of Swat Pathans, as studied in the 1950s by the Norwegian anthropologist Fredrik Barth. The ruler of Swat, the Wali, was relatively weak, allowing a system of local 'bosses' or 'big men' to flourish, the *khans*. The *khans* were competitors for land, status and power. They spent their wealth on gifts and hospitality in order to build up a following. The authority of each *khan* was personal; it was what he could 'wrest' from each of his followers. 'Followers seek those leaders who offer them the greatest advantages and the most security.' In return, they offered their services and their loyalty. A large number of followers gave a leader honour (*izat*) and the power to humiliate his rivals.

On the other hand, the need to satisfy their followers forced the *khans* to compete with one another. In Pathan society, where honour depends on appearances, a *khan* with economic problems would not reduce his hospitality and might even increase it, even if he had to sell land in order to feed his visitors and clients. The logic underlying this paradox is summed up in a remark made to Barth (1959) by one of the *khans*: 'Only this constant show of force keeps the vultures at bay.' Barth's case-study combines vivid description with penetrating analysis, looks at patronage from below as well as from above, and illuminates both the economics and the politics of reciprocity.

If we look for a moment at England in the fifteenth century, more especially at East Anglia as revealed in the correspondence of the Paston family, we find a society which resembled Swat in certain important respects. In England too the acquisition of land was one of the major goals for adult males, and the competition for land sometimes took a violent form, as in the case of the seizure of John Paston's manor of Gresham by his powerful neighbour Lord Moleyns. In England too the ties between local leaders ('lords' or 'masters') and their followers (known as 'friends' or 'well-willers') were fundamental to the organization of society.

The small men needed the 'good lordship' of the great. Followers courted leaders not only with deference but with gifts. As a correspondent of the Pastons once remarked, 'men do not lure hawks with empty hands'. On the other hand, leaders needed followers in order to increase their honour or 'worship' (their *izat*, as Pathans would say). Hence they kept open house and offered their followers 'livery' – in other words, presents of clothes in the colours associated with the lord's family, which were worn as a demonstration of loyalty and support. Social behaviour which historians once interpreted as no more than a reaction to the temporary breakdown of central authority during the Wars of the Roses turns out to be an example of a much more general social phenomenon.

The existence of patron–client relationships in political life is not news to some historians. It was indeed in the 1920s that Lewis Namier put forward his argument, shocking at the time, that the Whig and Tory parties were not important in eighteenth-century politics. What really mattered was 'faction' – in other words, a group of clients around a patron, a group united not by an ideology or a political programme but by a common relationship to a leader.

In his well-known account of the conspicuous consumption of the Tudor and Stuart peerage, Lawrence Stone, following Veblen, described their hospitality essentially in terms of waste, or the need 'to justify the existence of echoing halls and sumptuous state apartments, and to keep at bay the melancholia and loneliness of a half empty mansion' (Stone 1965: 555). A reading of Fredrik Barth, or of Marcel Mauss on the gift, suggests an alternative explanation. Could the patronage networks of the peerage have survived without this hospitality? If some peers kept open house when they could ill afford it, they were perhaps acting from the same motives as the *khans* who tried by this means to keep the vultures at bay (cf. Heal 1990: 57–61).

The great value to historians of the anthropological approach to these problems is in its emphasis on the order underlying what often looks – to modern Western observers – like disorder, a stress on the rules of the game and the pressures on all the actors, the leaders no less than the followers, to continue to play their roles. Some recent studies of seventeenth-century French politics have taken advantage of the growing anthropological literature on patronage. They note, for example, how Cardinal Richelieu, the virtual ruler of France in the early seventeenth century, chose his subordinates on personal rather than impersonal or 'bureaucratic' grounds. In other words, he did not look for the most able candidate to fill a given post, but offered it to one of his clients, or to use the expressive seventeenth-century phrase, one of his 'creatures'.

Richelieu's method of selection was a long way from the 'bureaucratic' model. However, it had its rationale. The cardinal might not have survived politically had he not acted in this way. He needed subordinates he could trust, and apart from relatives, he could only trust his creatures, just as princes could only trust their favourites (Ranum 1963). For similar reasons, the early modern popes, who were secular as well as spiritual rulers, surrounded themselves with their relatives and clients. This 'nepotism' was often condemned in the nineteenth and twentieth centuries, but we need to be aware of the positive aspects of the practice.

Another study of seventeenth-century France, focusing on patrons, clients and what the author calls (following the anthropologist Eric

Wolf) the 'brokers' between them, argues that patronage networks were parallel and supplementary to official political institutions, and that the social rituals of the gift served political purposes. Here too power depended on exchange. The system made a positive contribution to political integration at the price of encouraging conflict and 'corruption' (Wolf 1956; Kettering 1986, 1988).

The problem of 'corruption', which has surfaced several times already (in the case of Francis Bacon, for instance) deserves more systematic attention (J. C. Scott 1969; Peck 1990; Chabal and Daloz 1999: 95–100). Is the term anything more than a personal judgement, implying a decline of standards from a moral golden age at some point in the past? Is it simply a label used by members of so-called bureaucratic societies to dismiss other ways of organizing political life?

Suppose we define corruption in a relativistic manner as behaviour deviating from the formal duties of a public role, transgressing the 'moral boundaries' of a given society (Harding 1981). In what social situations does this kind of behaviour arise or flourish? Or better, in what social situations is it perceived to flourish? If we phrase the question in this way, we see that corruption is in part in the eye of the beholder. The more formally organized the society and the sharper the distinction between public and private domains, the clearer the cases of corruption will be.

As in the case of the 'favourite' (above, p. 47) it is also worth asking whether this form of behaviour fulfils a social function for the public as well as for the officials involved – whether, for example, it should be seen as a form of pressure-group activity. This question leads to others. Does corruption play a more or less important role in different cultures, less in Sweden (say) and more in Nigeria? Again, does corruption take different forms in different cultures? One might, for instance, distinguish the granting of favours by officials to their relatives and friends from the sale of such favours, in other words the exploitation of office in accordance with the rules of the market. The rise of corruption in the latter sense seems to be part of the general rise of market society from the eighteenth century onwards.

Power and Political Culture

The discussion of patronage and corruption has led us to the problem of power. 'Power' is a term so embedded in ordinary language, at least in the West, that it may seem unproblematic. However, the appearance of clarity is deceptive, a point which emerges from studies of the idea of power in other cultures, Java for instance, where it is regarded as a form of creative energy which competitors can take from one another (B. Anderson 1990: 20–2). A similar assumption underlies the idea of 'charisma'.

Whether regarded as energy or not, power is a concept which is often reified. It is easy to assume that one person, group or institution in a given society – the 'ruler', for example, the 'ruling class' or the political 'elite' – 'has' this power while everyone else lacks it. As the American political scientist Harold Lasswell once asserted in his usual trenchant style, 'Those who get the most are *elite*; the rest are *mass*' (1936: 13). Historians have often made this assumption.

However, the existence of a power elite in a given society is better regarded as a hypothesis than as an axiom. The problems involved in verifying the hypothesis, indeed in defining the concept, may be illustrated from a well-known controversy over the distribution of power in the United States. It was argued that the 'elite model' can be tested only when decisions are made on issues where there is an observable conflict of interests between different groups in society.

This formulation certainly brought more clarity and precision into the discussion. On the other hand, this 'one-dimensional' view of power may be criticized for concentrating on decision making and ignoring the ways in which a particular group or groups may be able to exclude certain issues or grievances from the political agenda (Dahl 1958; Bachrach and Baratz 1962; cf. Giddens 1985: 8–9). The critics were in turn criticized for their 'two-dimensional' view which included manipulation as well as decision making but ignored a good deal else, including the 'power to prevent people . . . from having grievances by shaping their perceptions, cognitions and preferences in such a way that they accept their role in the existing order of things' (Lukes 1974: 24). This type of cultural 'hegemony' will be discussed further below (p. 88).

More generally, the historical sociologist Michael Mann has suggested that 'Societies are constituted of multiple overlapping and intersecting socio-spatial networks of power'. He goes on to distinguish four sources of power – ideological, economic, military and political (Mann 1986–93: i. 518–21; cf. J. Scott 1994). Mann's concern with ideological power, like the reference to 'perceptions and cognitions' above, implies that a student of the topic must examine not only political structures but also political 'culture'.

This term – which entered the discourse of political scientists in the 1950s and that of historians in the 1970s – may be defined as the political knowledge, ideas and sentiments current in a given place and time. It includes 'political socialization' – in other words, the means by which this culture is transmitted from one generation to another, whether in the family, the school or the street (Almond and Verba 1963: 12–26; Baker 1987; Lucas 1988). In seventeenth-century England, for example, the fact that children grew up in patriarchal families must have made it easier for them to accept a patriarchal society without questioning it. They were told that obedience to the king was enjoined by the biblical commandment 'Honour thy father' (there was considerably less discussion of mothers) (Schochet 1975).

The concept of political culture, like that of social capital, has sometimes been criticized as implicitly normative and even ethnocentric, and it is true that some political scientists have judged political cultures according to their closeness to Western democratic values. All the same, the example of patriarchy, like that of the Pathans or the Pastons, suggests that the concept can be freed from this kind of assumption. It may be defined as a 'set of discourses and practices' concerning political ends and means (Baker 1987: pp. xi–xiii). In this sense of the term both north and south Italy, to return to Putnam's example, have political cultures. The problem for a united Italy is that these two cultures are incompatible.

One implication of this approach to politics is the need to take symbols seriously, to recognize their power in mobilizing support. Elections, for example, may be studied not only as an opportunity for the voters to make choices between parties but also as a form of ritual which concentrates on personalities rather than issues, because this makes for drama and popular appeal (Edelman 1971; Kertzer 1988; O'Gorman 1992).

Some recent studies of the French Revolution have also adopted this point of view, and treat the symbols of the Revolution as central rather than peripheral to the movement. Thus the French historian Mona Ozouf has devoted a book to the analysis of revolutionary festivals – the Festival of the Federation, the Festival of the Supreme Being and so on – paying particular attention to the ways in which the organizers of these events tried to restructure the participants' perceptions of space and time. There was a systematic attempt to create new sacred spaces, such as the Champ de Mars in Paris, for instance, in order to replace traditional Catholic ones.

Again, the American historian Lynn Hunt has pointed out that in France in the 1790s, 'Different costumes indicated different politics'. She emphasizes the importance of the tricolour cockade, the liberty cap, and the liberty tree (a kind of maypole which came to acquire a political meaning) in what theorists call the 'political mobilization' of the people. By May 1792, 60,000 liberty trees had been planted.

In ways like these, the ideas and ideals of the Revolution penetrated everyday life (Ozouf 1976; Hunt 1984; cf. Lucas 1988).

One implication of the new approach is that the term 'politics' needs to be extended in order to include the informal aspects of the exercise of power. The French philosopher-historian Michel Foucault was one of the first to advocate the study of the 'micro-physics' of power, in other words, its exercise in a variety of small-scale institutions including prisons, schools, hospitals and even families (above, p. 40). A bold suggestion when he uttered it, this view is now well on the way to becoming orthodox (Foucault 1980).

Another implication of this broader approach to power is that the relative success or failure of particular forms of political organization – Western-style democracy, for example – in different regions or periods will remain unintelligible without the study of the wider culture, especially what has become known as 'civil society' and the 'public sphere'.

Civil Society and the Public Sphere

'Civil society' is a term describing the ample domain between the state on one side and the family on the other, or, as Gellner put it, 'that set of diverse non-governmental institutions which is strong enough to counterbalance the state' (1994: 5). It is in this domain, inhabited by voluntary associations, that the political effects of 'social capital' are most visible.

Civil society is the topic of a famous study, now more than forty years old, by the German philosopher-sociologist Jürgen Habermas, on the transformation of what he calls the 'public sphere' (Öffentlichkeit) in the eighteenth century. Habermas discussed the invasion of the traditional public sphere, restricted to a small elite, by the bourgeoisie – in other words 'private people come together as a public'. This public developed its own informal institutions such as coffee-houses, theatres and newspapers, especially in large cities such as London and Paris. Thanks to these institutions, an arena of debate emerged which encouraged critical and rational thought (Habermas 1962; cf. Calhoun 1992).

Historians had long ago suggested that the late eighteenth century was the time of the rise of 'public opinion'. In a sense, Habermas was replacing an old label by a new one. However, the advantages of the new phrase 'public sphere' over the old phrase 'public opinion' are that it communicates more sense of debate, of an arena rather than an attitude, and also more sense of the locales in which debate was conducted.

After a considerable time-lag, the concept of the public sphere entered the discourse of historians, encouraging them to study not only the coffee-houses emphasized by Habermas but also other informal institutions such as academies, clubs and salons (Melton 2001). Take the case of clubs. London alone had some 3,000 clubs at the end of the eighteenth century, and their rituals, such as electing officers, taking turns to speak and keeping minutes of meetings, were modelled on the rituals and rules of Parliament. It was also in the eighteenth century that the Freemasons became important both as a network of voluntary associations and as a political pressure group (P. Clark 2000; cf. Melton 2001: 197–272).

Again, a study of colonial America by David Shields, inspired in part by Habermas, discusses forms of sociability and locales of conversation such as taverns, coffee-houses and clubs (for males) and tea-tables and assemblies (for both sexes). He emphasizes the 'verbal glue' that held these discursive communities together, the rules they followed in their choice of a manner or tone of speaking or a topic of conversation, and the ideals of civility and equality on which good talk was based. As an article in the *New England Weekly Journal* expressed it in the 1720s, 'Title and Distinction must be laid aside in order to talk and act sociably.' Turning from speech to writing, the author notes the importance of the 'civic sorority', a community of women 'constituted in letters' (Shields 1997: pp. xvi, 287, 319).

Shields is a professor of English, who entered the field of socio-cultural history in search of the contexts of the occasional poetry of the time, but he is well aware of the political implications of his study. Returning to the notion of social capital, it may be said that his book helps us to understand how the 'civil' and the 'civic' were connected, and how colonial elites were able to co-operate in collective action at the time of the American Revolution.

Another institution that deserves to be taken seriously in any account of the public sphere is the demonstration, which might be described as the utilization of public space for unofficial and sometimes anti-official purposes. The term 'demonstration' is recorded in English only in the early nineteenth century, but the practice is much older. In London in the 1640s, for instance, and again in the 1680s, ordinary people marched to Parliament carrying petitions (Zaret 2000). We need to put the 'demo' back into democracy, for two reasons in particular. In the first place, it is an example of non-violent collective action. In the second place, it 'demonstrates' wide support by the numbers of marchers or the number of signatures affixed to the petition.

Ironically enough, one of the historical studies which follows the Habermas model most closely in its concepts, methods and organization is sharply critical of Habermas himself for failing to discuss the place of women. Joan Landes argues that women tried to enter the public sphere in the course of the French Revolution (when the *Declaration of the Rights of Man* was quickly followed by the *Declaration of the Rights of Woman*), but found their way blocked. 'The Republic was constructed against women, not just without them' (Landes 1988).

At a more general level, Habermas's account is vulnerable to a number of criticisms. He has, for example, been accused of idealizing the bourgeois public sphere, and forgetting the ways in which media such as newspapers have always manipulated opinion as well as informing it. His lack of concern with religious debate has been noted, as well as his lack of interest in earlier public spheres – in seventeenth-century England, for example (Zaret 2000). Habermas may also be criticized for assuming that the public sphere is either present in a society or absent from it, as if the twentieth-century USA, for example, had a public sphere, while Russia, China and Syria did not.

The concept of a 'public sphere' is rather less clear than it looks, since different periods, different cultures and different social groups (men and women, for example) may well draw the line between public and private in different places. Perhaps we should speak and think in terms not of the simple presence or absence of a public sphere but of the different forms it may take and the relative importance it may have in different cultures. In different places and times, the role of the now famous coffee-house was filled by taverns, barber's shops or pharmacies.

One might have expected the female public sphere to be absent from strongly Islamic political regimes, but two recent books reveal that a little political space for women – sometimes in the most unlikely places – existed in both the Iran of the ayatollahs and the Afghanistan of the Taliban. The 'sewing circle of Herat', for instance, was a meeting of women in a private house to study Western literature, and so inevitably to discuss political issues as well. In that context even Jane Austen and Henry James were subversive (Lamb 2002; Nafisi 2003).

These examples are paradoxical ones, of public spheres which were kept secret, as well as small in scale, but they should not be forgotten.

They encourage us to think of public spheres and publics in the plural rather than the singular, permeating the culture in the manner of power as Foucault sees it.

Centres and Peripheries

Processes of centralization are a traditional object of study. The concept of 'periphery', on the other hand, became current relatively recently, as a consequence of debates among development economists such as Raul Prebisch, Paul Baran and André Gunder Frank in the 1950s and 1960s. Following the general lines of Lenin's analysis of imperialism and Marx's analysis of capitalism, these economists argued that the prosperity of the industrialized nations and the poverty of the so-called underdeveloped countries were opposite sides of the same coin, an illustration of what Marx called the structural 'contradictions' in the capitalist system. 'The metropolis expropriates economic surplus from its satellites and appropriates it for its own economic development' – hence the phrase 'the development of underdevelopment' (Frank 1967).

Historians from Poland and Hungary made use of this dependency theory to dissolve an apparent paradox in European history: the fact that the rise of the towns and the decline of serfdom in Western Europe took place at much the same time, the sixteenth and seventeenth centuries, as the decline of the towns and the rise of the so-called second serfdom in Eastern or 'East-Central' Europe, a central element in Kula's model of economic feudalism (above, p. 46).

The American sociologist Immanuel Wallerstein went one step further in his account of the rise of capitalism, combining the theories of Latin American economists and East European historians and arguing that the price of economic development in the West included not only serfdom in the East but also slavery in the New World as part of the new division of labour between the 'core' and the 'periphery'. Changes in what he called the 'semi-periphery', especially Mediterranean Europe, formed part of the same world system. Economic development in one part of the world was the result of increasing 'underdevelopment' elsewhere. Spatial concepts thus play a central role in Wallerstein's restructuring of the Marxist theory of social change (Wallerstein 1974; cf. Skocpol 1984: 276–317). (below, p. 151). The theory also has a political dimension, since the periphery is often comprised of former colonies. Underdevelopment is thus linked to 'colonialism', a term coined 100 years ago by the

French socialist Paul Louis but now part of the discourse of social theorists.

Centre–periphery models have also been employed in other areas, from politics to culture. For example, the American historian William McNeill organized his study of the Ottoman Empire in this way. The effectiveness with which he uses the model to account for change over several generations makes this an appropriate example to discuss in more detail. McNeill comes from the Middle West and taught at Chicago, and his study of what he calls 'Europe's steppe frontier' reveals an obvious debt to Frederick J. Turner. However, he is much more concerned than Turner with the nature of the relation between centre and periphery. His main thesis is that 'the centre could sustain organized military power on a large scale for an extended time only by preying upon peripheral communities'. The booty thus collected saved the regime from having to oppress the peasantry in its own central provinces. Conquest paid for itself. In addition – though McNeill does not lay much stress on this point – the so-called tribute of children (*devşirme*) collected from the Christian population of the conquered provinces encouraged a meritocratic system of administration (above, p. 65).

The empire was therefore geared to continuous conquest. The problem for the Ottomans was that conquest could not be sustained and the frontier expanded indefinitely. As McNeill argues persuasively, it was necessary to call a halt to this process of expansion for reasons which were fundamentally logistical. 'The only effective limit upon the expansion of Turkish power', he writes, 'was the distance the Sultan's army could travel from its winter quarters for the campaigning season.'

This limit was reached in the late sixteenth century, a time when the balance of power between the rival empires, Ottoman and Habsburg, led to a stalemate. The frontier zone between the empires was naturally ravaged by both sides, with the result that 'the very operations of the Turkish field armies tended . . . to create conditions at the extreme range of their effective radius of action that prevented them from going further'.

When expansion stopped, the political system began to disintegrate, and even the social structure began to change. The soldiers settled down on the land, and 'the drive toward hereditary succession among the military elite of the empire gathered strength'. One might add that the supply of Christian children available for recruitment into the elite probably dwindled. Taxes replaced plunder as the chief source of revenue, so that the burden on the peasantry increased. Local notables emerged, and the political system became less centralized. In short, the organization of the centre was transformed by changes which began on the periphery (McNeill 1964; cf. McNeill 1983).

Theorists and historians from Scandinavia, who often describe themselves as inhabitants of the periphery of Europe, have taken a particular interest in centres and peripheries in politics. For instance, the Norwegian political scientist Stein Rokkan has offered a typology of different possible relationships between territorial centres and their subject peripheries in the age of the formation of national states in Western Europe, examining the degree of 'centre distinctiveness', the degree of 'periphery integration', the strength of 'standardizing agencies' and so on (Tilly 1975: esp. 565–70).

The intellectual elegance of analyses in terms of a pair of opposed yet complementary concepts is extremely seductive. Using these concepts should encourage the pursuit of a fruitful yet relatively neglected line of historical enquiry. Historians are accustomed to study centralization, but they have scarcely begun to explore the process of 'peripheralization'. An obvious example comes from the history of language; the increasing political centralization of Britain and France in the nineteenth century was accompanied by the spread of English and French and the marginalization or peripheralization of Breton, Welsh, Irish, Occitan and so on. These languages did not disappear, but they did retreat, in the sense not only of being spoken by a smaller proportion of the population but also that of being excluded from certain domains – from schools, for example – or from the literary sphere, sometimes by the direct action of the state. Terms from dominant or central languages tended to invade the vocabulary of subordinate or peripheral ones (Certeau, Revel and Julia 1976; Grillo 1989).

On the other hand, there were counter-movements, movements of linguistic revival in the periphery, as in the case of the 'Renaissance' of Occitan and Catalan in the early nineteenth century. There were declarations of the independence of provincial or colonial forms of a language, as in the case of American English after 1776 and American Spanish after the wars of independence. The relationship between centre and periphery, in language and elsewhere, is rarely stable.

The history of knowledge is another domain that may be analysed in terms of centre and periphery. Information may take a long time to reach the periphery, as in the case of Spanish books exported to colonial Mexico and Peru. In some cases – Brazil, for instance – local universities did not exist in the colonial period. For higher education, students were expected to travel to the metropolis (more exactly, to Coimbra).

Again, the sociologist Bruno Latour has noted the importance of what he calls 'centres of calculation', usually located in cities, from ancient Alexandria to modern Paris, in which information coming in from different parts of the world is compared, criticized and classified. An analogy has been drawn between information flows and trade flows, the 'raw material' coming in from the periphery in order to be 'processed' at the centre. However, this is to diminish the importance of local informants whose contribution was not limited to specific concrete items. Whether or not their contribution was acknowledged, they sometimes provided the scholars at the centre with intellectual categories as well (Jacob 1992; Latour 1996; Burke 2000: 53–80).

'Periphery' is partly a matter of psychology, not just geography, a form of consciousness. Provincials often feel inferior, suffering from what Australians vividly describe as the 'cultural cringe' (Phillips 1958). They believe that their knowledge is out-of-date, just as their clothes are out of fashion. Xenophilia and the fashion for the foreign are recurrent features in Brazilian cultural history, for instance, though many other countries (from Russia to Argentina, or from Turkey to Japan) offer parallels.

Sometimes, though, the people of the periphery are self-consciously regionalist, and may resist the culture of the metropolis. They are not so much centripetal as centrifugal, creative and subversive. Revolts and heresies often start on the periphery, which may not have been fully conquered (in the case of imperial peripheries), and is usually controlled less closely. Peripheries are sometimes safe havens in the interstices between rival authorities. For this reason Voltaire decided to live in Ferney, on the border between France and Switzerland. At a time when book production in France was strictly controlled, the country was invaded by subversive books from across the border, in the seventeenth century from Amsterdam and in the eighteenth from Neuchâatel (Eisenstein 1992; Darnton 1995).

The concepts associated with 'centre' and 'periphery' have considerable value, then, in all sorts of contexts, but they also have their price – ambiguity, for instance. The term 'centre' is sometimes used in a literal (geographical) sense, but at other times in a metaphorical (political or economic) sense. As a result, statements like 'the centralization of France was the work of Louis XIV' are much less clear than they may seem at first sight.

Another problem arises from the fact that some analyses, Rokkan's for example, imply a view of society which stresses equilibrium, while others, such as Wallerstein's, emphasize conflicts. In the case of the theorists of underdevelopment, it has been argued that the crucial concept of 'surplus' needs clarification, and that insufficient evidence has been provided to demonstrate the economic dependence of the core on the politically dependent periphery. However, these criticisms do not imply that the concepts should be abandoned, only that they should be used with care, making discriminations between different types of centre – political, economic or even ideological.

For example, the American sociologist Edward Shils has analysed what he calls the 'central value system' of society and the central institutional system which it legitimates. 'It is central because of its intimate connection with what the society holds to be sacred; it is central because it is espoused by the ruling authorities of the society. These two kinds of centrality are vitally related. Each defines and supports the other' (Shils 1975: 2). For example, deference is allocated to individuals according to their closeness to the centre of society. In this way Shils links important (or even 'central') themes in the work of Durkheim (on the sacrality of the social order) and Weber (on the phenomenon of charisma).

Of the historical studies which make use of Shils's ideas, the most celebrated is surely that of divine kingship in nineteenth-century Bali by the anthropologist Clifford Geertz. In this study the author stresses what he calls the 'expressive nature' of the Balinese state and the theory of the 'exemplary centre' – that is, the idea that the ruler and his court are 'at once a microcosm of the supernatural order . . . and the material embodiment of political order'. The ruler sat immobile during court ceremonies in order 'to project an enormous calm at the centre of an enormous activity'. One of the most vivid illustrations of this enormous activity is the description of an elaborate procession ending in the cremation of a Balinese rajah who died in 1847, in which his concubines jumped into the flames, watched by a crowd of some 50,000 spectators. Yet the territory ruled by the rajah was small and his power limited. 'What was high centralization representationally was enormous dispersion institutionally' (C. Geertz 1980: 121, 122, 132).

The notion of a sacred or exemplary centre is equally relevant to Europe. In the seventeenth century, for example, the royal court was viewed as a microcosm of the universe. Planetary rooms in palaces and representations of kings as gods emphasized the analogy. Philip IV of Spain, for instance, was known as the 'planet king', and when he made his rare public appearances, he seemed to be as immobile as a statue – or a Balinese rajah. The Versailles of the 'Sun King' Louis XIV makes an even clearer example of an exemplary centre. The king's *lever* (which might be described as 'kingrise' on the analogy of sunrise) was an everyday ritual, like his eating and going to bed. The manners of the courtiers, their clothes and their vocabulary, were imitated in Paris and – with the usual few years' delay – in the provinces.

However, this imitation of the court does not imply that everyone in France admired or respected Louis XIV or the system of government he represented. Indeed, it may be argued more generally that Shils, like Durkheim, has overestimated social consensus and underestimated social conflict. By contrast, the Dutch sociologist W. F. Wertheim has emphasized the variety of value systems within the borders of a given society and the 'counterpoint' or clashes between them (1974: 105–20).

Another way of making this criticism might be to say that the fascinating analysis of centrality offered by Shils has not been matched by equal attention to the periphery, which appears to be little more than a residual concept, the 'non-centre'. In the words of a perceptive analysis of the historiography of Italian art, in many studies 'the periphery is only present as an area of shadow which serves to bring out the radiance of the metropolis' (Castelnuovo and Ginzburg 1979).

A more positive, constructive approach to the periphery might be to analyse it as the frontier has been analysed since the days of Frederick Jackson Turner, as a region favouring freedom and equality, a refuge for rebels and heretics. The Ukraine of the sixteenth and seventeenth centuries makes a good example of the frontier as a refuge. In the interstices between three powers (the Poles, the Russians and the Turks) an egalitarian community of Cossacks was able to flourish, recruiting its members from runaway serfs. In similar fashion, in seventeenth-century Brazil, slaves who fled from the harsh conditions of the sugar plantations of Bahia and Pernambuco found refuge in the uncolonized interior, where they set up free settlements known as *quilombos*.

If one takes a detached, global view of society, a periphery of this kind appears as a counterpart (perhaps a necessary counterpart) to the orthodoxy and respect for authority and tradition associated with the centre. To use the vocabulary of Albert Hirschman (1970), it adds a third option ('exit') to the conventional alternatives of protest ('voice') and conformity ('loyalty').

There seems to be a strong case for analysing the relationships between centres and peripheries in cultural as well as in economic and political terms (Wolf 1969: 278ff). For example, in the Ottoman Empire of the sixteenth and seventeenth centuries, high culture on the Persian model was predominant in the capital, Istanbul, and in the provincial centres. In frontier regions, on the other hand, what predominated was the popular culture of the warriors, together with the popular and sometimes unorthodox religion of the dervishes (Inalcik 1973). The boundary between Christianity and Islam was extremely permeable. Indeed, the frontier zone was the site of cultural exchanges, with Muslims visiting Christian shrines and paying reverence to Christian saints, and vice versa. Poles and Hungarians learned the use of light cavalry and the scimitar from their Turkish opponents, just as American and Canadian frontiersmen learned from the methods of warfare of the Native Americans. Indeed, it might be argued more generally (as it has been in the case of the French and Spanish Pyrenees) that – at least before the centralized states of the nineteenth and twentieth centuries – the men and women on each side of a political border have more in common with each other than they have with their respective centres (P. Sahlins 1989).

Hegemony and Resistance

One of the problems raised by the use of the paired concepts of 'centre' and 'periphery', as we have seen, is that of the relationship between the two, complementarity or conflict. A similar problem is raised by the use of the terms 'elite culture' and 'popular culture'. One possibility in this case is to replace the terms 'elite' and 'popular' by those of 'dominant' and 'subordinate' cultures, in order to analyse the relationship between the two in terms of 'hegemony'.

The question whether or not the values of the ruling class are accepted by the ruled at a particular place and time is obviously a difficult one to answer. If they are so accepted, why is resistance (not to mention open revolt) so frequent? If they are not accepted, how does the ruling class continue to rule? Does its power depend on coercion or consensus, or is there something in between? That there may be something of this kind was suggested by the Italian Marxist Antonio Gramsci. The key term he used, derived from the Russian Social Democratic movement, was 'hegemony' (*egemonia*) (P. Anderson 1976–7; Joll 1977; Femia 1981).

Gramsci's basic idea was that the ruling class did not rule only by force (or at any rate not by force alone) but also by persuasion, a combination of force and consensus. The persuasion was indirect: the subordinate or 'subaltern' classes (*classi subalterni*) learned to see society through their rulers' eyes thanks to their education and also to their place in the system.

The concept of hegemony did not attract much attention when Gramsci formulated it, but it has since enjoyed a revival. Indeed, it has been taken out of its original context to analyse a much wider range of situations, including the rule of elites at home and in empires, economic dominance within the world system and political dominance in the field of international relations (Lears 1985; Frank and Gills 1993). In the case of economic history, two complementary studies suggest that the period since 1970 may be described as one 'after hegemony' and the period before 1500 as 'before hegemony' (Keohane 1984; Abu-Lughod 1989).

In the case of culture, as a corrective to the inflation or dilution of the concept, it may be useful to ask the following three questions – questions which apply almost equally well to 'acculturation'.

1   Is hegemony a constant factor, or has it operated only in certain places and at certain times? If the latter, what are the conditions and the indicators of its presence?
2   Is the concept purely descriptive, or is it supposed to be explanatory as well? If the latter, is the explanation proposed one which refers to the conscious strategies of the ruling class (or of groups within it) or to what might be called the latent rationality of their actions?
3   How are we to account for the successful achievement of this hegemony? Does the ruling class simply impose its values on the subordinate classes, or is there some kind of compromise? Can hegemony be resisted with success? Can it be established without the collusion, connivance, collaboration or complicity of some at least of the dominated? Less glamorous than resistance, complicity has not attracted as much theorizing as it deserves.

In the last twenty years or so, the most important and influential employment and development of Gramsci's ideas has been in the field of Indian history, the work of a group of historians founded by Ranajit Guha who have published a series of collective volumes under the title *Subaltern Studies*. The group was founded in reaction against 'elitist' interpretations of the movement for Indian independence as the work of a small upper-class group (Chaturvedi 2000; Chakrabarty 2003).

By contrast, the subaltern historians stress the participation of the people, and especially the different forms of popular resistance to British rule in the age of Gandhi. Guha was dissatisfied with Eric Hobsbawm's description of the attitudes of peasants in pre-industrial societies as 'pre-political', and so, despite his concern with resistance rather than hegemony, he turned to Gramsci, whose view of the 'incalculable value' of 'every trace of independent initiative on the part of subaltern groups' has been an inspiration to this network of scholars (Guha 1983, 1997; Guha and Spivak 1990; Gramsci, quoted in Pandey 1995: 282).

In order to read popular resistance (riots, strikes and so on), and to reconstruct the attitudes underlying it, the subaltern historians, despite their original allegiance to Marxism, have drawn on later theorists ranging from Roland Barthes and Jacques Lacan to Michel Foucault and Jacques Derrida. Indeed, the Subaltern Studies Group is among the most theory-minded networks of historians to be found in the world today. In this respect it has been an inspiration to historians and critics in different parts of the world, from Ireland to Latin America.

All the same, it may be useful to range still more widely than Guha and his followers by introducing two more concepts into the discussion, 'symbolic violence' and 'negotiation'. 'Symbolic violence', another concept launched by Pierre Bourdieu, refers to the imposition of the culture of the ruling class on dominated groups, and especially to the process by which these dominated groups are forced to recognize the ruling culture as legitimate and their own culture as illegitimate (1972: 190–7). Examples range from the history of language – for instance, the pressure on dialect speakers to perceive their own speech as incorrect – to the history of popular healers who were turned into heretics or criminals by being labelled as 'witches' and forced to confess that their activities were literally diabolical.

As for the term 'negotiation', originally used by sociologists in a literal sense to analyse 'plea bargaining' by lawyers and their clients, it has been adapted to discuss the silent process of give and take between elites and subordinate groups. Thus an analysis of the British class system has argued that in general the underprivileged do not reject dominant values but 'negotiate or modify them in the light of their own existential conditions' (Strauss 1978: 224–33; Parkin 1971: 92).

Historians too have found the term useful, whether they are discussing the redefinition of the values of 'respectability' by the skilled workers of Victorian Edinburgh, or the relation between official and unofficial Catholicism in seventeenth-century Naples. The process by which saints were canonized in the Counter-Reformation Church was the result of such a process of negotiation between the periphery, in other words the region in which the cult of a local hero grew up, and the centre, Rome, where the ecclesiastical lawyers decided whether to accept or reject it. In the mission field, it has been argued that indigenous populations, in nineteenth-century Madagascar, for instance, were often able to influence the process of evangelization.

They were active agents, not just passive receivers of a new message. In other words, the form of Christianity that they adopted was the outcome of a process of negotiation (Gray 1976: Ch. 7; Burke 1987: 48–62; Larson 1997).

Alternatively, the subordinate classes – slaves, serfs, proletarians, farm hands and so on – may choose to resist rather than negotiate. The term 'resistance' covers a wide variety of forms of collective action, 'weapons of the weak' as the anthropologist James Scott calls them, such as 'pilfering, feigned ignorance . . . foot-dragging . . . sabotage . . . arson, flight', and so on. It has been described as 'Švejkism' after the 'good soldier Švejk' in the book by the Czech novelist Jaroslav Hašek describing the hero's resistance to the army by means of what another anthropologist, Frederick Bailey, describes as 'scrimshanking, flannelling, swinging the lead, wangling, fiddling, dodging' (J. C. Scott 1990: 188; F. G. Bailey 1993: 7–17).

As for foot-dragging, a remarkably vivid description of the process may be found in the reminiscences of the poet Gyula Illyés, who grew up on a large farm on the Hungarian plain, or *puszta*, at the beginning of the century. On the *puszta*, work for the farm servants was unremitting, long hours on weekdays and Sundays alike. Their reaction – like that of the farm animals – was to perform every action in slow motion. Illyés describes watching Uncle Róka fill his pipe with 'tortoise-like deliberation'. 'He handled the matches as if the matchstick in his hand were the last possible means of making fire and the fate of all mankind depended on it' (1967: 126–7). This style of behaviour may be seen as a form of resistance to excessive demands by the landowners and the overseers, 'an instinctive defence' as Illyés puts it. One wonders how many serfs and slaves in history have behaved in a similar manner.

Not only individual or group actions but cultural forms as well may be analysed in this way. Indeed, some students of popular culture go so far as to define it as a culture of resistance to the dominance of official or elite culture. The strategy adopted is defensive, appropriate to a position of subordination – subversion rather than confrontation, guerrilla tactics rather than open warfare – but resistance all the same (Certeau 1980; cf. Ahearne 1995: 162–4).

Resistance may take the defensive form of outward conformity plus concealment. When the slaves on the colonial plantations were obliged to accept Christianity, they concealed their traditional religion behind a Christian façade, finding equivalents for their gods among the saints, so that the West African god Legba, for instance, was equated with St Anthony, and Shango with St Barbara. In this way African cults were able to survive in the New World.

Alternatively, resistance may take the ambiguous form of mimicry – with differences which may be read from above as mistakes but viewed from below look more like mockery. Another way of describing this kind of mimicry is 'transgressive re-inscription', a phrase coined to draw attention to the way in which a subordinate or marginal group (the people, women, the colonized, gays . . .) adopts and adapts, or converts and subverts the vocabulary of a more respectable or powerful one (Bhabha 1994: 85–92; Dollimore 1991).

Social Protest and Social Movements

On occasion, of course, everyday resistance turns into open revolt or into some other form of 'social movement'. This term came into use among sociologists and political scientists in the United States in the 1950s, and has remained popular ever since (Tilly 1978; Tarrow 1994; Melucci 1996). One of the first historians to use it was Eric Hobsbawm, whose *Primitive Rebels* (1959) carries the subtitle 'Studies in Archaic Forms of Social Movement in the Nineteenth and Twentieth Centuries', and ranges from bandits to believers in the imminence of the millennium. His book was soon followed by a shelf of studies of millenarian movements in particular, the joint work of anthropologists, sociologists and historians.

A possible weakness in *Primitive Rebels* is its broad use of the term to include anything from a riot lasting only a few hours to permanent organizations, from the Carbonari to the Mafia. On the other hand, the value of Hobsbawm's study, and of the term 'social movement' more generally, is to direct attention to characteristics which are shared by religious and political movements, previously studied in isolation from each other.

Some of these movements may be described as 'active', taking the initiative in the pursuit of precise aims such as national independence, the abolition of slavery or votes for women. Although it is not customary to discuss the German Reformation as a social movement, it may be useful to follow the late Bob Scribner (1987) and to consider its early years in this way, stressing the importance of collective and popular action to change the existing order.

Other movements are better described as reactive, responding to changes that are already taking place and attempting to preserve a traditional way of life against threats from outside. Classic instances of such movements are the German Peasant War of 1525, responding to an increase in the demands made by landlords, and the Vendée of north-western France, reacting against the French Revolution. Still more defensive was the so-called revolt of Canudos, in the backlands of north-eastern Brazil, in 1896–7, a reaction against the establishment of the Brazilian Republic by a military coup in 1889. This reaction took the form of 'exit' rather than 'voice', of withdrawal and the foundation of a holy city rather than rebellion. All the same, the city was attacked and destroyed by the army (Levine 1992).

Among the questions one might ask about social movements are the following three.

(1)   In the first place, who is moving? What kind of person leads, and what kind of person follows? Many movements, religious and political alike, have leaders of the kind that Max Weber defined as 'charismatic', from St Francis or Martin Luther to Napoleon or Lenin. Weber defined charisma as a quality by virtue of which an individual is treated as 'endowed with supernatural, superhuman or at least specifically exceptional powers or qualities' (1920: i. 241).

In the case of Canudos, for instance, the charismatic leader was a wandering holy man, Antonio Conselheiro, an ascetic who made his reputation with prophecies of imminent disaster from which Brazil would be saved by the return of King Sebastian (who had died in 1578 fighting the Muslims in North Africa). Successful movements not infrequently have two leaders with complementary roles, the charismatic but unworldly leader who draws followers and the bureaucratic leader who takes charge of organization. Local leaders must not be forgotten, among them the clergy who played an important role in the Vendée and in similar movements elsewhere.

Weber has been criticized for overemphasizing the qualities of the leader, rather than the expectations of the followers who 'impute' these qualities (Shils 1975: 126–84; B. Anderson 1990: 78–93). One might ask whether there are kinds of follower who are particularly susceptible to charismatic leaders, the young for example. The young are often prominent in social movements, perhaps because their capacity for spontaneous action has not yet been dulled by routine, and because they have less to lose than their elders in the event of failure and repression. At all events, the young were prominent in the Reformation, the revolutions of 1848 and the movements of 1968 in Paris and Prague (Brigden 1982).

(2)   In the second place, what means are adopted to achieve the collective goals? A recurrent conflict within social movements is between participants who are prepared to use violence in pursuit of their goals and those, such as Gandhi in the movement for Indian independence,

who reject the use of force and attempt to find alternatives, from peaceful demonstrations to the boycott of foreign goods.

Following the sociologist Charles Tilly and others, we may speak of the different 'repertoires' of different movements. A recurrent element in peaceful movements is the signing of a petition and its presentation to the authorities. Another is the hunger strike, used by the suffragettes and the IRA alike to demand the status of political prisoners.

Even riots, however spontaneous in origin, draw on repertoires such as rituals which are familiar in a given culture, rituals which both legitimate popular action by presenting it as a procession or pilgrimage and also make it more persuasive by giving it dramatic form. Alternatively, they refer back to other riots by adopting traditional symbols such as the hanging of unpopular figures in effigy or placing a loaf on a spear as a protest against the price of bread.

(3) In the third place, what makes some movements more successful than others? A useful concept coined by social theorists is that of the successful 'mobilization' of resources such as arms, money and, above all, people (Tilly 1978: 69–84; Oberschall 1993; Melucci 1996: 289–312). One of the keys to mobilization is charismatic leadership, but another is the creation of organizations. In nineteenth-century Ireland, for instance, support for independence, or 'Home Rule', was mobilized by the creation of The Home Government Association, the Irish Republican Brotherhood, the Irish National League and even the Gaelic Athletic Association. Subscriptions from members not only helped to finance the movement, but also encouraged loyalty by the 'investors'.

The re-employment of organizations that are already in existence is a common procedure that helps explain why social movements are more successful in some places, with a strong 'culture of associations', than in others. In early modern Europe, religious confraternities formed the basic for the Catholic League, a militantly anti-Protestant organization which was a major player in the religious wars in sixteenth-century France. Indeed, the League, otherwise known as the 'Holy Catholic Union', may be regarded as a giant confraternity. A contemporary social movement that was originally based on pre-existing organizations is Silvio Berlusconi's Forza Italia, an organization of football supporters that turned into a political party, neatly illustrating Putnam's concept of 'social capital'.

Social movements are essentially fluid and informal, characterized by what Victor Turner called 'communitas'. As a result they cannot last very long in this form. Some of them wither away, while others are transformed by their own success. Growth leads to the 'routinization of communitas' – as Turner, adapting Weber's 'routinization of charisma', described it – or, more prosaically, to the development of permanent institutions such as the Franciscan Order, the Lutheran Church and the Communist Party. The 'movement' ceases to move (V. Turner 1969: 131ff).

Later, when successful organizations commission official histories of themselves, these histories generally give the impression that these bodies were consciously planned and institutionalized right from the start. It is prudent to be sceptical of such claims.

Mentalities, Ideologies, Discourses

The political problems of domination and resistance lead us back to the realm of culture, to questions of ethos, mentality or discourse. We have seen that the patron–client system depends on a culture of honour. The bureaucracies discussed earlier (p. 29) also depend on a particular ethos, including respect (some would say, excessive respect) for the formal rules which define this type of administrative system. Again, the hegemony of the ruling class depends on a certain degree of acceptance by the subordinate classes. In each case it is impossible to comprehend the workings of the system without understanding the attitudes and values of the participants.

One might therefore claim with some justice that it is impossible to write social history without the history of ideas, provided that the phrase is understood as the history of everyone's ideas rather than the ideas of the most original thinkers of a given epoch. This history of ideas in the wide sense is associated with two rival concepts, mentality and ideology.

The history of mentalities began as a Durkheimian approach to ideas, although Durkheim himself preferred the term 'collective representations'. It was developed by Durkheim's follower Lucien Lévy-Bruhl in studies such as *La Mentalité primitive* (1927) (Burke 1997: 162–82). Contemporary sociologists and anthropologists are more likely to speak of 'modes of thought', 'belief systems' or 'cognitive maps'.

Whatever the term used, the approach differs from conventional intellectual history in at least three features. In the first place, there is a stress on collective attitudes rather than individual ones, on what might be called 'communities of belief'. In the second place, there is an emphasis on unspoken assumptions rather than explicit theories

– in other words, on 'common sense' or, more exactly, what appears to be common sense in a particular culture. In the third place, there is a concern with the structure of belief systems, including the categories used to interpret experience and the dominant methods of proof and persuasion, categories and methods shared by individuals who may disagree about many things. There is an obvious parallel between these three features of the history of mentalities and the approach of Michel Foucault in *The Order of Things* (1966) to what he liked to call the 'archaeology' of systems of thought or 'epistemes'.

An example of the kind of problem which the mentalities approach helps to solve is the medieval ordeal. The fact that in the early Middle Ages guilt or innocence was sometimes determined by an ordeal such as carrying a red-hot iron or plunging the suspect's hand into boiling water has long been a stumbling-block to the understanding of the period. As the eighteenth-century Scottish historian William Robertson remarked, 'Among all the whimsical and absurd institutions which owe their existence to the weakness of human reason, this . . . appears to be the most extravagant and preposterous.'

In the later twentieth century, however, a series of studies appeared which took the custom of the ordeal seriously and tried to render it more intelligible by investigating the assumptions of the participants. The ancient historian Peter Brown (1975), for example, suggested that the ordeal functioned as an instrument of consensus. Other historians reject this particular conclusion, but share Brown's concern to replace the ordeal in its cultural context. It may indeed be concluded that the history of mentalities has survived its own trial by ordeal (cf. Morris 1975; Bartlett 1986).

A similar problem provoked a pioneering study by Marc Bloch, *The Royal Touch* (1924). Bloch, whose admiration for Durkheim has already been discussed, wrote the history of the belief that the kings of France and England had the miraculous power to cure sufferers from a skin disease, scrofula, by touching them. This power was a sign of their charisma, a concept which Weber had recently formulated but of which Bloch was probably not aware. The belief in the royal touch persisted for many centuries. In England, the practice lasted till the reign of Queen Anne (among the sufferers she touched was a small boy called Samuel Johnson). In France, it persisted until the Revolution, and was revived by Charles X in 1825.

Bloch started from the assumption that the kings and queens of England and France did not actually have the power to cure skin disease, and went on to consider why this 'collective illusion', as he called it, was able to persist for so long. He stressed the fact that people expected a miracle. If the symptoms of the disease disappeared, they therefore gave the king the credit. On the other hand, if the symptoms did not disappear, that only showed that the sick person needed to be touched again. Bloch also noted that the propensity to believe something which was contradicted by experience is 'an essential trait of the so-called "primitive" mentality', discussed by Lévy-Bruhl (Bloch 1924: 421 n.).

In France, the history of mentalities has been part of historical practice from the 1960s onwards. It was relatively slow to attract the British, however, and when it finally did so, it arrived by a somewhat roundabout route. The British anthropologist Edward Evans-Pritchard was inspired by Durkheim and Lévy-Bruhl to study the belief system of the Azande (who live in Central Africa). Evans-Pritchard emphasized the self-confirming character of the Zande poison oracles in a manner reminiscent of Bloch – whom he had read when he was a student of medieval history – on the royal touch (Evans-Pritchard 1937: 194). It was thanks to Evans-Pritchard and other anthropologists that modes of thought and belief systems came to interest British historians, notably Keith Thomas in his *Religion and the Decline of Magic* (1971).

The history of mentalities has proved itself to be an extremely fruitful approach to the past, and Bloch's book is only one of the masterpieces of the genre. All the same, in the course of solving traditional problems, new problems arose. The most serious of these may be called the problem of 'immobilization'. Historians have proved much more successful at describing mentalities at a particular point in the past than at explaining how, when or why they changed (G. E. R. Lloyd 1990).

Foucault's *Order of Things* also suffers from this weakness, as many critics have pointed out. The weakness is closely associated with one of the great strengths of the approach, the assumption of a belief system in which each part depends on the rest. As Evans-Pritchard wrote, 'In this web of belief, every strand depends on every other strand.' This assumption allows historians to explain the persistence of a certain mentality over time despite the existence of awkward empirical evidence. The more satisfying the explanation of persistence, however, the harder it is to explain a change of mentality when it eventually does occur.

A second major problem raised by the history of mentalities might be called the problem of 'homogenization'. To focus on collective mentalities is to forget that individuals do not think exactly alike. To this objection, one might respond in the words of the French historian Jacques Le Goff (1974), who suggests that the term 'mentality' be used only to describe the beliefs which individuals have in common with the rest of their group.

A still more serious problem arises from the fact that historians of mentalities easily slip into assuming the existence of a binary opposition between two belief systems, the 'traditional' and the 'modern', reproducing in different words the distinction made by Lévy-Bruhl between what he called 'prelogical' and 'logical' thought. Modern thought is viewed as more abstract, less dependent on context, and more 'open' in the sense that there are a number of competing systems available, with the result that individuals are more easily aware of alternatives to their own beliefs. By contrast, a Zande man, to quote Evans-Pritchard once more, cannot escape from his 'web of belief' because 'it is the only world he knows' (Horton 1967, 1982; Gellner 1974: 18).

To demonstrate the problems inherent in such an opposition, one might try a simple experiment, that of reading in quick succession two classics in the field, Marcel Granet's *La Pensée chinoise* (1934) and Lucien Febvre's *Le Problème de l'incroyance* (1942). The characteristics attributed to the traditional Chinese and the sixteenth-century French seem very much alike. They are both defined by contrast to the twentieth-century French intellectual, and the contrast between Them and Us reduces the variety of the 'other' to uniformity. This kind of reduction is the price of structural analysis (below, p. 134).

Some of the difficulties associated with the concept of collective mentalities are avoided by an analysis in terms of 'ideology', an approach to the history of thought built on Marxist foundations and developed by German 'sociologists of knowledge' such as Karl Mannheim (1936), who studied what he called 'styles of thought' and the bonds between kinds of knowledge and social situations. The rise of interest in this approach to ideas took place between the wars, in other words during the rise of the rival ideologies of communism and fascism.

'Ideology' is a term with many – too many – definitions. Some people use the term in a pejorative sense – I have beliefs, he (or she) has an ideology. Others treat it as neutral, as a synonym for 'world-view' (Geuss 1981: ch. 1; J. B. Thompson 1990: ch. 1). A useful distinction between two concepts of ideology was made by Mannheim. The first, which he called the 'total' conception of ideology, suggests that there is an association between a particular set of beliefs or view of the world and a particular social group or class, thus implying that Bloch and Febvre were wrong to discuss the mentality of the medieval or the sixteenth-century French without making social distinctions.

The second, which Mannheim called the 'particular' conception of ideology, is the notion that ideas or representations may be utilized to maintain a particular social or political order. For example, the idea of democracy may be used to 'mystify', to conceal the extent to which power is exercised by a small group. Alternatively, ideas may justify (or, as Weber would say, 'legitimate') the system, often by representing the political order as natural rather than cultural, the king for example as the sun. These conceptions of ideology were elaborated at the end of the 1960s by the French philosopher Louis Althusser (1970), who described ideology as referring to 'the imaginary [or 'imagined'] relationship of individuals to their real conditions of existence'. No longer limited to forms of what Marx called 'false consciousness', ideology has become virtually indistinguishable from the collective imagination.

The relationship between mentalities and ideologies may be in some need of clarification (Vovelle 1982: esp. 1–12). For this purpose it may be useful to return to the royal touch. Marc Bloch's classic study treated the belief in the royal touch as if it was 'innocent'. An analysis in terms of ideology, on the other hand, would stress the fact that it was in the interests of the royal regime that ordinary people should believe that the king had the power to work miracles. Charisma was not a natural property of the kings of France and England. It was in a sense manufactured, produced by royal robes, rituals and so on.

Although the contrast between mentalities and ideologies is a useful one, attempts to analyse the ways in which ideas sustain political systems have brought difficulties to light, not unlike the difficulties associated with the concept 'hegemony' (above, p. 88). Ideology has often been treated as a kind of 'social cement' holding society together. However, its importance in this respect has been challenged in a series of studies which criticize Marxists and Durkheimians alike. These studies suggest, for instance, that the social cohesion of liberal democracy is negative, rather than positive; in other words, that it depends not on a consensus over the fundamental values embodied in the regime but rather on a lack of consensus over criticisms of the government (Abercrombie, Hill and Turner 1980; J. B. Thompson 1990: 3).

A third concept, which occupies some of the same intellectual space as mentalities and ideologies and has come into regular use in the last twenty years or so, is 'discourse', displacing attention from thoughts to the media in which they are expressed – speech, images or texts. Linguists were already speaking of 'discourse analysis' in the 1950s to refer to the study of units longer than the sentence, whether they were fragments of conversation or paragraphs from a book. However, it was only when Foucault took up the term that it spread across the disciplines.

In his *Archaeology of Knowledge* (1969), Foucault introduced the word 'discourse' (*discours*) as part of his double critique of what he considered the illusions of 'truth' and the 'individual'. A discourse, he suggested, 'constructs' the topic with which it is concerned, so that there are different 'regimes of truth' expressed in different discourses, rather than objective descriptions of reality. This problem will be discussed below (p. 100).

Another reason for Foucault's introduction of the term 'discourse' was to criticize the common-sense notion of a text written by a certain individual and expressing his or her ideas. For Foucault, on the contrary, a discourse is a collective construction. A particular text should be viewed as part of a larger system or repertoire of texts, to which it consciously or unconsciously refers. It follows 'an ensemble of rules which characterize a discursive practice', selecting from a common store or repertoire (Foucault 1969: ch. 2; for a synthesis of the discourses of the linguists and of Foucault, see Fairclough 1995).

A similar point about what has become known as 'intertextuality' had been made earlier, without the term 'discourse', by the Russian literary theorist Mikhail Bakhtin (1981), who suggested that we should listen to texts as if they were in conversation with one another, responding to one another. This idea was part of a more general theory of 'dialogue' (cf. Morson and Emerson 1990: 52–62; Holquist 1990).

Foucault's concept was taken up by Edward Said, whose book *Orientalism* (1978) defined its subject as a discourse which created 'the Orient' as well as an institution employed by 'the West' to dominate the Near East. Trained as a literary critic, Said offered a close analysis of a number of Western texts about the East, whether by travellers such as Richard Burton, novelists such as Gustave Flaubert, or scholars such as Ernest Renan. His analysis draws attention to what he calls their 'schematization of the Orient' via stereotypes such as passivity, sensuality and degeneracy. In this way the texts legitimated Western rule by portraying Orientals as unfit to govern themselves, feminizing them in order to justify the intervention of aggressively masculine imperialists (Said 1978, criticized in MacKenzie 1995).

A generation earlier, Said might have written the same book but described it differently. He might have called his book a study of the 'rhetoric' of Orientalism, or even of 'the Orientalist mentality' – though these formulations would not have allowed him to emphasize the place of texts in the support of empires. He might also have described Orientalism as an 'ideology' rather than a 'discourse'.

'Discourse', like 'mentality', is an imprecise term. The imprecision may be part of the attraction in both cases (as in that of 'culture'), but it also leads to problems when one tries to work with the concept. When and where, for example, does one discourse end and another begin? Is there one 'colonial discourse', for example, or are there several? Is it useful to distinguish discourses according to social groups (rulers and ruled, clergy and laity, doctors and lawyers) as well as by place and time?

Where would this process of distinguishing stop? The individual, expelled through the door by Foucault, might return through the window as the author of a particular selection and combination from a cultural repertoire. As a sixteenth-century editor of a collection of texts on politics once wrote, 'nothing is mine' because the texts were written by others, but 'everything is mine', because he had arranged them and thus given them meaning.

Vagueness is not the only problem. To focus on discourse is to carry out an internal analysis of a text without concern for context. This context includes readers and listeners.

Communication and Reception

From discourse it is only a step to the idea of communication, which has long been a focus of interest in a number of disciplines, as four examples may illustrate. Coming from the study of politics, Harold Lasswell (1936) once defined the objects of such a study in his usual vigorous manner as 'Who says what to whom, and with what effects' (implying that these 'effects' were measurable). Coming from literature, Raymond Williams (1962) offered a slightly softer definition, with more emphasis on form: 'the institutions and forms in which ideas, information and attitudes are transmitted and received'. Coming from linguistics, Joshua Fishman offered another variation on the theme when he proposed 'the study of who speaks what language to whom and when', emphasizing the propensity of many speakers to switch languages or forms of language in different situations or 'speech domains'. Coming from anthropology, Dell Hymes took an even wider view of the topic, recommending an ethnography of communicative events which would take account not only of messages, senders and receivers, but of 'channels', 'codes' and 'settings' (Giglioli 1972).

Inspired by Hymes, Fishman and their colleagues, some historians are working on the social history of language, its changing forms and its various functions (Burke and Porter 1987, 1991). For instance, language, like consumption, is a means for some social groups to distinguish themselves from others. As a concrete example one might take Thorstein Veblen's (1899) assertion that the manner of speaking of the leisure class was necessarily 'cumbrous and out of date', because such usages implied a waste of time and so 'exemption from the use and need of direct and forcible speech'.

Sociolinguists have also had much to say about the use of language as a status symbol. One of the best-known examples is the discussion of upper-class and non-upper-class English usage ('U' and 'non-U') in the 1950s, in which it was claimed that the term 'looking-glass' was U, while 'mirror' was non-U; 'writing-paper' U, 'notepaper' non-U, and so on (Burke and Porter 1987: 4–5). In similar fashion in seventeenth-century France, François de Callières, who was private secretary to Louis XIV, pointed out differences between what he called 'bourgeois ways of speaking' (*façons de parler bourgeoises*) and the vocabulary characteristic of the aristocracy. In these cases, the choice of any particular term appears to be arbitrary, motivated by the desire of the aristocrats to distinguish themselves from the bourgeoisie, who in turn change their speech patterns to resemble the aristocracy, who are therefore constantly compelled to innovate.

An alternative strategy was the everyday use by certain elites of foreign languages, such as French in nineteenth-century Russia, eighteenth-century Prussia, and the Netherlands in the seventeenth century. This was at once a means of distinguishing them from people lower in the social scale and an expression of homage to Paris as the centre of civilization. Veblen might have added that communicating with native speakers of one's own language in a foreign language makes conspicuous the leisure of 'leisure classes'.

So far we have been considering the communicators, their intentions and strategies. What of the audiences and their responses? In this area literary theorists such as Hans-Robert Jauss (1974) and Wolfgang Iser have made an important contribution, emphasizing the role in the construction of meaning of readers and their 'horizon of expectations' (a phrase derived from the German philosophical tradition) (cf. Culler 1980: 31–83; Holub 1984: 38–63). In similar fashion the French theorist Michel de Certeau (1980) stressed the creativity of ordinary people and their active reinterpretations of the messages beamed at them by the television screen and other media. Central concepts in this discussion are 'appropriation', used by

Michel Foucault and Paul Ricoeur, and 're-employment', used by Certeau. An extreme case of this process is the 'transgressive re-inscription' mentioned above (p. 92).

Historians would obviously be ill-advised to take sides on the ultimately metaphysical question whether the 'real' meanings are to be found in the texts or whether they are projected on to them. On the other hand, the empirical question of the differences between the message transmitted and the message received by viewers, listeners or readers in different times and places is clearly of historical importance. Luther, for example, once complained that the German peasants misunderstood his teaching when they claimed that serfdom should be abolished because Christ died for all men.

The term 'horizon' has sometimes been criticized as too vague, but a concern with the expectations of receivers of messages is as illuminating as other forms of history 'from below'. These expectations are often collective, so that terms such as 'textual communities' and 'communities of interpretation' have come into use (once again, the indispensability of the term 'community' becomes apparent).

The problem of reception is central to what has become known as the 'history of reading'. In a famous passage of his *Cheese and Worms* (1976), Carlo Ginzburg discussed the mental 'grids' through which the heretical miller Menocchio read certain books and the discrepancies between his reading of the religious literature of the late Middle Ages and the orthodox readings of the Inquisitors (cf. Foucault 1971: 11). Roger Chartier (1987), who acknowledges his intellectual debt to Certeau, and Robert Darnton (1991) are among the historians who have made more systematic explorations of this kind, focusing on eighteenth-century France and reconstructing readers' views of particular texts via the study of annotations, the records of lending libraries, and letters from readers to famous authors such as Jean-Jacques Rousseau.

The growing interest in the history of translation and the differences between original works and the versions published in other languages is also part of the general shift of interest from production to reception. Art historians too are increasingly concerned with responses to images. Iconoclasm, for example, whether directed against images of devils or images of saints, has been studied as evidence enabling us to reconstruct the point of view of long-dead spectators (Freedberg 1989: 378–428). The greater the cultural distance between the receiver and the original sender, the more can be learned by studying the responses of readers, listeners and viewers.

Reception studies of this kind raise some difficult questions. If we accept Certeau's view of the creativity of reception, the distance between originals and copies or between messages sent and messages received, there is more than one way to explain the differences. If we speak of 'reinterpretation', we imply that the activity is conscious. If we speak of 'misinterpretation', we imply that it is unconscious (as well as incompetent). In many cases it is impossible to decide between these alternatives, and difficult to do more than register the fact that what from the sender's point of view is a misunderstanding, may be a creative adaptation in the eyes of posterity.

There remains the problem of differences in receptivity, not only at the level of the readers of a particular text, but at the level of whole cultures. What makes some cultures relatively open (or vulnerable) to influences from outside, while others are better able to resist these influences – indeed unable to do anything else? Africanists have gone furthest in explaining why some peoples – the Ibo, for instance – display remarkable receptivity to change, while others, like the Pakot, show equally remarkable resistance. They contrast highly integrated cultures, which tend to be closed, with others which have more internal conflicts and are therefore more open (Braudel 1949: ii. 704; Bascom and Herskovits 1959: 180–67).

It also appears that a tradition of receptivity to foreign influence can be built up over time. The Japanese, for example, were already accustomed to adapt Chinese ideas, practices and institutions long before their encounter with the West, and this helps explain the speed and success with which they appropriated different elements of Western culture, especially from the middle of the nineteenth century onwards. Yet it might be unwise to offer an explanation of this tradition of innovation in terms of the Japanese character, without investigating differences between social groups or indeed between cultural domains.

The problems of appropriation, receptivity and cultural distance are major themes in what has become known as 'Postcolonial Studies'.

Postcolonialism and Cultural Hybridity

'Postcolonialism' is a relatively new term, not yet accepted by the *Oxford English Dictionary*. 'Neocolonialism' dates from the beginning of the 1960s, as part of an argument by the Left that 'decolonization' was more apparent than real. Even the term 'Colonialism', used to describe a political system, goes back no further than the late nineteenth century (above, p. 82).

As for 'Postcolonial Studies', it is, like the 'Cultural Studies' on which it is modelled, a kind of interdisciplinary discipline dominated by specialists in literature, especially literature in English, who have turned to texts produced in the former colonies and also to theory, whether literary, linguistic, cultural, psychological, social, economic or political (Moore-Gilbert 1997; Young 2001). Why specialists in literature should have played such a central role in the cultivation of this field is an intriguing question. One answer might be that they are more open to theory than (say) historians are. Alternatively, it might be claimed that literary critics were looking for a new activity following the crisis of the 'canon' – that is, the loss of faith in an educational curriculum based on a selection of 'classic' texts, most of them written by DWMs (dead white males).

In any case, a new field has come into existence, combining a concern with literary texts and the cultures – colonial, neocolonial or postcolonial – in which they are embedded. The colonies or ex-colonies studied are usually British, despite a body of work on Latin America as well as attempts to extend the approach still further. Following Edward Said, the idea of 'discourse' in general, and 'colonial discourse' in particular, has become central in these studies (Washbrook 1999). Two major themes recur: identity and hybridity.

It was the Black American writer W. E. B. Du Bois who coined the term 'double consciousness' to describe his sense of being both American and African (Gilroy 1993: 30, 111–45). The problem of postcolonial identity has been studied with special reference to writers, and it has often been posed in terms of 'displacement'. Many writers who identify themselves as Indian, say, or African write in the language of their former colonial masters. What does this language mean for them? In a sense they are exiles in their own land, or indeed 'out of place' everywhere, as Edward Said put it in some of his poignant reflections on exile. A milder version of the problem surfaces in the work of writers whose mother tongue is English but to whom the English literary tradition is alien because they live so far from the metropolis. We have returned to the topic of centres and peripheries.

For an exemplary discussion of the problem we may turn to the Brazilian critic Roberto Schwarz. Writing about the great nineteenth-century novelist Machado de Assis, Schwarz launched the idea of 'ideas out of place', pointing to the contradiction between the enthusiasm for French and English ideas among the educated Brazilians of Machado's time and the realities of a society based on slavery. Machado was 'a master on the periphery of capitalism', writing in Portuguese, familiar with French and English literary traditions, but targeting a public in his own country. How could he avoid imitating the culture of the centre and find his own voice? By using the vocabulary of Europe, Schwarz suggests, but employing it to say something different (1992: 19–32).

It is this kind of difference that has been explored by the theorists of cultural hybridity. The anthropologists who first discussed what they called 'acculturation' made two assumptions about the process that have subsequently been challenged: in the first place, that change was one-way, that subordinate cultures imitated dominant ones; and in the second place, that change took the form of imitation rather than adaptation.

The Cuban sociologist Fernando Ortiz argued that 'acculturation' was a misnomer, and that a more appropriate term would be 'transculturation', implying that culture contacts affected both sides, in the Cuban case the dominant Spanish as well as the dominated African and Amerindian cultures (Ortiz convinced Malinowski to adopt this suggestion). In similar fashion, Gilberto Freyre noted that African and Amerindian cultures influenced the Portuguese in Brazil, as well as the other way round, a process of change that he described as 'interpenetration'. (Freyre 1933; Ortiz 1940). Today, it has become common to speak of cultural 'exchange'.

The idea of imitation has since been replaced by that of adaptation. Adaptation need not be conscious: one of Freyre's examples was that of black carpenters in Brazil copying Chippendale chairs and turning their angles into curves, thanks to the power of African cultural traditions. At times, though, adaptation is a conscious project. Machado de Assis – like many Asian, African and American writers after him – drew on the European tradition of the novel in order to say something about his own country. Again, some European missionaries deliberately followed a practice they called 'accommodation', in other words the adaptation of the Christian message to different cultures in China, Japan, India and elsewhere.

The result of these processes is the formation of texts, religions and whole cultures which are often described as 'hybrid' or 'mixed'. In the case of religion, where an earlier generation of historians spoke with confidence of 'conversion', scholars are increasingly inclined to see local forms of Christianity, for example, as drawing on (say) African or Japanese traditions as much as on European ones, as in the Malagasy example cited above. The traditional term in analysing this interaction between religions is 'syncretism'.

The term 'syncretism' suffers from certain disadvantages. It needs to be liberated from the pejorative overtones given it by missionaries who use it to describe unsuccessful Christianization. An impersonal term, it encourages us to overlook the role of individual agents in the interaction between religions. All the same, it remains useful as an 'umbrella term' covering a variety of processes that may be distinguished. For example, we might distinguish action from above by missionaries and rulers, and action from below, as in the case of the slaves who called their god Legba 'St Anthony' (above, p. 91). Or we might contrast a temporary coexistence of elements from different religions with a formal synthesis (Pye 1993; Stewart and Shaw 1994).

Outside the religious sphere, one of the most common terms for describing the results of cultural exchange is 'cultural hybridity' (Canclini 1989). 'Hybridity' is a metaphor from zoology which was used by anthropologists and others to speak of racial interbreeding before it was employed to discuss culture. Like 'syncretism', it suffers from the disadvantage of making the results of culture contact seem automatic, as if individuals had no place in the process. For this reason it seems preferable to employ a linguistic metaphor and to speak of cultural 'translation' (Pálsson 1993). Individual translators adapt exotic items (texts, religions, styles of building and so on) to local cultural contexts, and these adaptations are sometimes successful in the sense of being taken up by other people and eventually becoming part of local tradition.

Out of the process of mixing and adaptation arise new cultural forms and even new cultures. This was the aspect of hybridization emphasized by Mikhail Bakhtin, who seems to have developed the concept independently of the anthropologists. Writing about the rise of vernacular literatures in the European Renaissance, for instance, he emphasized their interaction with Latin and also with one another. This 'interanimation', as he called it, of languages and literatures encouraged the awareness of alternatives, and so stimulated creativity (Bakhtin 1965: 81–2; cf. Morson and Emerson 1990: 142–5, 325–44).

This creative process is not confined to language, although it is illuminating to describe it by means of another linguistic metaphor, 'creolization'. Generalizing from studies of the Caribbean, linguists have come to employ this term to describe the situation in which a former pidgin develops a more complex structure. Building on their affinities or congruences, two languages in contact become more like each other, 'converging' to create something new.

Generalizing from this model, the Swedish anthropologist Ulf Hannerz has described creole cultures as those that have had time 'to move towards a degree of coherence' and 'can put things together in new ways'. Historians of colonial Jamaica have illustrated this process of reshaping in studies of African-American religion, music, housing, clothing and cuisine (Hannerz 1987; Buisseret and Reinhardt 2000).

In some cases the theorists of adaptation have themselves adapted and re-employed the concepts of earlier critics of colonialism, including poets and novelists. (Moore-Gilbert 1997: 179–84). Such re-employment is characteristic of the development of new disciplines – it was noted above (p. 10), for example, that in the early years of sociology, Max Weber borrowed the idea of charisma from historians of the Church.

A more distinctive feature of studies of postcolonialism is the contribution made by scholars from outside the West, even if these scholars are often Westernized or even culturally hybrid, like the Palestinian-American Said or the expatriate Indians Homi Bhabha and Gayatri Spivak, who have all experienced the process of displacement that they analyse. The pioneering study of 'transculturation' was the work of a Cuban, Ortiz, and that of hybridity by a Brazilian, Freyre, who advocated what he called the 'tropicalization' of social theory, modifying generalizations that had been based on too narrow a range of human experience, mainly in the temperate zones of the world. Postcolonial studies offer an unusual opportunity for opposing the hegemony of Western theory and allowing other voices to be heard. They provide a supportive environment for what the Argentinian scholar Walter Mignolo (2000) calls 'border thinking', ideas that subvert or go beyond simple dichotomies.

Problems, as always, remain: the problem of deciding which cultures count as 'postcolonial', for instance (the term has sometimes been extended to Canada, to Ireland and to China); the problem of distinguishing between the deeper and the more superficial forms of Europeanization; the problem of making a synthesis between the approaches of literary critics, anthropologists and historians (perhaps we should speak of 'syncretism' in this context). All the same, the focus on exchange and mixture is renewing the study of cultural history.

Orality and Textuality

One form of hybridity that has not yet been discussed is the result of interaction between the oral and the written, or the oral and the printed. It has often been observed that African novelists, from Amos Tutuola to Chinua Achebe, keep closer to colloquial speech and oral traditions than most of their European colleagues.

Oral communication has its own style or styles. A famous study of rumour argued that in the course of oral transmission, messages are adapted to the needs of the receivers in a process which involves simplification ('levelling'), selection ('sharpening') and the assimilation of the unknown to the known (Allport and Postman 1947). An equally celebrated study of oral epics in Bosnia suggested that the stories were improvised by the singer thanks to the use of prefabricated elements, notably 'formulae' (set phrases like Homer's 'wine-dark sea') and 'themes' (recurrent episodes such as councils and battles). On the basis of studies of this kind, the media theorist Walter Ong has described the basic characteristics of 'orally based thought and expression', notably redundancy and a structure that adds one statement to another rather than subordinating one to another (Lord 1960: esp. 80–98; Ong 1982: 31–77).

These analyses and debates have had a somewhat delayed impact on historical writing. Studies of oral cultures in the past are only now beginning to appear (Fox and Woolf 2003). Even historical studies of rumour remain relatively rare, despite the example of Georges Lefebvre, who devoted a whole book to the spread of the so-called Great Fear of 1789. Lefebvre (1932) made a meticulous analysis of the chronology, geography and sociology of the propagation of rumours of an aristocratic plot and of imminent attacks by 'brigands', explaining these 'panics' in terms of the economic, social and political situation at a time when bread was scarce and discontent was turning into revolution. In similar fashion, the rumour current in Paris in 1750 that the government of Louis XV was kidnapping children has been interpreted as a concrete expression of a more diffuse discontent with the regime (Farge and Revel 1988).

Lefebvre had less to say about the different versions of these rumours, and we are still waiting for someone to analyse the anxieties of 1789 or (say) the English Protestant fears of a 'Popish Plot' in 1678 in terms of the 'levelling' and 'sharpening' processes, or of the assimilation of recent events to traditional themes of oral narrative such as plots, poisoning and kidnapping. Rumours of the return of a lost leader, from King Sebastian of Portugal to the Mexican revolutionary Emiliano Zapata or the Indian nationalist leader Subhas Chandra Bose, make another series of examples of the reactivation of a traditional folktale in a particular political situation to express collective discontents with the present and hopes for the future.

Despite the rise of 'oral history' in the last generation, it is only recently that historians have devoted serious attention to oral tradition as an art-form. It is instructive in this respect to compare the first edition of the study of oral tradition by the Belgian anthropologist-historian Jan Vansina, published in 1961, which concentrates almost exclusively on the problem of reliability, with the second edition of 1985, which is more concerned with the forms and genres of communication.

Writing too is increasingly investigated as a medium with special qualities and limitations. The British anthropologist Jack Goody, for example, has published a series of studies of the consequences of literacy, claiming that the traditional contrast between two 'mentalities', primitive and modern, is better described as one between two modes of communication, the oral and the written (Goody 1977). For example, it is much easier to rearrange a written list than a memorized one. In this way writing encourages abstraction. Again, writing promotes the awareness of alternatives, which transforms a closed system into an open one. In this sense 'writing restructures consciousness', as Ong puts it (1982: 78–116). In similar fashion the psychologist David Olson has put forward a theory of literacy, or at least a series of 'principles', noting that literacy heightens consciousness of speech, and that 'thought about assumptions, inferences and conjectures, concepts which depend critically upon the concept of literal meaning, is distinctive of literate discourse' (1994: 257–82).

These arguments have been criticized for overemphasizing the difference between oral and written modes, for neglecting the qualities of oral communication and for treating literacy as a neutral technique which can be detached from its context (Street 1984, 1993). The criticisms qualify rather than undermine the central thesis, but they imply that it would be more useful to speak of 'literacies' in the plural, allowing for differences between alphabetic, syllabic and ideographic systems, and also for the religious, commercial and other contexts in which literacy is learned.

The debate about the 'Great Divide', and the conclusion that we should think in terms of a continuum rather than a chasm between oral and literate cultures or mentalities, has suggested new directions for research, focusing on the interaction or 'interface' between the oral and the written (Goody 1987). For example, formulae and themes are to be found in written texts as well as in oral performances. Do they take different forms, or are they used in different ways? What is changed when a folktale is written down, especially when it is written down by a member of an elite?

Another relatively new focus of attention is writing at second hand. For example, illiterates have letters written for them by friends, the parish priest or the professional scribe, whether the clients dictate to the writer or simply explain what kind of letter they want. Public writers of this kind can be found today on Plaza Santo Domingo in

Mexico City, as they could be found in seventeenth-century Paris in the cemetery of the Innocents, where tombs were used as makeshift desks (Kalman 1999; Métayer 2000).

A striking feature of this debate is its contrast between orality and literacy at the expense of a third medium, print. In the case of West Africa, from which so many examples have been taken, literacy and print arrived at much the same time, so that their consequences are difficult to disentangle. In the case of Europe, on the other hand, there is a long-standing debate on the print 'revolution'. It used to be discussed simply in terms of the diffusion of books, ideas and movements (especially the Protestant Reformation), but attention has been turning from the message to the medium.

The American critic Marshall McLuhan, for example, claimed that printing was responsible for a shift of emphasis from the auditory to the visual (thanks in part to the increasing use of diagrams), and also for what he called a 'split between heart and head'. The American historian Elizabeth Eisenstein translated McLuhan into academically respectable form in her study of 'the printing press as an agent of change', which emphasized such features of 'print culture' as the standardization and the preservation or 'fixing' of texts (McLuhan 1962; Eisenstein 1979: 43–159).

In similar fashion, Ong (whose early historical work had inspired McLuhan in the first place), described the way in which print reinforces writing in bringing about the 'shift from sound to visual space' and encouraging 'a sense of closure', of a definitive text (Ong 1982: 117–38). For their part, scholars who have studied transmission by writing have been stressing the way in which scribes felt free not only to omit but also to add sections to a text, even in the age of printing, making manuscript what we would call an 'interactive' medium (Love 1993).

Recent research has ringed this simple account of standardization and fixity with a number of qualifications, by emphasizing the variation between different copies of the same edition of a book, for instance, or the competition between different standard forms of Italian by printers based in Florence, Venice or Milan (Johns 1998: esp. 10, 31, 91). A concern with the interaction between oral, written and printed communication is replacing the focus on print alone. All the same, the suggestion that printing encouraged the process of standardization and 'fixation' remains a plausible one (Briggs and Burke 2002: 21–2, 44–8).

The proposition that a document is a text which requires the skills of a literary critic to read it is another challenge to historians, from the so-called new historicists such as Stephen Greenblatt (1988).

Whether or not Greenblatt's interpretations of specific Elizabethan documents carry conviction, his general proposition about the rhetoric of documents deserves to be taken very seriously by historians, and it will be discussed in more detail below (p. 126).

Historians of images, or of what is coming to be known as 'visual culture', followed a similar approach to historians of orality. The cultural historian Aby Warburg noted the recurrence of what he called the 'pathos formula', a schema for the representation of emotions through particular gestures or facial expressions. E. H. Gombrich's classic *Art and Illusion* (1960), a study of the psychology of pictorial representation, drew on Warburg's work, as it did on the conclusions of Gestalt psychologists such as Wolfgang Köhler (1929), who argued that we perceive configurations rather than individual items.

Gombrich emphasized the ways in which the perceptions of artists and their publics, their visual 'levels of expectation', are shaped by what he variously called 'schemata', 'stereotypes', 'models' and 'formulae'. He claimed that 'All representations are grounded on schemata which the artist learns to use', and stressed 'the beholder's share' in the work of art. The parallel with the studies of orality and reception discussed in the last section will be obvious. In the case of painting as in that of performance, schemata may be regarded as at once constraints on and aids to cultural construction. The way in which they change will be discussed below (p. 160).

Myth and Memory

To take the discussion of rumour, orality and schemata a little further, it may be useful to introduce the term 'myth'. Positivist historians often use the term 'myth' to refer to stories which are not true, in explicit contrast to their own stories, which they call 'history'. It may be illuminating to compare and contrast this usage with that of anthropologists, literary theorists or psychologists, among others.

Malinowski, for example, claimed that myths were – primarily, if not exclusively – stories with social functions. A myth, he suggested, is a story about the past which serves, as he put it, as a 'charter' for the present. That is, the story performs the function of justifying some institution in the present and thus of keeping that institution in being. He was probably thinking not only of the stories told by his Trobriand Islanders, but also of Magna Carta, a document which was used to justify a variety of institutions and practices over the centuries. Because it was continually misinterpreted, or reinterpreted, the document was always up-to-date. Over the centuries the 'liberties' or privileges of the barons were transformed into the liberty of the subject. What was important in English history was not so much the text as the 'myth' of Magna Carta (Malinowski 1926).

In similar fashion the so-called Whig interpretation of history current in Britain in the nineteenth and early twentieth centuries – in other words, 'the tendency to write on the side of Protestants and Whigs, to praise revolutions provided they have been successful, to emphasize certain principles of progress in the past' – functioned as a justification of the contemporary political system (Butterfield 1931: p. v; cf. Burrow 1981).

An alternative definition of myth might be a story which has a moral – for instance, the triumph of good over evil – and stereotyped characters who, whether heroes or villains, are larger (or simpler) than life. In this sense one might speak of the 'myth of Louis XIV' or the 'Hitler myth', on the grounds that these rulers were presented in the official media of their day as heroic figures who were virtually omniscient or omnipotent (Burke 1992a; Kershaw 1989). An alternative myth of Hitler as a diabolical figure was also in circulation. In similar fashion, during the witch-hunts of early modern Europe, the common belief that the witches were servants of Satan may be described as a 'myth' (N. Cohn 1975).

These examples can of course be accommodated by Malinowski's definition. The myth of Hitler legitimated his rule, and the myth of the witches justified the persecution of old women whom posterity believes to have been harmless. All the same, it is illuminating to define myth in terms not only of functions but also of recurrent forms or 'plots' (the original meaning of the Greek term *mythos*). The Swiss psychologist Carl Gustav Jung called them 'archetypes' and explained them as unchanging products of the collective unconscious. A historian is more likely to view them as the products of culture, changing slowly over the long term (Samuel and Thompson 1990: 58).

In any case it is important to be aware that there are elements of archetype, stereotype or myth in all narratives, both oral and written. This includes written history – 'mythistory', as some call it – and also life stories which the narrators regard as the unvarnished truth, as no more than memories (McNeill 1986; Samuel and Thompson 1990: 36–48). The study of memory by historians has been booming in the last few years. It offers opportunities, which a few scholars have seized, for co-operation with anthropologists, sociologists, literary critics and psychologists.

One of the most important and controversial theoretical questions is whether it is legitimate to speak of memory as a collective phenomenon. The case for this approach was made as long ago as the 1920s by the French sociologist Maurice Halbwachs (1925, 1950). Halbwachs argued that memories are constructed by social groups or, in the language employed elsewhere in this chapter, by 'communities'. It is individuals who remember, in the literal, physical sense, but it is the community which determines what is 'memorable' and also how it will be remembered. Individuals identify with public events which are of importance to their group, and so they 'remember' a great deal that they have not experienced directly.

The idea of 'collective memory' is counter-intuitive, and it has often been rejected by scholars who declare that only individuals remember (the idea of 'collective mentalities' has been rejected on similar grounds). All the same, the phrase condenses an important insight into the influence of groups on individuals. Following Halbwachs, a number of historians have been exploring the problems of what they variously call 'social' or 'cultural' memory (Connerton 1989; Fentress and Wickham 1992; Assmann 1992, 1995; Burke 1997: 43–59; Confino 1997; Winter and Sivan 1999).

One such problem is the explanation of collective amnesia. Anthropologists became aware of the problem in investigating oral traditions, while historians encountered it in the course of studying events such as the Holocaust or the civil wars of the twentieth century in Finland, Ireland, Russia, Spain and elsewhere. The problem is not a loss of memory at the individual level, but the disappearance from public discourse of certain events, or of certain protagonists linked to particular interpretations of events. These events are in a sense 'repressed', not necessarily because they were traumatic, though many of them were, but because it has become politically inconvenient to refer to them (Peltonen 1999).

The work of specialists in literature has also inspired some historians of memory. Studies of texts – novels, letters or poems – show that participants in the Second World War often described their experiences by means of images taken (consciously or unconsciously) from accounts of the First. More generally, we may say that a real event is often remembered – and may have been experienced in the first place – in terms of another event, as narrated in a well-known text such as the Bible. To return for a moment to the rumours of kidnapping children that circulated in Paris in 1750, they echo the biblical story of the massacre of the innocents, and so imply that Louis XV was a new Herod (Fussell 1975; Samuel and Thompson 1990; Farge and Revel 1988: 108).

Again, the Swiss Protestant Pastor Johann Kessler recounted in his memoirs the story of how he met Martin Luther, who was in disguise, in an inn at Jena. 'We asked, "Sir, can you tell us whether Dr Martin Luther is in Wittenberg just now, or where else he may be?" He replied, "I know for certain that he is not at Wittenberg at this moment." ' Whether he did this consciously or not, Kessler modelled his story on a biblical prototype, that of the disciples who encountered Christ on the road to Emmaus.

Again, heroes are sometimes conflated with one another in popular memory, a process akin to what Freud, analysing dreams, called 'condensation'. On certain occasions it is possible to observe this process of 'mythification' at work, in a series of accounts of the past which come closer and closer to an archetype: in the case of rumours, for instance, or in the case of an individual's memory of the same event, recorded several times over the years. The process of 're-remembering' is influenced by changing situations in which past events are recalled.

Some critics – notably the American scholar Hayden White – would argue that written history itself is a form of the 'fictions' and 'myths' which have just been discussed (1973, 1978: 121–4). Similar points have been made by sociologists and anthropologists about the 'textual construction of reality' (Clifford and Marcus 1986; Atkinson 1990; Samuel and Thompson 1990: 28–35). The problem of 'constructivism', as it is sometimes called, will be addressed in the following chapter.

4

Central Problems

In many cases, some of them illustrated in the previous chapter, historians can increase the vocabulary – and, let us hope, the sophistication – of their analysis by borrowing concepts from other disciplines without making radical changes to their own intellectual traditions. Other ideas are more dangerous. They carry a heavier load of philosophical presuppositions. Hence they resist incorporation into an alien tradition – indeed, they threaten to transform any intellectual system into which they are introduced.

It is with these ideas, or some of them at any rate, that this chapter is concerned. It concentrates on four sets of intellectual contrasts and debates: in the first place, the debate between universalizing explanations of human behaviour in terms of rational choice and explanations which take cultural differences seriously; in the second place, the contrast between the view of society as essentially consensual and the idea of society as full of conflicts; in the third place, the contradiction between the traditional assumption that historians, sociologists, anthropologists and others present 'the facts' about societies and the view that what they offer is some kind of fiction; and finally, the opposition between the idea of function (or structure) on one side and that of human agency (the 'actors') on the other. The point is not to try to decide any of these issues – which would be presumptuous – but to encourage readers to be aware of different possibilities.

Rationality versus Relativism

Rationality is variously defined in terms of calculation, self-interest, a critical attitude or as following rules. Whichever of these definitions or aspects of individual behaviour or social organization concerns us, problems arise. In the first place, how rational are humans? In the second place, is there a universal standard of rationality, or are there different standards in different cultures? In this domain a vigorous debate is going on, opposing the universalists (especially economists and sociologists) and the relativists (especially anthropologists and historians).

The current form of universalism is known as 'Rational Choice Theory' (RCT for short). A textbook written from this standpoint is James Coleman's *Foundations of Social Theory* (1990). Society is viewed in terms of individuals following strategies (above, p. 67) based on the maximization of utility, even when they join revolutions, involve themselves in stock-market panics or form part of a violent crowd (Coleman 1990: 216–18, 220–9, 468–502). RCT is a form of cost–benefit analysis, based on the assumption that people make their decisions in the expectation of rewards or 'pay-offs' of some kind. In the case of difficult decisions, they make 'trade-offs' between the possible costs and benefits of buying a car, for example, or voting for a party that will increase taxes but also spend more on welfare than its rival. In short, RCT applies an economic model to the whole of human behaviour.

On the other side we find the relativists. Cultural relativists do not claim that 'anything goes', but they do argue that what counts as rational depends on the local circumstances and the wider culture. They point out that knowledge is socially situated and note the impossibility of standing outside one's own culture when studying another one. Their main conclusion is the need for scholars to avoid making judgements based on their own standards of rationality (or morality) about the peoples they study – in history, the avoidance of anachronism and in anthropology the avoidance of ethnocentrism.

In commenting on this debate, it may be useful to make four points. In the first place, since Freud wrote, it has been difficult to claim that individuals are rational all the time. What about groups? Take the case of panics. In a section on financial panics, Coleman puts forward the ingenious but (to me at least) unconvincing argument that even here individuals attempt 'to maximize utility by making a unilateral transfer of control' over their actions (1990: 203).

In the second place, we should distinguish the rationality of actions, on which RCT concentrates, from the rationality of beliefs, which has exercised philosophers and anthropologists (Wilson 1979; Hollis and Lukes 1982). Witchcraft, for instance, has often been dismissed as irrational. However, if the belief in witches forms part of a coherent belief system, it can hardly be rejected so easily. Given the information available and the assumptions common in a particular place and time, it is often possible to offer plausible arguments in support of the belief in witchcraft. Indeed, it has been argued that the rise of demonology in the sixteenth and seventeenth centuries was associated with 'development and indeed, "advancement" rather than with stagnation and decay' (S. Clark 1997).

In any case, there is something odd about describing a whole belief system as irrational, although it might be helpful to describe some systems as more rational than others in the sense of offering a larger place for alternatives, thus allowing individuals to make conscious choices (despite the social pressure on individuals to accept beliefs that are important to a given community) (Horton 1967, 1982).

In the third place, we should distinguish the rationality of individual decision making from the rationality of a social or political system. Weber argued that what he called the 'bureaucratic' system of government is more rational than its predecessor, the 'patrimonial' system, because it is more consistent. Decisions are made according to rules, so that similar problems receive similar solutions. In the bureaucratic system, appointments, for example, are made according to public criteria such as efficiency as measured by examinations and interviews. The system is impartial – as well as inhuman, in the sense of ignoring the differences between individuals.

On the other hand, to take another example discussed above, Cardinal Richelieu made appointments to office on the basis of private criteria, choosing his relatives, friends and clients as his assistants. In Weber's terms these decisions appear to be irrational, or at any rate non-rational. However, as we have seen, they had their own rationale. Given the circumstances – in this case the seventeenth-century French cultural system, in which loyalty to relatives and patrons was considered important – Richelieu found an effective means for maintaining himself in power and having his orders carried out. In short, different kinds of rationality are in conflict. In the short term, Richelieu was acting rationally, but the consequence of his actions was to delay the process of political 'rationalization', as Weber calls it.

Finally, turning to actions, RCT assumes that 'individuals evaluate the possible outcomes associated with their choices in accordance with their preferences and values', whether they are growing rice, shopping or voting (Popkin 1979: 31). Expressed like this, the

assumption sounds uncontroversial, but there are at least two difficulties here. The first difficulty, or series of difficulties, concerns the
practice of evaluation. Is it always individuals who evaluate? The discussion of family strategies (above, p. 56) suggests that small groups
take some important decisions. Is the process of evaluation subject
to constraints? Yes, since it may be based on inadequate information,
so that it may be necessary to speak of 'bounded' rather than un-
limited rationality' (Simon 1957: 241–60). The evaluation of commodities or candidates for office may also be subject to manipulation
by powerful means of persuasion such as advertising.

The second difficulty concerns 'preferences and values'. In practice
the theorists concentrate on a narrow range of preferences and values,
especially the material welfare of the individual as opposed to fear,
shame, sympathy for others, commitment to moral norms or loyalty
to organizations. In its extreme version, RTC reduces social interaction to the pursuit of egocentric self-interest and works with a model
of human nature that Amartya Sen (1977) has described as the
'rational fool' (cf. Gellner 1985).

At this point we might attempt a cost–benefit analysis of
cost–benefit analysis. RCT offers a clear, sharp and rigorous mode of
studying individual actions. The price of this mode is to ignore an
important part of the range of human motivation, as well as differences between cultures. In this sense RCT is reductionist.

Cultural analysis, on the other hand, is an approach that stresses
the variety of preferences and values, and their unequal importance
in different cultures. In some cultures, for example, avoiding shame
is more important than gaining material rewards. The practice of calculation is valued differently as well as taking different forms in different cultures. The individual, central to the model of action in RCT,
is taken less seriously in some cultures than in others. The idea of the
individual, or the category of the person, varies from one culture to
another, as Marcel Mauss (1938) argued in a famous essay (cf.
Carrithers, Collins and Lukes 1985). In short, RCT itself may be
viewed as an expression of the values of North American culture,
especially its stress on calculation and the individual. It is difficult to
imagine this approach originating in Brazil, for instance, or in Japan.

Concepts of Culture

'Culture' is a concept with an embarrassing variety of definitions. In
the nineteenth century, the term was generally used to refer to the

visual arts, literature, philosophy, natural science and music. At the same time, it expressed a growing awareness of the ways in which the arts and sciences are shaped by their social milieu. This growing awareness led to the rise of a sociology or social history of culture. This tendency was essentially Marxist, or at least Marxian in the sense of treating art, literature, music and so on as a kind of superstructure, reflecting changes in the economic and social 'base'.

A typical example of the genre is the famous *Social History of Art* by Arnold Hauser, which characterizes the art of fifteenth-century Florence, for example, as 'middle-class naturalism', or explains Mannerism as the artistic expression of the economic and political 'crisis' which followed the discovery of America and the invasion of Italy by France in 1492 and 1494 respectively (Hauser 1951: 2, 27, 96–9; criticized in Gombrich 1969). This approach was undermined by two parallel and connected developments.

In the first place, the term 'culture' widened its meaning as historians, sociologists, literary critics and others widened their interests. Increasing attention was devoted to popular culture, in the sense of the attitudes and values of ordinary people and their expression in folk art, folksongs, folktales, festivals and so on (Burke 1978). The concern with popular artefacts and performances – the popular equivalents of easel paintings, operas and so on – was in turn criticized as too narrow.

The current tendency is to turn away from the so-called operahouse definition of culture and to use the term in the wide sense favoured by American anthropologists such as Clifford Geertz, whose *Interpretation of Cultures* (1973) has inspired scholars in a wide range of disciplines (Kuper 1999; Burke 2004c). Even specialists in literature, at least the so-called New Historicists in the USA, have moved in this direction, emphasizing what they call the 'poetics of culture', in other words the conventions underlying the meaning of all texts – not just literary ones – and of informal performances such as cock-fights as well as formal ones such as plays (Stallybrass and White 1986; Greenblatt 1988).

If we define culture in terms of attitudes and values and their expression or embodiment in social practices, then cultural analysis offers an alternative or, at the very least, a necessary supplement to RCT. To return to Cardinal Richelieu, we might say that his appointment of relatives as assistants was rational in the 'circumstances' in which he found himself, circumstances which included the attitudes to family and the norms of loyalty current in his culture.

Again, take the case of food riots in eighteenth-century Britain, once dismissed by historians as eruptions of blind fury, an attitude described by Edward Thompson as 'a spasmodic view of popular history' (1991: 185). RCT theorists would reject the spasmodic view and see the individuals in the crowd as pursuing their self-interest, taking violent action in order to force the authorities to lower prices and weighing the cost of violent action (the possibility of imprisonment or execution) against the benefit of cheap bread.

There is certainly something to be said for this view, but it does not seem to be the whole story. In his famous account of 'the moral economy of the English crowd', Thompson interpreted food riots in terms of values, mentalities, 'the political culture, the expectations, traditions and, indeed, superstitions of the working population', especially the traditional values of a moralized economy of reciprocity (described above, p. 69). A cultural account of food riots would also give weight to their expressive or symbolic aspects, viewing them as a form of social drama that borrowed from the repertoire of ritual (E. P. Thompson 1991: 260; cf. N. Z. Davis 1975: 152–88).

Other cases of collective violence are more difficult for RCT to explain – ethnic cleansing, for instance, which is often dismissed as irrational or 'senseless'. It may be rational in the sense that violence is a means to the end of expelling the 'other' ethnic group from the territory, but what is the benefit from the expulsion? It seems more plausible to view violence as a kind of symbolic action, which takes different forms in different cultures, as well as targeting different groups – in other words, to ask questions about the meaning of the violence for the community rather than about its rewards for individual participants.

In cases such as these, it is surely necessary to consider fears as well as interests, and unconscious as well as conscious motivation. Psychologists might discuss the projection of aggressive parts of the self on to the 'other', while students of culture focus on cultural repertoires, including the re-enactment of traditional narratives of conflict (Kakar 1990; Blok 2001: 108–14).

Anxiety brings us to the so-called moral panic, a technical term for another phenomenon that does not fit the rational choice model. The term came into use following a study by the sociologist Stanley Cohen of public attitudes to two British youth groups of the 1960s, the Mods and the Rockers. In a moral panic, as Cohen (1972) defines it, a threat to society is identified, the threatening individual, group or event is presented in an exaggerated and stereotyped manner in the media of communication, and for a short time at least there is considerable public anxiety.

This concept certainly has its uses in the study of the past. Whatever the rationality or non-rationality of the idea of witchcraft, the recurrent attacks on so-called witches in early modern Europe followed the model of moral panics. A similar point may be made about accusations made against the Jews in the late Middle Ages, including desecrating the host, kidnapping children and murdering them for ritual purposes. Contemporary cultures are no more immune to moral panics than earlier ones, witness the recent wave of accusations of child abuse and child murder by worshippers of Satan (La Fontaine 1998).

The recent accusations are a kind of a recycling of traditional stories about Jews and witches, reactivating elements from the European cultural repertoire. Moral panics occur in other cultures, but they take different forms. In China in 1768, for example, the panic concerned 'soul-stealers'. Rumour spread to the effect that people were writing the names of their enemies on slips of paper and nailing them to the piles of bridges. The paper would assist the hammering of the piles but in the process destroy the victim. The story then expanded to include the theme of clipping 'queues', the pigtails that the Qing regime made compulsory for men in China. Thanks to these political overtones, the emperor himself took a personal interest in the spread and eventual decline of the panic, which, like European stories about the servants of Satan, revealed something about the anxieties prevalent in the culture (P. A. Kuhn 1990).

Consensus versus Conflict

'Culture' is often defined as a system of shared meanings. However, this conception is problematic, especially in the case of large groups such as nations. This approach to culture has the defects as well as the merits of the Durkheimian model of society, which stresses consensus at the expense of conflict (above, p. 62). Edward Thompson went so far as to suggest that 'the very term "culture", with its cosy invocation of consensus, may serve to distract attention from social and cultural contradictions'(1991: 56; cf. Sewell 1999). Both the defects and the merits of the model of culture as shared meanings are visible with particular clarity in Simon Schama's description and interpretation of Dutch culture in the seventeenth century, *The Embarrassment of Riches* (1987).

Schama is at his best when discussing the attempts of the Dutch to construct a collective identity by distinguishing themselves from their neighbours. However, the socio-cultural divisions within the republic of the United Provinces – between rich and poor, towns-people and peasants, Calvinists and Catholics, Hollanders and Frisians – are scarcely visible in his work. *The Embarrassment of Riches* is vulnerable to the criticisms levelled against the anthropo-logical concept of culture on the grounds that an emphasis on shared values is, to say the least, 'not very effective for understanding class-based societies', and needs to be replaced by a stress on cultural con-flict (Sider 1986: 5, 109).

To this criticism it might very well be replied that the concept of conflict implies that of solidarity, and that the critics have simply replaced one community, the region or nation, with another, social class. What is to be done? One possibility is to make use of the soci-ological concept of 'subculture', defined as a partially autonomous culture within a larger whole (no implications of inferiority are intended by this concept) (Hebdige 1979).

Sociologists generally study the more visible subcultures, such as ethnic or religious minorities, 'deviants' from the norms of a given society such as criminals or heretics, and youth groups. Historians too have often studied groups such as the Jews in medieval Spain or the beggars in Elizabethan London, but they have not always paid attention to the relationship between the culture of these minorities and that of the surrounding society.

There is a whole series of questions to ask about the relationship between subcultures and the culture at large. How sharp are the boundaries? Does a subculture include all aspects of the life of its members, or only some? Is the relationship between main culture and subculture one of complementarity or conflict? Was there more in common in the sixteenth century between two Jews, one of whom was Italian, or two Italians, one of whom was a Jew? Are occupa-tional subcultures less autonomous than ethnic or religious subcul-tures? How long can the subculture of a new group of immigrants, such as the French Protestants in seventeenth-century London or Amsterdam, remain autonomous?

It might reasonably be argued that the most important subcultures have rarely been studied as such: the cultures of social classes. A vivid contrast between the middle class and the working class emerges from Pierre Bourdieu's (1979) well-known study of social distinction. It may be illuminating to compare and contrast this classic study of the later twentieth century with Edward Thompson's equally classic study of the English working class in the early nineteenth century. Where Bourdieu studies structure, Thompson focuses on change, on 'making'. Thompson looks at the working class more or less by itself, but Bourdieu compares and contrasts two classes, each of which defines itself against the other. In that sense he offers an exemplary study of subcultures.

In recent years the term 'subculture' seems to have been dropping out of use, perhaps because it sounds pejorative. All the same, the problems discussed above remain, however we choose to describe them. One possibility is to speak of different 'cultures' within the same society, but even this is problematic, as the anthropologist Gerd Baumann shows in a study of five ethnic groups in a part of London in which he found 'cultures across communities' so that 'The equation between community and culture, dominant as it is in much public discourse about ethnic minorities, disintegrated' (1996: 10).

Facts versus Fictions

Historians, like sociologists and anthropologists, used to assume that they dealt in facts, and that their texts reflected historical reality. This assumption has crumbled under the assaults of the philosophers – whether or not they may be said to 'mirror' a broader, deeper change in mentality (Rorty 1980). Hence it is necessary to consider the claim that historians and ethnographers are as much in the business of fiction as are novelists and poets; in other words, they too are producers of 'literary artifacts' according to rules of genre and style (whether they are conscious of these rules or not) (White 1973, 1978; Clifford and Marcus 1986).

Recent studies of the 'poetics of ethnography' have described the work of sociologists and anthropologists as the 'textual construction' of reality, and compared it to the work of novelists. The work of the expatriate Pole Bronisław Malinowski, for example, is frequently compared with that of his compatriot Joseph Conrad – whose stories he read in the field – while the anthropologist Alfred Métraux has been described as an 'ethnographic surrealist' (Clifford 1988: 92–113, 117–51).

In the case of historians, the main challenge to traditional assumptions has come from Hayden White, who has accused his professional colleagues of living in the nineteenth century, the age of the system of literary conventions known as 'realism', and of refusing to experiment with modern forms of representation. Although this pronouncement was made as long ago as 1966, the shock waves that followed are still spreading (White 1978: 27–50).

White also claims, like the Canadian literary theorist Northrop Frye, that historians – like poets, novelists or playwrights – organize their accounts of the past around recurrent plots or *mythoi* – in other words, narrative schemata. For example, 'the Comic mythos served as the plot structure for most of Ranke's historical works,' in the sense that when writing about the French or English civil wars, for example, he told a three-part story which moved like a comedy (or tragicomedy) 'from a condition of apparent peace, through the revelation of conflict, to the resolution of the conflict in the establishment of a genuinely peaceful social order'.

Ranke's story thus contained an irreducibly fictive or creative element. His documents did not tell him when to start his story or when to end it (White 1973: 167, 177). To claim, as Ranke did – and as some historians still do – to be writing down 'what actually happened', no more and no less, is to fall victim to what an anthropologist (neatly turning the historians' use of the term 'myth' against themselves) has recently called 'the myth of realism' (LaCapra 1985: 15–44; Samuel and Thompson 1990: 25–35).

In other words, the boundary between fact and fiction, which once looked firm, has been eroded (alternatively, it is only now that we see that the boundary was always open). In this border area we find writers who are attracted by the idea of the so-called non-fiction novel, such as Truman Capote's *In Cold Blood* (1965), which tells the story of the murder of the Clutter family, or Norman Mailer's *The Armies of the Night* (1968), about a protest march to the Pentagon, subtitled 'History as a Novel/The Novel as History'.

We also find novelists who incorporate documents (decrees, newspaper cuttings and so on) into the text of their story, or who explore alternative pasts, as in Carlos Fuentes' *Terra Nostra* (1975), or who build their narrative on the obstacles to the attainment of historical truth, as Mario Vargas Llosa does in *The Real Life of Alejandro Mayta* (1984), in which the narrator is trying to reconstruct the career of a Peruvian revolutionary – perhaps for a novel, perhaps for a 'very free history of the period', in the face of contradictory evidence. 'Why try to find out everything that happened?,' asks one informant: 'I wonder if we really know what you call History with a capital H. . . . or if there's as much make-believe in history as in novels.'

On the other side, a small group of historians and others have responded to White's challenge and have been experimenting with 'creative non-fiction', in other words narrative techniques learned from novelists or from film-makers. The historian Golo Mann, for example, a son of the novelist Thomas Mann, published in 1971 a biography of the seventeenth-century general Albrecht von Wallenstein which he described as 'an all too true novel', in which he adapted the stream-of-consciousness technique to historical purposes, especially when evoking the last months of his hero's life, when the general, ill and embittered, appears to have been considering changing sides (Mann's footnotes, however, were more conventional than his text). Carlo Ginzburg, who also happens to be the son of a novelist, Natalia Ginzburg, is another historian remarkable for the self-consciously literary way in which he writes.

It remains a pity that the majority of professional historians have so far been reluctant to recognize the poetics of their work, the literary conventions they follow. There is a sense in which it is difficult to deny that historians construct the objects they study, grouping events into movements like 'The Scientific Revolution' or 'The Thirty Years War', which are only visible by hindsight. A more fundamental question was raised long ago by the American literary theorist Kenneth Burke in *The Rhetoric of Motives* (1950), the question whether human action as well as speech and writing does not follow the rules of rhetoric, an idea which also informs the dramaturgical perspectives of Erving Goffman and Victor Turner.

It is equally difficult to deny the role of fiction 'in the archives', as Natalie Davis puts it in a study in which she engaged with some of the problems raised by the literary critic Stephen Greenblatt. In this analysis of 'pardon tales' in sixteenth-century France she was essentially concerned with the place of rhetoric and narrative techniques in the construction of texts such as the depositions of witnesses, the interrogation of suspects, or pleas for pardon – in other words, documents which positivist historians had traditionally treated as relatively trustworthy evidence. Davis begins her study with the remark that she was taught like other historians 'to peel away the fictive elements in our documents so that we could get at the hard facts', but goes on to confess her discovery – perhaps a result of the challenge from Greenblatt and White – that the craft of storytelling is itself a historical theme of great interest (N. Z. Davis 1987: 3).

On the other side, it is an equal pity that White and his followers – not to mention the theorists of narrative – have not yet seriously engaged with the question whether history is a literary genre or cluster of genres of its own, whether it has its own forms of narrative and its own rhetoric, and whether the conventions include (as they surely do) rules about the relationship of statements to evidence as well as rules of representation. Ranke, for example, was not writing pure fiction. Documents not only supported his narrative, but discouraged the narrator from making statements for which evidence was lacking.

Similar points might be made about sociologists and anthropologists. Whether they use documents or construct their accounts out of interviews, conversations and personal observation, they follow a research strategy which includes criteria of reliability, representativity and so on. What needs to be discussed is the compatibility or conflict between these criteria and different forms of text or rhetoric, rather than the old oppositions between fact and fiction, science and art. This middle ground, that of the 'fictions of factual representation' (the mask of impartiality, the claim to inside knowledge, the use of statistics to impress the reader, and so on), is beginning to be explored in a systematic way (Siebenschuh 1983; Nelson, Megill and McCloskey 1987: 221–38).

Structures versus Agents

The extent to which human beings make their own decisions or make their own history has long been a matter for debate. Within social theory, it has taken the form of a conflict between two schools, between the so-called methodological individualists who reduce the social to the individual, and their opponents, the holists, who view specific actions as embedded in a system of social practices and explain suicide, for instance, independently of the individuals who kill themselves.

A classic statement of the individualist position comes from the *System of Logic* by the nineteenth-century English philosopher John Stuart Mill. 'Human beings in society have no properties but those which are derived from, and may be resolved into, the laws of the nature of the individual man' (book 6, section 7). The sociologist Herbert Spencer held similar views, attacked as 'psychologism' by Durkheim, who defined his own position on the priority of the collective or social over the individual against what he called 'the method followed by Monsieur Spencer'.

Methodological individualism has been particularly strong in the English-speaking world, while the most famous holists have been French or German (Durkheim and Lévi-Strauss, Weber and Simmel). As we have seen, French sociologists, historians and anthropologists speak of collective mentalities and collective memory (above, p. 114), concepts that are often rejected in Britain. The contrast is so striking as to suggest that we should interpret the debate itself in structural terms, as a clash of cultures.

Functionalism

'Function' is a key concept in the social theory of the holists. It seems harmless enough, implying only that institutions have their uses. Defined more precisely, however, there is a cutting edge to the idea which makes it at once more interesting and more dangerous. The function of each part of a structure, so the definition goes, is to maintain the whole. To 'maintain' it is to keep it in 'equilibrium' (an influential analogy between the world of nature, from mechanics to biology, and the world of society). What makes the theory both attractive and dangerous is the fact that it is not just descriptive but explanatory as well. The reason for the existence of a particular custom or institution, according to the functionalists, is precisely the contribution it makes to social equilibrium.

The idea of social equilibrium is not completely strange to historians. In the seventeenth and eighteenth centuries, the idea of the 'balance' of power, property and trade was central to political and economic analysis. When Gibbon, for example, explained the decline and fall of the Roman Empire in terms of its 'immoderate greatness', he was thinking in terms of a balance or see-saw. More recently, the Brazilian historian Gilberto Freyre (1933), who was also a sociologist, described his own society in terms of what he called an 'equilibrium of antagonisms', a phrase he took from Herbert Spencer. On the other hand, many social theorists have treated 'equilibrium' not as a metaphor to employ occasionally but as a basic assumption underlying the kinds of question they ask and the kinds of answer they regard as acceptable.

Functionalism has often been criticized as a complicated way of saying the obvious. In some cases, however, functionalist explanations flout common sense rather than confirm it, as in the case of Georg Simmel's (1908) analysis of the social function of conflict as 'an integrative force in the group'. One of the most brilliant discussions of these issues occurs in a book which deliberately avoids the terms 'structure' and 'function'. The book is explicitly concerned with Africa, but it has much wider implications (Gluckman 1955).

The author, the anthropologist Max Gluckman, constructed his book around a series of paradoxes. For example, a chapter entitled 'The Peace in the Feud' argued that the feud is not a threat to peace, as common sense might assume. On the contrary, it is an institution with the function of preserving peace and maintaining social cohesion. The point is that individuals often find themselves bound to both sides by ties of blood or friendship, and this conflict of loyalties gives them an interest in keeping the peace. Again, Gluckman argued that 'rebellions, far from destroying the established social order, work so that they even support this order'; that is, their function is to maintain this order by acting as a safety-valve. Yet again, discussing certain Zulu rituals of reversal, the author made the point that the annual lifting of the customary taboos 'serves to emphasize them'.

As we have seen (above, p. 12), the functionalist approach dominated sociology and social anthropology from about 1920 to about 1960. Even today, it might reasonably be argued that the functionalist tradition leads a submerged existence in sociology and anthropology, and even that it continues to exercise an influence all the more important for being more or less unconscious.

Historians on the other hand, despite the example of Gibbon, have been slow to adopt this approach. Indeed, it was only in the 1960s, at the very time that some sociologists were becoming unhappy with the idea of function, that a number of practising historians began to experiment with this kind of explanation.

In his classic study of witchcraft and magic, Keith Thomas, for instance, argued that 'witch-beliefs served to uphold the traditional obligations of charity and neighbourliness at a time when other social and economic forces were conspiring to weaken them' in English village communities, because the more prosperous villagers feared being cursed or bewitched by the poorer ones if they turned them away from the door empty-handed (Thomas 1971: 564–6).

Alan Macfarlane also suggested that 'the fear of the witch acted as a sanction in enforcing neighbourly conduct', though he was also tempted by an alternative (indeed opposite) functional explanation, to the effect that witchcraft prosecutions were 'a means of effecting a deep social change' from a more neighbourly society to a more individualistic one (Macfarlane 1970: 105, 196). The fact that these opposite explanations are compatible with the same evidence ought to make us uneasy. Functional explanations are easy to impute and difficult to verify (or falsify).

The value of functionalism to historians is that it compensates for their traditional tendency to explain too much of the past in terms of the intentions of individuals. An example in which traditional 'intentionalism', as it has been called, has come into open conflict with functionalism is the historiography of the Third Reich (Mason

1981). Attempts to explain the structures of the National Socialist State and the events of the period 1933–45 completely in terms of the intentions of the Führer looked increasingly implausible after research turned to the regions, the 'periphery' of the system. There has been a tendency to consider political and social pressures on Hitler, as well as his conscious plans. Although this concern with pressures may not be functionalist in the strict sense of the term, it serves to illustrate the need for a political history which is not confined to the actions and thoughts of leaders.

If it solves problems, functionalism also raises problems: in the first place, the problem of equilibrium. The anthropologist Edmund Leach once declared that 'real societies can never be in equilibrium'. It is only fair to note that Pareto, for instance, did not view societies in terms of a 'perfect' or static equilibrium, but rather of a 'dynamic' one, defined as 'such a state that if it is artificially subjected to some modification . . . a reaction at once takes place, tending to restore it to its real, its normal state' (1916: sect. 2068).

A second problem is the problem of social consensus, a consensus implied whenever it is claimed that the function of a particular practice or institution is to maintain the social system. This problem may be highlighted by considering a concept that once played an important role in sociology, 'social control'. 'Social control' is the traditional sociological phrase to describe the power which society exercises over individuals via law, education, religion and so on. However, it begs a very large question: who is 'society'? The use of the phrase depends on the acceptance of a view which has already been questioned more than once in these pages: the view that a social consensus exists, and that society has a centre. If we were to accept these assumptions, we might define social control as the enforcement of the consensus over norms, and the mechanism for the re-establishment of an equilibrium threatened by social 'deviants'. If, on the other hand, we think of society as composed of conflicting social groups, each with its own values, the phrase 'social control' will appear to be dangerous and misleading.

The concept is most useful in the situations in which the question, Who is society? is easiest to answer – in other words, in the analysis of face-to-face situations in which a non-conformist confronts the community, as in the case of the factory worker who produces more than his colleagues, the student who tries too hard to please the teacher, or the soldier whose equipment is too clean and tidy (it is ironic but revealing that in all these cases the 'deviant' in the face-to-face situation is the one who is following the official norms).

In the case of early modern Europe, one of the most striking forms of this kind of social control was the charivari. The old man who married a young girl, or the husband who allowed himself to be beaten by his wife, was considered to have transgressed the norms of the community. Hence the 'rough music' played outside the window, the satirical verses, or even the mock-procession of the victim through the streets of the neighbourhood. The masks worn by the players and singers hid their individuality and implied that they acted in the name of the community (N. Z. Davis 1975: 97–123; E. P. Thompson 1991: 467–538).

Despite the small scale of these incidents, however, it is not altogether clear who the community were: everyone in the village or parish, or just the young men who organized the charivari? Did they really express a consensus? Were the older men or the women of the neighbourhood likely to see the incident in the same light as the organizers?

Outside these face-to-face situations, the concept of social control becomes still more slippery. Some historians have used it to describe the activities of eighteenth-century English squires enforcing the game laws against poachers, or nineteenth-century town councils banning popular recreations like the football played in the streets of Derby and other cities on Shrove Tuesday and other festive occasions. The objection to this usage is that the term has become 'a label for what one class does to another', treating the values of the dominant class, squirearchy or bourgeoisie, as if they were the values of society as a whole (Yeo and Yeo 1981: 128–54).

The Example of Venice

A historical example which might seem almost to have been invented to demonstrate the strengths of functionalism is the Venetian Republic of the sixteenth and seventeenth centuries (Burke 1974). Venice was much admired at the time for the unusual stability of its social and political system. The Venetians themselves explained this stability, which they claimed was eternal, in terms of their mixed or 'balanced' constitution, in which the monarchical element was provided by the Doge, the aristocratic element by the Senate, and the so-called democratic element by the Great Council, which was composed of some 2,000 adult male nobles. In practice, Venice was ruled by an oligarchy of some 200 leading nobles (known at the time as the *grandi*), who took turns to hold the key political offices. The idea of the mixed constitution might therefore be described as an 'ideology', or a 'myth' (in the Malinowskian sense of that term), serving to keep the system in being.

It is unlikely that the myth was powerful enough to perform this function by itself, persuading the lesser nobles, the citizens and the commoners that all was well, but other institutions existed to defuse, or to stay with our central metaphor, to 'counter-balance' opposition from these quarters. In Venice, as in Gluckman's Africa, conflicting loyalties served the cause of social cohesion. The lesser nobles were pulled one way by group solidarity, but they were tugged in the opposite direction by the ties of patronage (above, p. 73) which bound them as individuals to individual *grandi*. Caught in this conflict, they had a stake in compromise.

What about the rest of the population? The most articulate group of commoners who might have challenged the Venetian oligarchy were the citizens, a relatively small group of 2,000–3,000 adult males. They enjoyed certain formal or informal privileges to compensate for their exclusion from the Great Council. Certain offices in the administration were reserved for them alone. Their daughters not infrequently married nobles. Certain religious fraternities were open to nobles and citizens alike. It might be argued that these privileges made the citizens feel that they were close to the nobles, and so detached them from the rest of the commoners.

These commoners, about 150,000 of them, were pacified like the populace of ancient Rome by a combination of bread and circuses. Corn was subsidized by the government, which also sponsored splendid public rituals. Carnival, which was unusually elaborate in Venice, was a ritual of reversal in which the authorities could be criticized with more or less impunity, a safety-valve like the Zulu rituals analysed by Gluckman. The fishermen of Venice were allowed to elect their own Doge, who was solemnly received and kissed by the real Doge, a ritual which might be described as serving the function of persuading ordinary people that they participated in a political system from which they were effectively excluded (Muir 1981).

There remained the population of the territories subject to Venice, including a substantial part of northern Italy (Padua, Vicenza, Verona, Bergamo and Brescia). The patricians of these cities probably resented their loss of independence, but they had opportunities for employment as officers in the Venetian army. As for the ordinary people, in many cases their hostility to their own patricians made them pro-Venetian. One might therefore say that the stability of the system depended on a complex balance of power, another example of the equilibrium of antagonisms.

There seems to be an elective affinity between this example of stability and the method of functional analysis. All the same, the example may serve to illustrate the weaknesses of the method, as well as its strengths. In the first place, the problem of change: all the world is not Venice, and the frequent conflicts and crises in the sister-republics of Florence and Genoa – to go no further afield – are difficult to explain in functionalist terms. Even in the Venetian case the system was not eternal. The Republic was abolished in 1797, and even in earlier centuries it passed through a number of crises which led to structural change – the closing of the Great Council to new recruits, the increasing importance of the Council of Ten, the shift from a maritime empire to an empire in northern Italy, and so on.

Change is often the result of conflict, a reminder that even in its more sophisticated versions the functional approach remains tied to a Durkheimian, consensual model of society. Historians of Italy have effectively recognized this point by coining the phrase the 'myth of Venice' to refer to the image of a stable, balanced society, implying that this image was a distorted one. It would indeed be unwise to assume that ordinary people shared all the values of the ruling class, or that they were easily manipulated by rituals such as the inauguration of the fishermen's Doge. Social stability need not imply consensus. It may depend on prudence or inertia rather than a shared ideology (above, p. 99). It is also assisted by particular types of political and social structure.

To sum up: the concept of 'function' is a useful item in the toolkit of historians and theorists alike, provided that it is not blunted by indiscriminate use. It carries with it temptations to neglect social change, social conflict and individual motives, but these temptations can be resisted. There is no need to assume that every institution in a given society has a positive function, without any costs ('dysfunctions'). There is no need to assume that a given institution is indispensable to the performance of a given function; in different societies or periods, different institutions may act as functional equivalents, analogues or alternatives (Merton 1948: 19–82; Runciman 1983–9: ii. 182–265).

However, functional explanations should not be viewed as replacements for other kinds of historical explanation, which they complement rather than contradict, since they tend to be answers to different questions, rather than different answers to the same question (Gellner 1973: 88–106). What is being suggested here is not that historians throw intentionalist explanations overboard, but simply that they take on board something for which they have no 'functional equivalent'.

Structuralism

Functional analysis is concerned not with people but with 'structures'. In practice, different approaches to society have utilized different conceptions of structure, of which it may be useful to distinguish at least three: the Marxian approach, in which the architectural metaphor of 'base' and 'superstructure' is central, and the base or infrastructure tends to be conceived in economic terms; the structural-functionalist approach, in which the concept 'structure' refers to a complex of institutions – the family, the state, the legal system and so on; and the approach of the so-called structuralists, primarily concerned with structures or systems of thought or culture.

The fundamental model or metaphor underlying structuralism is the model of society or culture as a language. Theorists of language provided the inspiration for this 'semiotic' or 'semiological' approach to culture as a 'system of signs'. The famous distinction between *langue* (the resources of a given language) and *parole* (a specific utterance, selected from these resources) was generalized into a distinction between 'code' and 'message'. The point which structuralists stress is that the meaning of a message depends not (or not only) on the intentions of the individual transmitting it, but also on the rules which make up the code – in other words, its structure (Culler 1980).

In France in particular, these ideas were taken up and applied, or adapted, in a number of different fields, giving rise to a structuralist anthropology (Claude Lévi-Strauss), a structuralist literary criticism (Roland Barthes), a structuralist version of psychoanalysis (Jacques Lacan), and a structuralist version of Marxism (Louis Althusser). In Russia, there was an independent development, leading from the linguists to the studies of the folktale by Vladimir Propp and the studies of Russian literature and culture by Juri Lotman. Propp, for example, studied what he called the 'morphology' of the Russian folktale, identifying thirty-one recurrent elements or 'functions' – the hero is prohibited from doing something, the prohibition is ignored, and so on (Propp 1928; Lotman and Uspenskii 1984).

What has all this to do with history? Structural history is well known, whether it follows the model of Marx or that of Braudel. Is there a place for structuralist history as well? It may well seem that an opposition to history is built into the structure of structuralism which deliberately privileges structure (the 'synchronic') over change (the 'diachronic'). However, the opposition between structuralism and history must not be exaggerated. Lévi-Strauss devoted attention to such topics as the comparative history of marriage. Barthes entered the territory of the historians to offer a structuralist analysis of historical discourse. As for Lotman, he devoted much of his time to the study of eighteenth-century Russian culture (Lotman and Uspenskii 1984: 231–56).

For their part, a few historians were tempted by the structuralist approach in the years of its intellectual dominance, especially in the study of myth. Ancient Greek myths, for example, have been analysed in the manner of Propp and Lévi-Strauss, emphasizing recurrent elements and binary oppositions (Vernant 1966).

One of the most impressive structural analyses carried out by a historian is a study of another historian, François Hartog's essay on Herodotus, which concentrates on the ways in which Herodotus represents the 'other', in other words non-Greeks. The Scythians, for example, are represented not only as different from, but in many respects as the inverse of, the Greeks. Greeks live in cities, for instance, while the Scythians live in the wilderness. Greeks are civilized, Scythians are 'barbarians'. However, when Herodotus comes to describe the attack on the Scythians by the Persians, who also attacked Greece, this event inverts the inversion, and the Scythians appear in a more favourable light. Hartog's work, like that of Roland Barthes and Hayden White, illustrates the textual strategies of historians and also what White calls 'the content of the form', its effects on the message (Hartog 1980).

In the course of working with structuralism, certain problems have become apparent. Some linguists and literary critics, including Mikhail Bakhtin (1952–3), expressed their discomfort with an idea of meaning abstracted from the context of place, time, speaker, hearer and situation. Others – notably Jacques Derrida and the so-called Poststructuralists – reject and undermine the binary oppositions built into structuralism. Derrida is also opposed to structural determinism, as opposed to the free play of meanings on the part of transmitters and receivers alike, a point which has come up already and will be discussed again below (Culler 1980; Norris 1982).

One of Propp's examples may serve to illustrate some of the difficulties with the structuralist method. He compares two Russian folktales, in one of which a magician gives Ivan a ship which takes him to another kingdom, while in the other a queen gives Ivan a ring with the same results. For Propp, these examples illustrate what he calls function 14, 'a magical object is put at the hero's disposition'. It is indeed difficult to deny the similarity in the structure of the two episodes. To analyse stories in this way is surely illuminating. All the same, something significant in a story is lost when an element like a ring or a horse, rich in associations in many cultures, is reduced to an algebraic x or y. Historians, like linguists and literary critics, wish to attend to objects and associations such as these, to the surface of the story as well as the structure. They cannot accept structuralism without reservations.

For a strongly expressed example of such reservations we may return to Jan Vansina, who goes so far as to describe structuralism as a 'fallacy', a method which is 'invalid' because its procedures 'are neither replicable nor falsifiable' (1985: 165). I would not go so far myself. For one thing, I doubt whether any analysis of texts or oral traditions can be as scientific as Vansina would like it to be. For another, I continue to believe that – although binary oppositions are not the only patterns to be found in culture – an increased sensitivity to such patterns is something we all owe to the structuralist movement.

The Return of the Actor

In the last generation, there has been a reaction against the dominance of structural explanations of different kinds. The French sociologist Alain Touraine (1984), for example, has called for the 'return of the actor' and suggested that the study of social movements is central to sociology. The American anthropologist Jonathan Friedman criticizes accounts of globalization (below, p. 186) that speak of the mixing of cultures. 'Cultures don't flow and mix with each other,' he says, but actors view the world in these terms (1994: 195–232).

Historians too have reacted against the notion of structures. The supporters of Marx and Braudel have been accused – not for the first time – of leaving people out of history, and even of being 'unhistorical', in the sense of studying immobile structures at the expense of change over time. Although these charges are generally exaggerated, attempts to combine structural with historical analysis raise problems which demand discussion, notably the problem of determinism versus freedom. It will be obvious that a problem of this kind – one of the perennial problems of philosophy – is not going to be solved in a brief discussion in a book such as this. All the same, the issue needs to be raised.

One way of linking structure and agency is via individual and collective psychology. So far, psychology has played a somewhat marginal role in this book. However, in the United States in the 1950s, a new term came into circulation to denote an exciting new approach: 'psychohistory'. A study of the young Luther by the psychoanalyst Erik Erikson (1958) led to a lively debate, while the president of the American Historical Association, a respected elder statesman of the profession, surprised his colleagues by telling them that the 'next assignment' for historians was to take psychology more seriously than they had done (Langer 1958). Journals devoted to psychohistory were founded, and leaders such as Gandhi or Hitler were studied from this point of view (E. Erikson 1970; Waite 1977).

All the same, the advertised meeting between history and psychology seems to have been adjourned indefinitely. Even today, despite the efforts of leading historians such as Peter Gay (one of the few members of the profession to have undergone a training analysis), it remains the next rather than the current assignment.

One reason for the reluctance of historians to come to grips with psychology – besides the empiricists' resistance to theory – is surely the variety of competing versions – Freudian, neo-Freudian, Jungian, developmental and so on. Another is the obvious difficulty of applying Freud's methods to the dead, of psychoanalysing documents rather than people. Yet another is the fact that the encounter between history and psychology took place at an inauspicious moment, at a time when historians were distancing themselves from 'great men', and focusing on the rest of the population. At this point, the important problem was not so much the personality of Hitler, say, as the susceptibility of the German people to his style of leadership.

What then of collective psychology? In the 1920s and 1930s, some historians, notably two Frenchmen – Marc Bloch and Lucien Febvre – preached and tried to practice what they called a 'historical psychology' of groups. However, their successors as historians of mentalities generally turned their attention from psychology to anthropology.

Anthropologists and sociologists also kept their distance from psychology. Durkheim defined sociology, the science of society, by contrast to psychology, the science of the individual. In the 1930s and 1940s, there were attempts at rapprochement, like the work of the American 'culture and personality' school (including Margaret Mead and Ruth Benedict), the synthesis of Weber and Freud offered by Norbert Elias, and the synthesis of Marx and Freud offered by Erich Fromm. The relevance of this approach to historians is obvious. If 'basic' personality varies from society to society, it must also have varied from one period to another. The work of the culture and personality school – its contrast between 'shame cultures' and 'guilt cultures', for example – underlies the classic study of ancient Greece by E. R. Dodds (1951), who cited both Benedict and Fromm. In general, however, these works had remarkably little impact on historical practice.

In any case, the rapprochement did not last. Anthropologists grew increasingly unhappy with the idea of national or 'social character', preferring to work with the more flexible notion of culture. The rise of a historical anthropology centred on this notion of culture has been one of the most fruitful interdisciplinary developments of recent years. Yet its success should not blind us to the potential of that abandoned project, historical psychology. Psychological theory can be of use to historians in at least three different ways.

(1)   In the first place, in freeing them from the 'common-sense' assumptions about human nature, assumptions all the more powerful for being unacknowledged, if not unconscious in the precise Freudian sense of the term. As Peter Gay puts it, 'The professional historian has always been a psychologist – an amateur psychologist' (1985: 6). Theory (more precisely, rival theories) may reveal the rational roots of apparently irrational behaviour, and vice versa, thus discouraging historians from assuming too easily that one individual or group acts rationally, while dismissing other individuals or groups as irrational ('fanatical', 'superstitious' and so on).

(2)   In the second place, psychological theory has a contribution to make in the process of source criticism. To make proper use of an autobiography or diary as historical evidence, it is necessary, so a distinguished psychoanalyst has suggested, to consider not only the culture in which the text was written and the literary conventions of the genre, but also the age of the author and his or her position in the life cycle (E. Erikson 1958: 701–2). In similar fashion, a social psychologist has suggested that all of us rewrite our biographies all the time in the manner of the notorious *Soviet Encyclopaedia*.

Oral historians too have begun to consider the element of fantasy in the testimonies they collect and the psychological needs underlying such fantasies (Samuel and Thompson 1990: 7–8, 55–7, 143–5). It is only a short step from daytime fantasies to dreams. The example of psychoanalysts of various schools might encourage historians to utilize a type of source rarely studied: dreams (or, more precisely, records of dreams).

A suitable case for study in this way is that of William Laud, archbishop of Canterbury, and – together with his master Charles I – a hammer of the Puritans. Laud appears to be a classic instance of an inferiority complex, since he was a man of low stature, low birth and aggressive behaviour. But how can a historian possibly show that Laud actually felt inferior, anxious or insecure? At this point dreams may have something to tell us.

Between 1623 and 1643 Laud recorded thirty dreams in his diary. Two-thirds of these dreams present disasters, or at least embarrassing situations. For example, 'I dreamed marvellously, that the King was offended with me, and would cast me off, and tell me no cause why.' For some psychologists, a dream of a king signifies the dreamer's father. For others, all figures in dreams represent aspects of the dreamer's personality. All the same, in this particular case it is hard to resist the conclusion that Laud was indeed anxious about his relationship with the king, and that the arrogance about which contemporaries complained expressed a fundamental lack of confidence (Burke 1997: 23–42).

(3)   In the third place, psychologists have a contribution to make to the debate on the relationship between the individual and society. For example, they have considered the psychology of followers as well as that of leaders – the need for a father-figure, for example. From this perspective, the imputation of charisma discussed above (p. 93) becomes somewhat easier to understand.

Another way in which psychologists have helped redefine the relationship between the individual and society is by discussing child rearing in different cultures, and this discussion too may illuminate historical problems. For example, a study of colonial America, inspired by Freud and Erikson, distinguishes three basic 'temperaments' and explains their genesis in terms of child rearing. The 'evangelicals', characterized by hostility to the self, were the product of strict discipline. The 'moderates', whose main characteristic was self-control, had undergone a more moderate discipline, their wills bent rather than broken in childhood. Finally the 'genteel', defined by their self-confidence, had been treated with affection and even indulgence when they were children. Of course these character types can be found in other cultures too, and comparative studies might add nuances to the picture. So far, however, comparative studies of childhood have not been historical, while few historical studies have been comparative (Greven 1977).

There is one field in which historians concerned with culture and society have been drawing closer to psychologists of different persuasions: the history of emotions. Nietzsche complained that historians neglected emotions, and Febvre urged them to study the topic, but his advice was not heeded by many scholars until the 1980s. Since then there has been a rise – one might almost say an explosion – of interest in the historicity of love, jealousy, anger, fear, tears and so on (Stearns and Stearns 1986; Naphy and Roberts 1997; Rosenwein 1998; Gouk and Hills 2004).

The study of what is sometimes called 'emotionology' raises some difficult problems. For example, what counts as an emotion? The psychologist Paul Ekman has claimed that it is possible to identify six basic emotions in all cultures: happiness, sadness, anger, fear, disgust and surprise. Reacting against this view, the Polish linguist Anna Wierzbicka has stressed the difficulty of translating descriptions of particular emotions into other languages, and the danger of treating the folk categories of our own native language as if they were universal (Ekman and Davidson 1994; Wierzbicka 1999).

To avoid these dangers, it may be best to concentrate on the ways in which emotions were 'managed' in different cultures. This is the approach of the historian William Reddy. Drawing on anthropology and psychology and attempting to bridge the gap between them, Reddy (2003) works with concepts such as the 'regime' and the 'performance' of emotions. Theatrical metaphors pervade recent discussions of the topic: the 'emotional repertoire', for instance, the 'scripts' available in a given culture, and the 'scenarios' – in other words, associations between particular situations and particular emotions (cf. Burke 2004b).

All these discussions of the relationship between individuals and societies occupy a middle ground between conventional assertions of freedom or determinism. They are concerned with the possible 'fit' between public reasons and private motives or emotions. They point to social pressures on individuals, which are more or less difficult (rather than impossible) to resist. They note the existence of social constraints, but view them as reducing the area of choice rather than requiring the individual to behave in a certain way. In any case, structures may be seen as empowering as well as constraining both individual and collective agents (Sewell 1992).

In Britain, Anthony Giddens has suggested that the apparent opposition between agency and structure can be resolved or dissolved by concentrating on the role of social actors in the process of 'structuration' (1979: cf. 2; cf. Bryant and Jary 1991). The idea of structuring as a process raises the question of social change, to be discussed in the following chapter.

5

Social Theory and
Social Change

Time and again in earlier chapters, particular approaches, from functionalism to structuralism, have been criticized because they fail to account for change. How does one account for change? Can the task be left to the historians and to their traditional concepts, or do social theorists also have a contribution to make? Is a theory of social change, or at least a model, actually available?

It needs to be stressed from the start that the term 'social change' is an ambiguous one. It is sometimes used in a narrow sense, referring to alterations in the social structure (the balance between different social classes, for example), but also in a considerably wider sense that includes political organization, the economy and culture. The emphasis in this chapter will fall on the wider definition.

Like philosophies of history, from which they cannot be completely distinguished, models or theories of social change fall into a number of main types. Some emphasize internal factors in change, and often describe society in terms of organic metaphors such as 'growth', 'evolution' and 'decay'. Others stress external factors and use terms like 'borrowing', 'diffusion' or 'imitation'. Some models are linear, like Judaeo-Christian philosophies of history or the 'modernization' model, while other models are cyclical, like the classical views of change revived by Machiavelli and others at the Renaissance, or the ideas underlying the work of the great fourteenth-century Arab historian Ibn Khaldun.

No model of social change is ever going to satisfy historians completely, because of their professional interest in variety and difference. Hence, as the English sociologist Ronald Dore once put it, 'You can't

make sociological omelettes without breaking a few historical eggs.'
All the same, historians have something to learn from the debate over
rival models, since an awareness of alternatives is a stimulus to the
imagination.

The two principal models of social change are the conflict model
and the evolution model, or, for simplicity's sake, Marx and Spencer.

Spencer's Model

'Spencer' is a convenient label for a model which stresses social
change which is gradual and cumulative ('evolution' as opposed to
'revolution'), and essentially determined from within ('endogenous'
as opposed to 'exogenous'). This endogenous process is often described in terms of 'structural differentiation' – in other words, a shift
from the simple, unspecialized and informal to the complex, specialized and formal, or in Spencer's own words, a shift from 'incoherent
homogeneity' to 'coherent heterogeneity' (Sanderson 1990: 10–35;
on Spencer himself, Peel 1971). This is, broadly speaking, the model
of change employed by both Durkheim and Weber.

Durkheim, who disagreed with Spencer on fundamental issues, as
we have seen (above, p. 127), followed him in describing social change
in essentially evolutionary terms. He emphasized the gradual replacement of simple 'mechanical solidarity' (in other words, the solidarity
of the similar) by a more complex 'organic solidarity', the solidarity
of the complementary, thanks to the increasing division of labour in
society (Durkheim 1893; cf. Lukes 1973: ch. 7). As for Weber, he
tended to avoid the term 'evolution', but all the same he viewed world
history as a gradual yet irreversible trend towards more complex and
impersonal forms of organization such as bureaucracy (above, p. 30)
and capitalism. It has therefore proved possible to make a synthesis
of the ideas of Durkheim and Weber on social change.

The result is what is known as the 'modernization' model, in which
the process of change is viewed as essentially a development from
within, and the outside world enters only to provide a stimulus to
'adaptation'. 'Traditional society' and 'modern society' are presented
as antithetical types along the following lines.

1   The traditional social hierarchy is based on birth ('ascription'),
and social mobility is low. The modern hierarchy, by contrast, is
based on merit ('achievement'), and mobility is high. A society of
'estates' (above, p. 61) is replaced by a society of 'classes', in which
there is greater equality of opportunity. Again, in traditional society,

the basic unit is a small group in which everyone knows everyone, a 'community'. After modernization, however, the basic unit is large and impersonal, 'Society' with a capital S. In the economic sphere this impersonality takes the form of the market, with its 'invisible hand', as Adam Smith called it; in the political sphere it takes the form of what Weber called 'bureaucracy'. Universal standards of behaviour replace standards viewed as applicable only to particular groups ('universalism' versus 'particularism'). Of course face-to-face groups do not disappear, but they adapt to the new situation. In order to act on the wider society, they take the form of voluntary associations for specific ends – professions, churches, clubs, political parties and so on, thus illustrating the rise of 'social capital' (above, p. 70).

2   These antithetical modes of social organization are associated with antithetical attitudes (if not 'mentalities'); attitudes to change, for example. In traditional society, where change is slow, people tend to be either hostile to it or unaware that it has taken place ('structural amnesia', above, p. 114). On the other hand, members of modern societies, in which change is rapid and constant, are well aware of it, expect it and approve of it. Indeed, actions are justified in the name of 'improvement' or 'progress', while institutions and ideas are condemned as 'out-of-date', and more traditional societies are dismissed as 'backward'. There is a shift from a situation in which 'new' is a term of abuse to one in which it is a recommendation in itself. The future is perceived not as a mere reproduction of the present, but as a space for the development of projects and trends (Koselleck 1985: 3–20).

3   To these basic contrasts, a number of others may be added. The culture of traditional societies has often been described as religious, magical and even irrational, while that of modern societies is viewed as secular, rational and scientific. Weber, for example, considered both secularization and rationalization to be central characteristics of the modernization process. He stressed the role of 'this-worldly asceticism' (*innerweltliche Askese*) and the 'disenchantment of the world' (*Entzauberung der Welt*) in the rise of capitalism. He also viewed bureaucracy as a more rational form of political organization than the one it replaced. It is worth noting that his use of the term 'rational' did not mean that Weber whole-heartedly approved of bureaucratization. He feared what he called the 'iron cage' of the modern world in which individuals have to submit to inflexible rules.

The parallel between this model of socio-cultural change and certain well-known models of economic growth and political development will be obvious enough. For example, theorists of economic growth have emphasized the 'take-off' from a pre-industrial society viewed as static to an industrial society in which growth is the normal condition. 'Compound interest becomes built, as it were, into its habits and institutional structure' (Rostow 1958). In similar fashion theorists of political development have stressed the spread of political participation as well as the rise of bureaucracy, and have noted the rise of social movements in the West from the late eighteenth century onwards (Lerner 1958; Tilly 2004).

The contrast between traditional and modern societies has been elaborated with the help of contributions from other disciplines. Geographers, for example, have suggested that modernity is associated with changes in conceptions of space, which comes to be treated as abstract or 'emptiable', in the sense of being available for a variety of purposes rather than tied to a particular function (Sack 1986). Social psychologists have described the development of a 'modern' personality, characterized by increasing self-control and also by the capacity for empathy with others. Social anthropologists have contrasted traditional modes of thought, relatively concrete and closed, with modern ones, more abstract and more 'open' (in other words, aware of alternative ideas) (Horton 1967, 1982).

For the last thirty years or so, however, social theorists have become increasingly uncomfortable with the assumptions underlying this model, such as the idea of backwardness and the inevitability and the benefits of a certain kind of social change (Tipps 1973; Knöbl 2003). Even in the field of economic history, the idea of progress towards an ever more affluent society has been challenged, and an alternative, ecological model proposed, according to which economic innovation is explained as essentially a reaction to the disappearance of a particular resource and the consequent need to find a substitute (Wilkinson 1973). As for cultural historians, they object to the notion of tradition as a residual concept, defined as what is not modern, as a consensual concept, ignoring conflicts within traditions, and as a static concept, ignoring the ways in which traditions are adjusted to changing circumstances, even if people do not always admit to themselves that this adjustment is taking place (Rudolph 1967; Hobsbawm and Ranger 1983; Heesterman 1985: 10–25).

Indeed, the evolutionary model has been criticized so severely in the last few years that it is only fair to begin by pointing to its merits. The idea of a sequence of social changes which, if not inevitable, are at least likely to follow one another, is not something to be rejected out of hand. The idea of 'evolution', with its echoes of Darwin, is not to be dismissed lightly either. For example, W. G. Runciman has argued that 'the process by which societies evolve is analogous, although by no means equivalent, to natural selection', emphasizing what he calls the 'competitive selection of practices' (1983–9: ii. 285–310). A good deal of military and economic history in particular, areas where the idea of competition is at its clearest, falls into place if it is approached in this way.

Another striking illustration of the merits of the model is Joseph Lee's (1973) study of Irish society since the Great Famine of the 1840s. It is organized around the concept of modernization in the hope, as the preface puts it, that this term will 'prove immune to the parochial preoccupations implicit in equally elusive and more emotive concepts like gaelicization and anglicization'. In this case, the comparative perspective allows the general to be seen in the particular, and suggests more profound or structural explanations for local changes than local historians had previously given.

For another illustration of the advantages of the model we may turn to Germany. Historians as different in their approach to the past as Thomas Nipperdey and Hans-Ulrich Wehler have discussed changes in German society from the late eighteenth century onwards in terms of modernization. Nipperdey, for example, has explained the growth of voluntary associations in the years around 1800 as part of the general shift from a traditional 'estate society' to a modern 'class society' (1976: 174–205).

As for Wehler (1987), he made his own contribution to theory with his concept of 'defensive modernization', employed to characterize the agrarian, administrative and military reforms carried out in Prussia and other German states between 1789 and 1815, on the grounds that they were essentially a response to what the ruling class perceived as the threat of the French Revolution and Napoleon.

The idea of defensive modernization is clearly capable of a wider application. The traditional notion of the 'Counter-Reformation', for example, modelled on that of 'counter-revolution', suggests that the Catholic Church reformed or modernized itself in the mid-sixteenth century as a reaction to the Protestant Reformation. Again, a number of movements for reform in the nineteenth century, from the 'Young Turks' in the Ottoman Empire to the Meiji 'restoration' in Japan, may be seen as responses to the threat posed by the rise of the West.

It is time to turn to the theory's defects. Formulated in industrializing countries in the late nineteenth century, the modernization model was elaborated in the 1950s to account for change in the Third World (the 'underdeveloped' countries, as they were called at the time). It is scarcely surprising to find that historians of pre-industrial Europe in particular should have found discrepancies between the model and the particular societies they study. They have expressed three main kinds of misgiving, about the direction, the explanation and the mechanics of social change.

(1)   In the first place, widening our horizons beyond the last century or two makes it clear that change is not unilinear, that history is not a 'one-way street'. In other words, society does not always move in the direction of increasing centralization, complexity, specialization and so on. Some adherents of modernization theory, Shmuel Eisenstadt (1973) for example, are aware of what he calls 'regression to decentralization', but the thrust of the theory is in the opposite direction. Regression has not yet received the thorough analysis it surely requires (cf. Runciman 1983–9: ii. 310–20).

An example of a regressive trend which is very well known to historians is that of Europe at the time of the decline of the Roman Empire and the invasions of the 'barbarians' (a category which itself deserves to be re-examined in the light of historical anthropology). The structural crisis of the Roman Empire in the third century CE was followed by a collapse of central government, a decline of the towns and an increasing tendency to local autonomy at both the economic and the political level. Lombards, Visigoths and other invaders were allowed to live under their own laws, so that a shift from 'universalism' to 'particularism' took place. The attempt by emperors to ensure that sons followed the occupation of their fathers suggests that there was also a shift from achievement to ascription. At the same time, Christianity became the official religion of the Empire following the conversion of the emperor Constantine. The Church became increasingly important in cultural, political and even economic life, while secular attitudes yielded to other-worldly ones (Brown 1971).

In other words, the case of the late Roman Empire illustrates the opposite of the process of 'modernization' in almost every social domain. The completeness of the reversal may be taken as evidence that the different trends are connected, as Spencerians assume, and in that sense support theories of social evolution. All the same, these theories have too often been put forward in a form implying that regressions do not take place. The fact that the terms 'urbanization', 'secularization' and 'structural differentiation' have no opposites in the language of sociology tells us more about the assumptions of sociologists than about the nature of social change.

The very term 'modernization' gives the impression of a linear process. However, intellectual historians are well aware that the word 'modern' – which was, ironically enough, already in use in the Middle Ages – has been filled with very different meanings in different centuries. Even the way in which the concept was used by Ranke and

Burckhardt, who both believed that modern history began in the fifteenth century, seems curiously old-fashioned today. Ranke stressed state building, and Burckhardt stressed individualism, but neither of them had anything to say about industrialization. This absence is hardly surprising, since the Industrial Revolution had not yet penetrated the German-speaking world at the time when Ranke wrote his *Latin and Teutonic Nations* (1828) or even when Burckhardt wrote his *Civilization of the Renaissance* (1860).

This absence means that the modernity of Ranke and Burckhardt is not ours. The trouble with modernity, in other words, is that it keeps changing (Kołakowski 1990; Latour 1993). As a result, historians have been forced to coin the self-contradictory term 'early modern' to refer to the period between the end of the Middle Ages and the beginning of the Industrial Revolution. More recently, sociologists and others have adopted another problematic term, 'postmodern', to describe the social and cultural changes of the last generation (below, p. 172).

(2) In the second place, historians have doubts about the explanation of social change built into the modernization model, notably the assumption that change is essentially internal to the social system, the development of potential, the growth of a branching tree. This assumption might work if one could isolate a particular society from the rest of the world, but in practice social change is often provoked by encounters between cultures (below, p. 162). In the cases of conquest and colonization in particular, the violent impact of forces external to a given society makes it inappropriate to discuss them in terms of mere stimuli to adaptation, the only function allotted to external factors in this model (Foster 1960).

(3) If we want to understand *why* social change takes place, it may be a good strategy to begin by examining *how* it takes place. Unfortunately, the Spencer model makes little reference to the mechanics of change. This lack of reference encourages the false assumption of a movement in one direction, and gives the process of change the appearance of a smooth and virtually automatic sequence of stages, as if all that people had to do was to step on to the escalator. An unusually explicit example of what we might call the 'escalator model' is the economist Walter Rostow's study of the stages of economic growth, from the 'traditional society', through the 'take-off', to 'the age of high mass-consumption'.

By contrast, the economic historian Alexander Gershenkron argued that late industrializers, such as Germany and Russia, diverged from the model of early industrializers, notably Britain. In the later cases, the role of the state was greater, and the profit motive was less important. The earlier model was inappropriate for latecomers precisely because they were in a hurry to catch up with their predecessors (Rostow 1958; Gershenkron 1962: 5–30). Latecomers had both advantages and disadvantages compared with early industrializers, but in both cases their situation was a different one.

The advantages of latecomers were generalized into a theory of change by the Dutch historian Jan Romein, who formulated what he called the law of the 'retarding lead', to the effect that an innovating society was usually 'backward' in the preceding generation. The argument for this leapfrog effect, or 'dialectics of progress', is that an innovating society tends to invest too heavily – metaphorically as well as literally – in a particular innovation, and so it fails to adapt when diminishing returns set in (Romein 1937: 9–64). It might be argued that the cultural history of the West illustrates Romein's theory rather well, with the Renaissance occurring in Italy (a culture which had not invested heavily in Gothic or scholasticism, as the French had done), while Romanticism developed in Germany (a culture which had not invested much in the Enlightenment).

In similar fashion, an economic historian, E. A. Wrigley (1972–3), has contrasted the process of social change in Britain and the Netherlands. By the middle of the eighteenth century, the working population of one rural region in the Netherlands, the Veluwe, were already involved in the production of paper and textiles as well as in agriculture. A region which lacked towns and factories was 'modern' in the sense that structural differentiation had taken place and that most adults were literate. In other words, the Veluwe is an example of modernization without industrialization. Conversely, the north of England in the early nineteenth century is an example of industrialization without modernization, since towns and factories coexisted with illiteracy and a strong sense of community.

The moral of these examples seems to be that we should be looking not for the consequences of industrialization (assuming them to be uniform) but rather for the 'fit' or compatibility between different socio-cultural structures and economic growth. The example of Japan points in the same direction, revealing the association of a remarkable economic performance with values and structures very different from those of the West. Hence the search by Weberian sociologists for a functional analogue of the Protestant ethic. One of them, the American Robert Bellah, found evidence for this-worldly asceticism (including a concept, *tenshoku*, much like that of the 'calling'), although he also drew attention to the 'penetration of the economy by political values' in Japan, in stark contrast to the history of the West (1957: 114–17).

The most important work of historical sociology in the Spencer tradition is Norbert Elias's (1939) study of 'the process of civilization'. This study had an unusual fate. First published in German in 1939, it was virtually neglected for decades. Only in the 1970s (or in the English-speaking world, in the 1980s) was this work taken as seriously as it deserved, by sociologists and by historians (cf. Elias 1970: 158–74; Mennell 1989; B. G. Smith 2001).

Elias's book was intended as a contribution to sociological theory. However, the author was also extremely interested in history, and his work is rich in concrete detail. The book is a monograph in the sense that the first volume in particular concentrates on certain aspects of social life in Western Europe, especially in the late Middle Ages. Indeed, Elias's second chapter could hardly be more concrete. Divided into sections on 'behaviour at table', 'blowing one's nose', 'spitting' and so on, it argues the case for a major change in behaviour at the Renaissance. New material objects, such as the handkerchief and the fork, came into use at this time, and Elias argues that these objects were instruments of what he calls 'civilization' and defines as a shift in the thresholds or 'frontiers' of embarrassment and shame. At a time when the history of material culture and the history of the body are supposed to be new discoveries, it is worth reminding ourselves that Elias's pages on this subject were written in the 1930s.

The picturesque descriptions of medieval noblemen wiping their noses on their sleeves, spitting on the floor and so on are not cited for their own sake. The condemnation of such behaviour in treatises on good manners in the fifteenth and sixteenth centuries is supposed to illustrate what Elias calls the 'sociogenesis of Western Civilization'. It is also intended to support a general theory of change. This theory may be regarded as a variation of the modernization model, but one which is not vulnerable to some at least of the objections discussed above.

In the first place, the theory is multilinear. Elias distinguishes what he called 'two main directions in the structural changes of society . . . those tending toward increased differentiation and integration, and those tending toward decreased differentiation and integration'. There is therefore no problem in principle in fitting the decline of the Roman Empire (say) into the model, though Elias might have said more than he did about the conscious rejection of traditional 'civilized' behaviour in certain periods of European history, whether by noble hooligans in Restoration England or by the Hungarian nobles of the Renaissance, anxious to define their identity by contrast to other nobilities and to establish their claim to descent from the 'barbarian' Huns (Klaniczay 1990; cf. Bryson 1998: 248–75).

In the second place, Elias is very much concerned with the mechanics of change, the 'how' as well as the 'why'. The most original section of his book is not the vivid description of changes in table manners, which has perhaps attracted a disproportionate share of readers' attention, but the argument in the second volume to the effect that the rise of self-control (and more generally, of social integration) is to be explained in political terms. Elias presents these changes as unintended consequences of the monopoly of force of the increasingly centralized state. The rise of this centralized or 'absolute' state, which turned the nobles from warriors into courtiers, is explained in its turn as an unintended consequence of the competition for power between small states in the Middle Ages.

The work of Elias has become increasingly influential in historical as well as sociological circles in recent years. All the same, it is vulnerable to certain criticisms. Unlike Weber, Elias illustrates his theory from European history alone, leaving the reader in doubt about its generality. One wonders whether a similar process of civilization might be identified in China (say) or in India (both arenas of competition between small states at some periods in their history). Again, despite his awareness of 'decreased integration', Elias had nothing to say about 'de-civilizing' processes, although he was writing his book at the time of the rise of Nazism (Elias and his followers later incorporated the ideas of 'informalization' and 'de-civilization' into their system) (Wouters 1977; Mennell 1990; Goody 2002).

A more serious criticism is that the central concept in this study, 'civilization', is problematic. If civilization is defined simply in terms of the existence of shame or self-control, then it is difficult to find any society which is not civilized. Indeed, it is impossible to demonstrate that medieval warriors, or the members of the so-called primitive societies, felt less shame or embarrassment than Westerners, rather than exhibiting these qualities in different situations (Duerr 1988–90). On the other hand, if 'civilization' is defined with more precision, a different kind of difficulty arises. How can one chart the rise of civilization in Europe if the standards of civilization were themselves changing? Despite these disagreements, the continuing relevance of Elias's study to any theory of social change is suggested by the wide range of recent studies, ranging from Japanese samurai to Russia under Stalinism, that draw on his work (Ikegami 1995; Volkov 2000).

If there is one general conclusion to be drawn from this variety of examples, it is that social change is multilinear rather than unilinear.

There is more than one path to modernity. These paths are not necessarily smooth, as the examples of France after 1789 and Russia after 1917 remind us. For an analysis of social change which emphasizes crisis and revolution, we may turn to Marx's model.

Marx's Model

'Marx', like 'Spencer', is a convenient piece of shorthand which will be used here to refer to a model of social change to which Engels, Lenin, Lukács and Gramsci (among others) all made contributions. In a sentence, it may be described as a model or theory of a sequence of societies ('social formations') which depend on economic systems ('modes of production') and contain internal conflicts ('contradictions') which lead to crisis, revolution and discontinuous change. There are of course ambiguities in the theory, allowing different interpreters to stress the importance of economic, political and cultural forces respectively, and to debate whether the forces of production determine the relations of production, or vice versa (G. Cohen 1978; Rigby 1987).

In some respects Marx offers little more than a variety of the modernization model. Like Spencer, the model assumes the existence of a sequence of forms of society – tribal, slave, feudal, capitalist, socialist and communist. Feudalism and capitalism, the social formations which have been discussed in most detail, are virtually defined – like traditional and modern society – as opposites. Like Spencer, Marx explains social change in fundamentally endogenous terms, emphasizing the internal dynamic of the mode of production (Sanderson 1990: 50–74). However, in some of its versions at least, the Marx model does stand up to the three main criticisms of Spencer summarized above.

In the first place, there is a place in the model for change in the 'wrong' direction, for example the so-called 'refeudalization' of Spain and Italy and the rise of serfdom in Central and Eastern Europe at the same time as the rise of the bourgeoisie in England and the Dutch Republic. Indeed, some Marxist analyses, as we have seen, emphasize the interdependence of economic and social development in the centre and the 'development of underdevelopment' on the periphery (Frank 1967; Wallerstein 1974) (above, p. 82).

In the second place, there is a place in Marx for exogenous explanations of social change. In the case of the West, this place is generally agreed to have been a subordinate one. In the famous controversy among Marxists of the 1950s over the transition from feudalism to capitalism, Paul Sweezy's explanation of the decline of feudalism in terms of external factors such as the reopening of the Mediterranean and the consequent rise of trade and towns met with a chorus of rejection (Hilton 1976). On the other hand, Marx himself regarded Asian society as devoid of internal mechanisms of change. Writing about the British in India, he suggested that the function of the conquerors (or, as he put it, their 'mission') was to destroy the traditional social framework and thus to make change possible (Avineri 1968).

Generally speaking, where the Spencer model presents the process of modernization as a series of parallel developments in different regions, Marx offers a more global account which stresses connections between changes in one society and changes in others. In similar fashion the Marxist Wallerstein, as we have seen, studies not the rise of individual European states or economies but the 'world economy', in other words an international system. He emphasizes the exogenous aspects of change (Frank 1967; Wallerstein 1974).

In the third place, Marx is much more concerned than Spencer with the mechanics of social change, especially in the case of the transition from feudalism to capitalism. Change is viewed in essentially dialectical terms – in other words, the emphasis falls on conflict and on consequences which are not only unintended but the very opposite of what was planned or expected. Thus social formations which once unleashed productive forces later 'turn into their fetters', and the bourgeoisie dig their own graves by calling the proletariat into existence (Marx and Engels 1848; cf. G. Cohen 1978).

On the question of unilinear versus multilinear development, Marxists disagree. The tribal–slave–feudal–capitalist–socialist sequence is obviously unilinear. However, Marx himself considered this schema to be relevant to European history alone. He did not expect India, or even Russia, to follow the Western path, although he did not make clear what paths he did expect them to take. Some analyses within the Marxist tradition are firmly multilinear. Perry Anderson (1974), for example, emphasizes the variety of possible paths to modernity by choosing the ballistic metaphor of 'trajectory' in preference to that of 'evolution', and describing 'passages' from antiquity to feudalism and 'lineages' of the absolutist state (cf. Skocpol 1984: 170–210). Again, Barrington Moore (1966) distinguishes three main historical routes to the modern world. There is the 'classic' route of bourgeois revolution, as in the cases of England, France and the United States; that of peasant (rather than proletarian) revolution, in the cases of Russia and China; and finally conservative revolution, or revolution from above, in the cases of Prussia and Japan (cf. Skocpol 1984: 318–55).

The emphasis on revolution (discussed above, p. 29) is of course a salient characteristic of Marx's model. In the Spencer model change is smooth, gradual and automatic, and the structures evolve as it were by themselves. In the Marx model, by contrast, change is abrupt, and the old structures are smashed in the course of a sequence of dramatic events. In the French Revolution, for example, the abolition of the monarchy and the feudal system, the expropriation of the Church and the aristocrats, and the replacement of provinces by departments all took place in a relatively short time (cf. Sewell 1996).

The tension, not to say 'contradiction', in the Marxian system between economic determinism and the collective voluntarism of revolution has often been remarked, and battles have ensued between different schools of interpretation. Marx's model thus raises, even if it does not solve, the problem of the relationship between political events and social change, as well as the problem of human agency, summarized in the famous phrase, 'Men make history, but not in circumstances of their own choosing'. Followers of Marx have been divided into 'economic', 'political' and 'cultural' Marxists on the basis of their different interpretations of this epigram.

Despite – or because of – these tensions, the Marx model seems to meet the criticisms of historians better than Spencer's alternative. This is not altogether surprising, since the model is much better known to historians, and many of them have modified it. It is difficult to think of a major contribution to social history (as opposed to historical sociology) which utilizes modernization as a framework. On the other hand, the Marx model is used in classic studies such as Emilio Sereni's *Capitalism in the Countryside* (1947), which deals with Italy in the generation after its unification in 1860; Edward Thompson's famous *The Making of the English Working Class* (1963), Maurice Agulhon's *The Republic in the Village* (1970), a study of eastern Provence in the first half of the nineteenth century, and the anthropologist Eric Wolf's *Europe and the People without History* (1982), a study of the interaction of world cultures from 1492 onwards, in which the title (taken too literally by Edward Said) both contrasts and links 'the people who claim history as their own and the people to whom history has been denied' (Wolf 1982: 29).

It may not be a coincidence that these three books, and others which might have been cited, deal with Marx's own century and with the transition which he knew and analysed best, the rise of capitalism. The Marx model is considerably less satisfactory as an interpretation of the old regimes of pre-industrial societies.

It fails, for example, to deal with demographic factors, which may well have been the most important motors of change in these societies (below, p. 159). Nor does it have much to offer to the analysis of social conflict in these societies. In practice, Marxist historians of old regimes use a weak version of the model when a modified version is needed. Social conflict in seventeenth-century France, for instance, has been presented as a foreshadowing of the conflicts of the nineteenth century (above, p. 61). It is only relatively recently that Marxist historians have taken serious account of social solidarities other than those of class, and the title of one of Edward Thompson's articles, 'Class Struggle without Class', illustrates not only the author's love of paradox but also the difficulty of finding an alternative conceptualization (Hobsbawm 1971; E. P. Thompson 1991: 16–91).

A Third Way?

Given the existence of two models of social change, each with its particular strengths and weaknesses, it is worth investigating the possibility of a synthesis. This may appear something like an alchemical wedding, in other words a union of opposites. However, in some respects, at least, the models are complementary rather than contradictory, and a number of studies of concrete situations mediate between them.

Essays in Synthesis

For example, Alexis de Tocqueville's famous account of the French Revolution, which presents it as a catalyst of changes which had already begun to take place during the old regime, might be said to mediate between the evolutionary and revolutionary models of change. Again, an examination of the important role played by political clubs during the French Revolution, notably that of the Jacobin Club, suggests that an emphasis on the role of voluntary associations and a stress on discontinuous change are perfectly compatible. Even Thompson's *The Making of the English Working Class*, which begins with an assault on sociology in general and structural differentiation in particular, includes a fascinating account of the place of trade unions and friendly societies in early nineteenth-century England, the 'rituals of mutuality' of the Brotherhood of Maltsters, the Unanimous

Society and so on, thus lending empirical support to one aspect of the theory of modernization that it sets out to undermine (E. P. Thompson 1963: 418–29).

A number of historical sociologists have drawn on both Marx and Spencer (especially the Weberian variety of the model) and attempted a synthesis. Barrington Moore's account of the making of the modern world is fundamentally Marxist in orientation, but incorporates insights from modernization theory, while Moore's former pupil Charles Tilly is a 'modernizer' able to respond to some of the Marxist criticisms of this approach. Wallerstein combines a fundamentally Marxian approach with elements from the evolutionary theory in which he was trained, notably the stress on competition between states, whether for profit or for hegemony. In her study of revolutions, Theda Skocpol confessed a debt to both Marx and Weber.

However, even a synthesis of Marx and Spencer could not deal with all the objections which have been raised to these models, which share serious limitations of perspective. Both were developed in order to account for industrialization and its consequences, and they are much less satisfactory in their account of changes before the middle of the eighteenth century. For example, 'traditional society' in Spencer and 'feudal society' in Marx are essentially residual categories, looking-glass worlds in which the principal characteristics of 'modern' or 'capitalist' society are simply reversed. The use of terms such as 'pre-industrial', 'pre-political' and even 'prelogical' is extremely revealing in this respect. They signify a failure to engage with the particularities of societies that do not fit a particular model.

Is there a third way, a model or theory of social change which will go beyond both Marx and Spencer? The revival of historical sociology in the 1980s included a number of attempts to do just this, on the part of Anthony Giddens (1985), for example, Michael Mann (1986–93), and Charles Tilly (1990), all of whom stress politics and war. Giddens, for example, introduced his study of *The Nation-State and Violence* with a critique of social evolutionism precisely on the grounds that it stresses economic factors ('allocative resources') at the expense of political ones (1985: 8–9). Mann offers what he calls a 'history of power', in which he suggests that 'The growth of the modern state, as measured by finance, is explained primarily not in domestic terms but in terms of geopolitical relations of violence' (1986–93: i. 490). Tilly is concerned with 'capital' as well as 'coercion', but describes himself as going beyond his predecessors precisely 'by placing the organization of coercion and preparation for war squarely in the middle of the analysis' (1990: 14).

In this respect all three sociologists converge not only with one another (and with Perry Anderson, whose volume *Lineages of the Absolutist State* had much to say about war), but also with historians of early modern Europe. For some time, a group of these historians have been arguing that political centralization in the sixteenth and seventeenth centuries, the age of the Habsburgs and the Bourbons, was little more than a by-product of the demands of war, thus illustrating a general theory dear to German historians early this century, that of 'the primacy of foreign policy'.

The argument runs roughly as follows. The sixteenth and seventeenth centuries were an age of 'military revolution' in which armies grew larger and larger. To pay for these armies, rulers had to squeeze more out of their subjects in taxes. The armies in turn helped to enforce the collection of the taxes, thus setting up what has been called the 'extraction-coercion cycle' (Tilly 1975: 96). The rise of the centralized state was not so much the result of a plan or a theory (such as 'absolutism') as an unintended consequence of competition for power in the international arena. In complementary fashion, in her comparative study of revolutions, Skocpol gave more explanatory weight to international conflicts, including wars, than her predecessors had done.

The idea that crises such as wars and revolutions act as catalysts or accelerators, speeding up social change rather than initiating it, has been explored in more detail by two historians who look at the First World War from opposite sides. Arthur Marwick (1965) suggests that the events of 1914–18 encouraged the 'blurring' of social distinctions in Britain, while Jürgen Kocka (1973) argues that in Germany, the 'same' events made social distinctions still more sharp (cf. Mann 1986–93: ii. 740–802). The two societies reacted to the war in opposite ways, because their pre-war structures were very different.

However, the most important contribution to a third way is surely that of Michel Foucault in *Discipline and Punish* (1975) and other studies. Focusing on Western Europe in the period 1650–1800, Foucault tells the story of a major shift in theories of punishment, from retribution to deterrence, and also in the practice of punishment, from 'spectacle' to 'surveillance'. The author rejected explanations of the abolition of public executions in humanitarian terms, as he had rejected such explanations of the rise of lunatic asylums.

Instead, Foucault stressed the rise of what he called the 'disciplinary society', increasingly visible from the later seventeenth century onwards in barracks, factories and schools no less than in prisons. As a vivid illustration of this new type of society he chose the famous early nineteenth-century project for a 'Panopticon', an ideal prison in which one warder can see everything while himself remaining unseen. At times, Foucault seems to be turning modernization theory on its head, writing about the rise of discipline instead of the rise of liberty.

There is obviously no place for the 'process of civilization' in Foucault's account of social change. Elias is turned on his head along with Spencer. All that changes, according to Foucault, is the mode of repression, physical repression in the old regime, psychological repression later. The cooler and more clinical term 'displacement' is substituted for the conventional idea of 'progress'. All the same, this vision of a repressively bureaucratic society has something important in common with that of Max Weber (O'Neill 1986).

Foucault's work has often been criticized by historians, both fairly and unfairly. In the case of *Discipline and Punish*, the conclusions have been said to have 'no base in archival research' (Spierenburg 1984: 108). Another criticism of Foucault by historians fastens on his insensitivity to local variation, his tendency to illustrate generalizations about Europe with French examples, as if different regions did not have their own time-scales. If, on the other hand, we think of Foucault as offering a simple model of change rather than telling the whole story, these criticisms become virtually irrelevant.

This redefinition of the author's purpose does not dispose of a third damaging criticism of his work, its failure to discuss the mechanics of change. A leader in the movement which proclaimed the 'death of man', or at least the 'decentring of the subject' (below, p. 179), Foucault seems to have shrunk from testing the theory by examining the intentions of the reformers of punishment, demonstrating that the new system which resulted had nothing to do with these intentions, and revealing what had really produced it. The task is of course an extremely intractable one, but if someone claims to be sweeping away traditional historical explanations, it is not unreasonable to expect that person to perform it.

In my own view, what is most valuable in Foucault's work in general, and in *Discipline and Punish* in particular, is the negative rather than the positive side. After his corrosive criticisms of the conventional wisdom, the history of incarceration, sexuality and so on will never be the same again. Nor will the theory of social change, since Foucault has revealed its associations with the belief in progress which he has done so much to undermine. As in the case of Nietzsche (one of Foucault's favourite philosophers), those who reject his answers remain unable to evade his questions.

Patterns of Population

Other discussions of social change break with both Marx and Spencer, because they are cyclical rather than linear. Oswald Spengler's *Decline of the West* (1918–22) and Arnold Toynbee's *Study of History* (1935–61) both viewed history as the story of a succession of cultures which went through the same cycle of growth, maturity, decline and fall. Cyclical theories of more limited application include the 'long waves' of the Russian economist Nikolai Kondratieff, the shorter cycles of the French economist Clément Juglar, and Pareto's account of the 'circulation of elites'.

Toynbee's massive study, which took a quarter of a century to write and ran to more than 6,000 pages, discussed twenty-one discrete 'civilizations' as the protagonists of history, examining their origins as responses to the 'challenges' of their environments, their 'growth', and above all their crises and declines, in which war and the rise of a proletariat (including an 'external' proletariat such as the barbarians who invaded the Roman Empire) played crucial parts. Institutions such as universal states and churches allowed civilizations to 'rally', sometimes more than once, but could not fend off a 'final dissolution'. These general theses were based on a series of vivid examples taken from Toynbee's amazingly wide historical reading, not to mention his use of assorted geographers, anthropologists, sociologists and psychologists (notably Carl Gustav Jung).

The first response to Toynbee was generally one of admiration, but after a time more and more serious criticisms were made of his project. Toynbee was faulted for being unduly schematic, for failing to engage with the ideas of historical sociologists such as Max Weber and Vilfredo Pareto, for virtually ignoring the place of natural science in civilization, and above all for treating 'civilizations' as bounded entities that could be counted and saying too little about their interaction.

Whereas Toynbee wrote about the whole of human history, the French historian Fernand Braudel concentrated on the sixteenth and seventeenth centuries. All the same, he offered some broader conclusions. In *The Mediterranean and the Mediterranean World in the Age of Philip II* (1949), one of the most famous studies of the past to have been published in the twentieth century, Braudel argued that historical changes take place at different speeds, three in particular. There was the long term of 'geohistory', 'a history of constant repetition'; the medium term of 'economic systems, states, societies and civilizations'; and finally the short term of events. In the first two cases, Braudel endorsed the cyclical model, describing geohistory as a time of 'ever-recurring cycles' and contrasting ages such as the sixteenth century, which favoured the creation of large empires like that of Philip II, with ages that encouraged their fragmentation. Like the economist François Simiand, whose work was an inspiration to him, Braudel saw history as the alternation of phases of expansion and phases of contraction ('A phases' and 'B phases').

In the second half of the twentieth century, cyclical theories were reinforced by the work of historical demographers, who argued that the most important factor in social change is the growth or decline in population.

In his study of the province of Languedoc in south-western France in the early modern period (1966), Emmanuel Le Roy Ladurie, a former student of Braudel's, drew on Kondratieff's concept of 'long waves' in the economy. However, for Le Roy Ladurie the real motor of social change is population. He wrote the history of what he called 'a great agrarian cycle, lasting from the end of the fifteenth century to the beginning of the eighteenth'. The basic pattern was one of growth followed by decline, which was followed in its turn by recovery. In the phase of expansion, a population explosion took place, followed by land clearance, the subdivision of farms, a price rise and what Le Roy calls 'a victory of profit' at the expense of rent and wages, in other words a victory of the class living from profit, the entrepreneurs. In the seventeenth century, however, agricultural productivity hit a ceiling, and as a result, all the main economic and social trends went into reverse.

As Malthus predicted, the population began to press on the means of subsistence. Growth was followed by decline, the result of different factors such as famine, plague, emigration and a later age of marriage. Profit was defeated by rent, the speculator – in the language of Pareto – by the rentier. Holdings which had been fragmented were united once more. Looking at the period 1500–1700 as a whole, Le Roy Ladurie suggests that the region functioned as a 'homeostatic eco-system', or, in a phrase that was taken out of context and became notorious, 'immobile history'. The obvious question to ask at this point is, What breaks the cycle? In many cases it is the intrusion of something external to the system, one of the 'encounters' to be discussed below (p. 162).

Le Roy Ladurie's Malthusian model (or 'neo-Malthusian model', as he prefers to call it) has been criticized by some Marxists, who argue that scholars who employ this model underestimate the importance of class conflict in the societies they study. However, other Marxist historians, especially in France, have revised their own models to take more account of demography, using population trends to solve the classic problem of the transition from feudalism to capitalism. Studies of revolution, such as that of Goldstone on the early modern world, have begun to take seriously the pressure of population on resources as a pre-condition for the breakdown of states.

In economic history, Braudel's (1979) history of early modern capitalism distinguished a succession of economies dominated by particular cities: Venice, Genoa, Antwerp, Amsterdam. In political history, Paul Kennedy's *Rise and Fall of the Great Powers* (1987) studied the succession of imperial hegemonies over the last 500 years, from China and Spain to Britain and the USA, stressing what he called 'imperial overstretch' as a key factor in decline. He focuses on the interaction between economics and strategy, especially the diversion of resources from the creation of wealth to the establishment and maintenance of hegemony, a diversion that leads to political decline over the long term. Expansion makes empires 'top-heavy', with too many soldiers and officials for the economic base to support. In similar fashion, recent studies of the world system on the model of Wallerstein are increasingly concerned with cycles and 'hegemonic shifts' over the long term, or, as some would say, a succession of world systems rather than one (Abu-Lughod 1989; Frank and Gills 1993: esp. 143–99, 278–91).

Patterns of Culture

Another criticism of both the Marx and the Spencer models is that they give too small a place to culture, treating it more or less as a superstructure, the icing on the cake, rather than treating it as a force for social change (as many scholars do today).

How do cultural patterns change? Two famous discussions of the question may be found in the work of the art historian Ernst Gombrich and the historian of science Thomas Kuhn, both of them concerned with 'culture' in the traditional sense of the arts and sciences, and especially with the history of cultural traditions.

As we have seen, one of Gombrich's key concepts was what he called the visual 'schema'. The use of schemata explains very well the persistence of artistic traditions over the long term, but what about change? To solve this problem, Gombrich introduced the idea of the 'correction' of the schema by artists who note discrepancies between the traditional model and the reality they observe. This solution raises in its turn the question of circularity. How can artists check a schema against reality if their view of reality is itself a product of the schema?

A possible answer to this question is that in some places and periods, at least, artists are aware of alternative schemata. As in the case of the history of mentalities (above, p. 95), it may be suggested that an awareness of alternatives diminishes the power of tradition and gives individuals more freedom to make choices. A striking example that supports this amendment to Gombrich comes from China in the seventeenth century. Some Chinese landscape painters changed their style at this time, after having had the opportunity to view some European prints brought into the country by Christian missionaries. They did not imitate the Western style, but awareness of it helped them to free themselves from traditional ways of representing landscape (Cahill 1982).

For his part, Thomas Kuhn analysed what he called 'the structure of scientific revolutions'. Whereas Foucault pointed to epistemological breaks without trying to explain them, Kuhn focused on the process of change. Whereas Gombrich spoke of the 'schema', Kuhn employed the parallel notion of the scientific 'paradigm', a view of the world of nature that influenced what he called 'normal science', the everyday practice of the scientific community. An obvious example is the traditional view of the universe with the earth at the centre, a paradigm associated with Aristotle and Ptolemy.

Kuhn argued that major changes, or 'revolutions', in scientific paradigms come about in a series of stages. In the first place, individual observers become aware of anomalies – in other words, information that is inconsistent with the paradigm. Secondly, to deal with these anomalies, the paradigm is modified or patched up, as in the case of the famous 'epicycles' introduced into the Ptolemaic system to allow more accurate predictions of the position of the planets. In the third place, discrepancies between specific observations and the general paradigm multiply, leading to a state of 'crisis'. New theories emerge, like the Copernican theory that the centre of the universe is the sun. Finally, in a dramatic 'revolution', a kind of 'Gestalt switch', one of these competing theories is adopted by the scientific community and becomes a new paradigm. Once again we see the uses of the term 'community', however difficult it is to define (T. S. Kuhn 1962, 1974: 239–319).

Kuhn's work itself presented a paradigm for the history of science. It has sometimes been criticized as a cyclical model that denies scientific progress. Kuhn certainly denied that science develops by accumulation. All the same, he claimed that there was progress, even if the path was zig-zag rather than linear, towards what he called 'an increasingly detailed and refined understanding of nature'. Although his ideas were put forward in a strictly scientific context, it is worth asking whether Kuhn's notion of a paradigm might be useful in discussing other kinds of cultural change. In the history of anthropology and historical writing, for example, Kuhnian revolutions have been identified. In the case of geography, it is well known that Columbus set sail with the traditional paradigm of three continents firmly in his head, and when he discovered Hispaniola, he thought that it must be part of Asia. It took some years for the paradigm to be revised and for America to be treated as a fourth continent.

Similar points might be made about stereotyped perceptions of the 'other' – cannibals, witches, Jews, lunatics, homosexuals and so on. Edward Said viewed Orientalism as, among other things a set of paradigms for research. It was an art historian in the tradition of Warburg and Gombrich, the Australian Bernard Smith, who suggested that eighteenth-century Europeans viewed the peoples of the Pacific whom they encountered for the first time through classical stereotypes such as the noble savage (in the second edition of his book, the author observed that his argument could be translated into Kuhnian terms (B. Smith 1960)).

Like scientific paradigms, these stereotypes or prejudices are often the basis for everyday action. Like scientific paradigms, they are subject to refutation, and they are sometimes modified or even abandoned. The formation, modification and abandonment of stereotypes of this kind, together with other kinds of social and cultural change, are particularly visible in the case of encounters between people from different cultures, especially in cases where the encounters are prolonged, as in the case of conquest or colonization.

Encounters

Both the Marx and the Spencer models concentrate on social change that is generated within a given society. However, there are many cases in history of change which was initiated from outside, by encounters of different kinds, from trade to invasion. It was to discuss the consequences of encounters, especially with American Indians, that anthropologists, whose very discipline was created and developed in the context of culture contact and imperialism, introduced the concept of 'acculturation', sometimes defined as the assimilation of a weaker or subordinate culture to the values of a dominant one (Dupront 1965; Spicer 1968).

A generation later, some historians took up the concept. The pioneer in this regard was the American Oscar Handlin, whose book *Boston's Immigrants*, subtitled 'A Study in Acculturation', goes back to 1941. More recently, the French historian Robert Muchembled (1978) has applied the term to cultural encounters within Europe, discussing what he called the 'acculturation of the rural world' in north-east France at the end of the sixteenth century. He noted that the rise in witch-trials coincided with the Counter-Reformation attack on 'idolatry' as well as the spread of literacy. The centre (or the clergy) was trying to change the values of the periphery (or the laity).

The problem with this extension of the concept is the assumption that clergy and people belonged to different cultures, an assumption which is surely exaggerated. The cultural distance between the two may have been increasing at a time when a greater proportion of the clergy were being educated in seminaries, but this distance is unlikely to have been anything like as great as that between the Amerindians and the European settlers. In this sense the use of the term 'acculturation' by historians of Europe is misleading. It is probably more useful to approach attempts to evangelize ordinary people during the Reformation and Counter-Reformation as cases of the 'negotiation' of meanings between groups (Greyerz 1984: 56–78).

In any case, as we have seen (above, p. 106), to do justice to the complexity of the results of cultural encounters, the concept of 'acculturation' should be joined by 'transculturation', 'cultural hybridity' and 'cultural translation'. The value of concepts such as these has been neatly illustrated in a discussion of the contacts between Christians and Muslims in medieval Spain. Up to a certain point, historians might be described as doing the same job as the anthropologists, while using different terms. Where the concepts of anthropologists proved their value was in explaining what happened, and in particular in discussing the mechanisms of social and cultural change, the particular ways in which it came about (Glick and Pi-Sunyer 1969).

For their part, historians can make a contribution to the development of social theory by introducing a greater variety of examples. Conquests, for instance, are a particular dramatic class of encounters between cultures, rarely discussed by social theorists (Foster 1960). Thus the Norman conquest of England in 1066 has been described as 'the classic example in European history of the disruption of a social order by the sudden introduction of an alien military technology' (White 1962: 38).

Outside Europe, the Spanish conquest of Mexico and Peru and the British conquest of India are equally clear examples of social change induced from outside (in both cases with the aid of a new military technology). In all these cases traditional elites were pushed aside by newcomers. The changes at the bottom of the social hierarchy were no less profound, and seem to have been at least in part the result of misunderstanding, a factor in social history which, like ignorance, has not received the attention it deserves.

The officials of the East India Company, for example, viewed the Indian social structure through English spectacles, as a system of landlords and tenants. They perceived the *zamindars*, who were more or less tax-collectors, as landlords. In the language of Kuhn, they stuck to their paradigm and ignored anomalies. However, the practice of conquest differs from the practice of science in a crucial respect. The conquerors had the power to turn their perceptions into reality by treating the *zamindars* as landlords. We might say that they 'translated' Indian society into terms that were intelligible to them. In a classic case of cultural 'construction' or reconstruction, a misunderstanding of the social structure led to change in the social structure (Neale 1957; B. Cohn 1962).

Although there is less evidence available in the case of the Norman conquest, it may be suspected that something of the same kind happened in England after 1066. The Normans failed to understand the complex social system of the Anglo-Saxons, in which status was expressed in terms of different amounts of 'wergild' – in other words, the amount of compensation to be paid to the victim's relatives if different kinds of people were killed. By failing to understand the local system, the Normans reduced Anglo-Saxon England to a society of serfs, freemen and knights. Like the previous example, this one suggests that some groups may be more important than others in the cultural 'constitution' of society (below, p. 175). It also suggests the importance of a relatively brief period of innovation, after which society 'crystallizes' into relatively inflexible structures.

In his study of colonial Peru, the French historian Nathan Wachtel (1971) focused on the crisis provoked by the Spanish conquest. The key terms in his account of social and cultural change between 1530 and 1580 are 'acculturation' and 'destructuration' (a term he appropriated from the Italian sociologist Vittorio Lanternari). In similar fashion Le Roy Ladurie described the revolt of the Protestants of the Cévennes at the beginning of the eighteenth century (a reaction to the outlawing of Protestantism by Louis XIV) as a protest against 'deculturation'.

By 'destructuration', Wachtel means the snapping of the links between different parts of the traditional social system. Traditional institutions and customs survived the conquest, but the old structure disintegrated. Tribute survived, for example, but without the old system of redistribution by the state of which it had formed a part. Local chiefs also survived, but their relation to the central government was no longer what it had been in the days of the Incas. Traditional religion survived, but it was now an unofficial, indeed a clandestine cult, regarded as 'idolatry' by the Spanish missionaries, who did all they could to uproot it. Specialists in what Bourdieu calls 'symbolic violence', the Spanish clergy were in effect missionaries of socio-cultural change or restructuration.

An important feature of Wachtel's version of acculturation is that it is concerned not only with 'objective' culture contact, but also with what he called, following the Mexican historian Miguel León-Portilla (1959), the 'vision of the vanquished' – in other words, the view of the dominant culture from below. His concern for the political context of culture contact and his interest in the ways in which members of the two cultures perceived one another give the old acculturation model a new, sharp cutting edge, making it explanatory as well as descriptive.

The Spanish conquest of the New World was accompanied by the spread of European diseases, such as smallpox, to which the indigenous population was extremely vulnerable. Estimates vary, but it is agreed that several million people, probably the majority of the population, died in the first generations after the conquest of Mexico (McNeill 1976; Crosby 1986). More generally, major epidemics offer a different kind of example of social change resulting from penetration from outside. In 1348, for example, the Black Death, a plague carried by rats, invaded Europe from Asia and killed about a third of the population in a short space of time. The consequent manpower shortages led to important long-term changes in the European social structure.

The Importance of Events

Plagues, like cultural encounters and revolutions, offer striking examples of the role of events in the process of social change, a role that some sociologists and historians used to deny or at any rate to minimize.

Like his compatriots Durkheim and Simiand, Braudel regarded traditional narrative history (*histoire événementielle*) as superficial. For Braudel events were nothing but froth and foam, interesting only for what they revealed about the underlying currents of history.

He viewed individuals as prisoners of destiny, their attempts to influence the course of affairs as ultimately futile. The 'hero' of his major work, Philip II, is more of an anti-hero, powerless to change the course of history. Suppose, however, that Braudel had chosen to write about Russia in the age of Lenin. Would he have found it so easy to ignore the role of the individual in history?

Braudel both inspired his successors and provoked them to react against his model of social change. For example, Le Roy Ladurie found a place in his history for the events which Braudel dismissed, presenting vivid vignettes of social conflict and social protest in order to show how contemporaries perceived and responded to economic and social change. In the phase of expansion, he described the carnival of Romans in Dauphiné in 1580, during which craftsmen and peasants declared that the elite of their town 'had grown rich at the expense of the poor people' (the author later made this dramatic event the focus of a book-length study in micro-history). In the phase of contraction, he discussed the revolt of the Vivarais in 1670 as an example of 'a more instinctive than rational reaction to the rural crisis'. All the same, the term 'reaction' is revealing. Like Braudel, Le Roy Ladurie assumed that events reflect structures rather than changing them.

An alternative approach emphasizes what may be called the 'management' of change. Two contrasting examples from the history of Japan may help to illuminate this problem. It is obvious that rulers are no more able to hold back social change than Canute was able to hold back the waves (this was actually the point that the king was making to his courtiers by taking them to the seashore). All the same, rulers have attempted to do this in Byzantium (above, p. 64) and also in Japan. In seventeenth-century Japan, at a time when towns were growing and trade expanding, the Tokugawa regime tried to freeze the social structure with a decree that the four main social groups should rank in the following order: samurai, peasants, craftsmen and merchants. As one might have expected, the decree did not prevent wealthy merchants from achieving an unofficial social status higher than many samurai.

On the other hand, the abolition of the samurai by the Meiji regime which replaced that of the Tokugawa in 1868 was a decree with important social consequences. For example, many ex-samurai went into business, a career previously closed to them (Moore 1966: 275–90). Why did the Meiji succeed while the Tokugawa failed? The obvious answer is that one regime tried to resist change, the other to assist it. However, it might be worth exploring the possibility that the Meiji were doing more than assist the inevitable; that the regime was concerned with what might be called the 'management' of social change – not so much giving orders to the waves as diverting the stream in the direction they preferred.

In Giuseppe de Lampedusa's great historical novel *The Leopard* (1958), set in Sicily in the middle of the nineteenth century, one aristocrat remarks to another that 'in order to keep everything as it is we have to change everything'. Some aristocracies (notably the British) seem to have had a talent for this kind of adaptation to new circumstances, for making sacrifices or tactical concessions in the interests of a strategy for the survival for the family or the class over the long term. Such activities surely deserve a place in any general theory of social change.

One might also hope that the theory would specify the types of situation in which a strategy of this kind has a chance of success. Two independent studies of aristocratic behaviour, concerned respectively with nineteenth-century England and twentieth-century Rajasthan, offer remarkably similar accounts of one such situation. Both studies describe a ruling class which was split between an upper group which was more sympathetic to change and a lower group which had more to lose from it. However, in both cases the lower group traditionally looked to the upper group for leadership. In this situation it was very difficult for the group with most to lose to organize resistance to change. Hence the ruling class as a whole followed the 'adaptation' policy of its leaders, and social change took place without violence (F. M. L. Thompson 1963; Rudolph and Rudolph 1966).

If individuals, groups and events have an important place in the process of social change, the form no less than the content of the analysis (whether it is offered by social historians, sociologists or social anthropologists) may be in need of revision. In fact, the turn (or return) to narrative has been the object of much recent discussion in all three disciplines. The problem might be posed in the form of a dilemma. The analysis of structures is too static and does not allow either writers or readers to be sufficiently aware of change. On the other hand, traditional historical narrative is unable to accommodate these structures at all. A search is therefore under way for new forms of narrative appropriate to social history.

One might call this the search for a 'braided' narrative, since it interweaves analysis with storytelling (Fischer 1976). Alternatively, one might speak of 'thick' narrative, on the model of Geertz's 'thick description', on the grounds that the new forms need to be constructed to bear a heavier weight of explanation than the old (concerned as they were with the actions of prominent individuals). In any case, we find some historians turning to literary theory, especially the theory of narrative, in order to find the literary form most appropriate for their needs (Abbott 2002).

The new forms – new for historians at any rate – include stories which present the same events from multiple points of view (below, p. 179) or deal with the experience of ordinary people at the local level in what might be called 'micronarratives' (Burke 1991).

The turn to micro-history was discussed in chapter 2. Sometimes it takes the form of a description, as in Le Roy Ladurie's study of the community of Montaillou, but it can also take the form of a story. One of the most dramatic of such stories concerns Martin Guerre.

Martin was a peasant from south-western France who ran away from the family farm to serve in the wars with Spain, returning to discover that his place had been taken by an intruder, a man who claimed to be him. The story has been retold by the historian Natalie Davis (1983) not only for its dramatic qualities, but also to shed light on social structures, including the structure of the family, and on the way in which these structures were experienced in everyday life. In her account the central figure is not so much Martin as his wife Bertrande de Rols. Abandoned by her husband, she was neither wife nor widow. Davis suggests that Bertrande's decision to recognize the intruder, for whatever reason, as her long-lost husband, was the only honourable way for her to escape from this impossible situation.

The return or revival of historical narrative in the last generation is also associated with a recognition of the power of certain events to undermine structures, most obviously in the case of revolutions. In the study of revolutions there has been a shift away from a preoccupation with the pre-conditions or 'triggers' and towards a concern with what Noel Parker calls 'the revolutionary narrative', defined as the form 'within which the events and actions that constitute one revolution or another are interpreted and acted upon' (1999: 111–59, at 112). The point is that the narrative is part of the experience of the agents themselves before it is taken up and modified by later scholars. It is shaped by, but in turn shapes, the experience of events, and so the next stage of action.

In some cases at least, past revolutions provide a model or paradigm for the present. In certain respects, for example, the French Revolution was perceived as a re-enactment of the English Revolution of the 1640s, down to the beheading of the king, while the Bolshevik Revolution was perceived by Trotsky and other participants as a re-enactment of 1789. As in the case of scientific paradigms, anomalies may be perceived, differences between the new event and the old model, but even in the case of revolutions, cultural traditions retain their power.

The tension between new events and old perceptions is all too rarely studied. One of the exceptions to this rule, as well as one of the most original discussions of cultural and social change to have appeared in the last generation, is a study of Hawaii by the Chicago anthropologist Marshall Sahlins, beginning with the arrival of Captain Cook in 1779 and moving from narrative to interpretation and from analysis of a specific situation to general theory.

On his visit to Hawaii, so we are told, Cook received an enthusiastic welcome on the part of some thousands of people, who came to meet him in their canoes. He was escorted to a temple and participated in a ritual in which he was worshipped. A few weeks later he returned to the island, and his reception was much cooler. The Hawaiians committed a series of thefts, and in attempting to put a stop to them, Cook was killed. Some years later, however, the new chief Kamehameha decided on a policy of friendship and commercial relations with Britain, perhaps as a way of managing social change.

Sahlins interprets Cook's reception (or more exactly, the various accounts of these incidents) through the hypothesis that the Hawaiians saw Cook as an incarnation of their god Lono, since he arrived at the time when the god was expected. He goes on to suggest that the murder, as well as the worship, of Cook was a ritual act, the slaying of the god. He interprets the pro-British policies of Kamehameha as appropriate for the man who had inherited Cook's *mana* (M. Sahlins 1985: 104–35; contrast Obeyesekere 1992).

Sahlins utilizes this interpretation to comment in a more general way on what he calls the interaction between systems and events, making two complementary points. In the first place, the events which took place were 'ordered by culture'. The Hawaiians perceived Cook through the lens of their own cultural tradition and acted accordingly, thus giving the events a distinctive cultural 'signature'. In other words, Sahlins emphasizes the 'fit' between endogenous and exogenous factors, in a similar way to the reception theorists discussed earlier. His discussion is reminiscent of Braudel's view of events as a litmus paper revealing structures, as well as Gombrich's concern with cultural schemata.

On the other hand, unlike Braudel and Gombrich, Sahlins goes on to suggest that in the process of assimilating these events, of 'reproducing that contact in its own image', Hawaiian culture 'changed radically and decisively'. For example, the tension between chiefs and commoners increased, because the distinction between the two groups was overlaid by the distinction between European and Hawaiian. The response of the chiefs was to adopt English names such as 'King George' or 'Billy Pitt', as if to make the point that chiefs are to people as Europeans are to Hawaiians – in other words, the dominant partner in the relationship. In a final discussion of social or historical change, Sahlins notes how every conscious attempt to prevent change or even to adapt to it brought other changes in its train, and concludes that all cultural reproduction involves alteration. Cultural categories are always at risk when they are used to interpret the world (M. Sahlins 1981, 1985: pp. vii–xvii, 136–86; W. H. Sewell 1996: 879).

These general suggestions offer a possible paradigm for studies of change elsewhere, or at least prompt us to ask whether Hawaii was a privileged or an eccentric example of culture contact, and whether culture contact is a privileged or an eccentric way of studying social change. Are Sahlins's generalizations about the relationship between structures and events valid, or at least suggestive, in contexts as remote from his 'field' as the German Reformation, say, or the French Revolution?

Generations

The idea of a 'generation' has long fascinated historians and sociologists alike. One reason for the fascination is that the concept seems to reflect our own experience of growing up and defining ourselves collectively in contrast to older people. Another is that it promises to link changes in structures to individuals and events via the sense of belonging to a particular age-group: the generation of 1789, for example (as the young Wordsworth wrote, 'Bliss was it in that dawn to be alive / But to be young was very heaven'), or the Spanish generation of 1898, which experienced the end of an empire.

There are some important discussions of what might be called the theory of the generation, notably Karl Mannheim's emphasis on the place of what he called 'a common location in the social and historical process' in creating a particular world-view or mentality (1952: 276–320). The theory has often not been translated into practice, however, and the few case-studies are mainly concerned with the history of art and literature (Pinder 1926; Peyre 1948; Burke 1972: 235–43; Ramsden 1974).

An interesting exception to this rule is an anthropological study of a small town in Aragon, carried out in the 1960s, which distinguished three groups, the 'declining', 'controlling' and 'emerging' generations, in terms of reactions to the formative – not to say traumatic – events of the Spanish Civil War. The first group formed their attitudes before the Civil War, the second participated in the fighting, while the third was too young to remember it. Although these contrasts extended well beyond the political sphere, it is tempting to explain them in political terms. A problem remains: to assess the importance of the events of 1936–9 in the formation of generations in this town, it is at once necessary and impossible to examine a 'control group', a similar community which did not experience the Civil War (Lisón-Tolosana 1966: 190–201).

It may be useful to approach generations, like nations, as examples of imagined communities. The members of a given generation share certain experiences and memories which help to bond them in a sort of alliance against the generation of their parents and, later, against that of their children as well. They may not share beliefs or values, but in their different ways they are responding to the same situation.

Whether they like it or not, many readers of this book belong to what may be called the 'postmodern' generation, marked by the events of 1968 or 1989. The consequences of postmodernity for history and theory will be discussed in the following chapter.

6

Postmodernity and Postmodernism

Some analysts of contemporary society have come to describe it not only as 'post-industrial' and 'late capitalist' but also as 'postmodern'. One of the first to use the concept was the historian Arnold Toynbee (for the history of the idea, P. Anderson 1998). Since Toynbee's day, however, historians – unlike economists, geographers or sociologists – have made a surprisingly small contribution to the debate on the nature of postmodernity. I say 'surprisingly' since periodization is one of the central concerns of historians. One contribution that they could make is a sceptical one. To a historian, especially to one concerned with trends over the long term, the term 'postmodern' is bound to look like yet another example of the hyperbole to which generations of intellectuals have resorted, from the Renaissance onwards, to persuade others that their period or generation is a special one. The rhetoric of any one generation would sound extremely plausible, were it not for the examples of their predecessors.

In any case, the concept 'postmodern' is an ambiguous one. Some people use the term in opposition to 'modern', as the description of a completely new epoch, while others think of postmodernity (in French, *surmodernité*) as an intensification or acceleration of modern trends or, in the words of the German sociologist Ulrich Beck, a 'second modernity' (Giddens 1990; Beck 2000).

Whatever adjective we use to describe it, a major shift in attitudes has occurred in the last generation among historians and social theorists as well as in the culture at large. There is a tendency to take structures less seriously, associated with a dizzy sense of liberty and also of uncertainty and precariousness. The shift is surely a response to the acceleration of social change. Just as we realize that opportunities for secure long-term employment are declining or that there is more and more movement of people, goods and messages across political frontiers, so we are increasingly aware of what Sahlins calls the 'risk' to categories whenever they are used in everyday life (M. Sahlins 1985: 149). As the Polish sociologist Zygmunt Bauman (2000) memorably puts it, we live in an age of fluidity, in a 'liquid' world where even personal relationships seem to be less constant than they used to be.

It is in this new social and cultural environment that the historians and theorists to be discussed in this chapter are working. Their conscious responses to postmodernity may be described, like much of contemporary art and literature, as examples of postmodernism. However, in the cases of history and social theory it is more precise and may be more illuminating to speak of 'postmodernism', and more especially of the twin movements of destabilization and decentring.

Destabilization

By 'destabilization', I mean a shift from the assumption of fixity to the assumption of fluidity, or, to vary the metaphor, the collapse of the traditional idea of structures, whether they are economic, social, political or cultural. Concepts such as 'structure' have been largely replaced by concepts such as 'flow' and 'transformation'.

One sign of change is the rise of network analysis in anthropology, sociology and history. Network analysis is a method, but one that is associated with a certain image of society. Instead of examining more or less firm social structures, network analysts concentrate on social relationships centred on a single individual. The theory they often use in their work is 'social exchange'. The idea of social exchange is not new, as we have seen (above, p. 68), but it has become associated with a view of society as the sum of the actions of individuals following strategies based on expectations of returns. What we see is a revival of methodological individualism (above, p. 127).

The example of gossip provides a vivid illustration of the difference between the functional and the individualist approaches. Whereas a functional analysis of gossip notes how this activity binds the members of a given group together, a more recent approach focuses on individual gossipers, their competition with one another and their use of this medium to acquire information or to impress their neighbours (Gluckman 1963; Paine 1967).

When Mrs Thatcher declared that 'there is no such thing as society', she was putting into words a current trend as well as expressing an old-fashioned English individualism. The historical sociologist Michael Mann agrees: 'I would abolish the concept of "society" altogether.' Instead of structures or 'bounded totalities' Mann operates with the idea of networks, especially what he calls 'multiple overlapping and intersecting socio-spatial networks of power'. Discussing ancient Greece, for example, he distinguishes three such networks: that of the city-state, that of the Greek state system, and finally the ancient idea of humanity.

In similar fashion the anthropologist Eric Wolf denied the existence of entities such as tribes, nations or 'the West', so many bounded systems, and preferred to speak of 'bundles of relationships' or 'a totality of interconnected processes' (Wolf 1982: 3–7; Mann 1986–93: i. 1–2, 223–7). Some, at least, of the micro-historians who are studying networks in the past (above, p. 41) are doing so for similar reasons to Mann and Wolf.

There are some sociological precedents for this attempt to replace or reconceptualize the idea of structure. Georg Simmel, for instance, claimed that 'Society is merely the name for a number of individuals connected by interaction'. Norbert Elias, who is taken more seriously as a social theorist today than he was in his own time, developed this point with his concept of the 'figuration', a pattern of social relationships which is exemplified on a micro level by a football match, on a medium level by an eighteenth-century court (one of Elias's favourite historical examples), and on a macro level by a nation, which might be regarded as a network of networks. According to Elias, people are bound together in different ways in different kinds of society (1969: 18, 208–13; 1970: 128–33).

A similar approach was adopted by Pierre Bourdieu, who criticized the approaches of both Durkheim and Lévi-Strauss as too rigid and mechanical. He preferred the more flexible notion of a 'field'. More precisely, Bourdieu distinguished a series of fields – the religious field, the literary field, the economic field and so on. Social actors are 'defined by their *relative positions* in this space', which Bourdieu also described as a 'field of forces' imposing certain relations on those who enter, 'relations which are not reducible to the intentions of individual agents or even to direct *interactions* between agents'.

Interesting attempts have been made to use Bourdieu's concept of a field to analyse the 'birth' of French writers and French intellectuals as self-conscious groups in the seventeenth and nineteenth centuries respectively (revealing in the process the difficulty of defining 'literary' or 'intellectual' space) (Bourdieu 1993; Viala 1985; Charle 1990). Again, Jesuit science has been analysed as a 'cultural field' in a study of the relationship between the discourse, its institutional setting and the wider political context. The author of this analysis argues that a discourse, sometimes taken to be static (above, p. 99), 'is never fixed but rather constantly negotiated, constituted and reconstituted' under pressures coming from the field (Feldhay 1999).

Cultural Constructions

Another aspect of destabilization is the increasing interest shown by historians and theorists alike in what might be called the 'constructibility' of culture or society. The spread of the compound 'sociocultural' is a sign of an increasing awareness of this plasticity or malleability. There is a tendency to think of culture as active rather than passive. The structuralists had already moved in this direction a generation ago, and it might well be argued that Lévi-Strauss, in particular, turned Marx on his head (in other words, returned to Hegel), by suggesting that the really deep structures are not economic and social arrangements but mental categories.

Today, however, both structuralism and Marxism are frequently rejected as determinist, and the emphasis falls on collective creativity (Certeau 1980). What used to be assumed to be objective, hard social facts, like gender or class or community, are now assumed to be culturally 'constructed' or 'constituted' (Hacking 1999; Burke 2004c: 74–99). In contrast to the structuralists, poststructuralists emphasize human agency and also change, not so much construction as reconstruction, a process of continuous creation. For this reason the term 'essentialism' is one of the greatest insults in their vocabulary.

In this regard Foucault's studies of changing Western views of madness (1961) and sexuality (1976–84), and his critique of impoverished conceptions of the 'real' which omit the reality of what is imagined, have been extremely influential. However, Foucault's work is part of a wider and also a longer trend. Gestalt psychologists, for example, viewed perception as a kind of construction (above, p. 99). Phenomenologists have long emphasized what is sometimes called the 'social construction of reality' (Berger and Luckmann 1966). 'Cultural' Marxists such as Louis Althusser (1970) and Maurice

Godelier are among the theorists who have stressed the importance of thought and imagination in the production of what we call 'society' (1984: 125–78). The critical theorist Cornelius Castoriadis (1975) has also been influential in this regard, although the launching of the term *l'imaginaire* probably owes most to the example of the psychoanalyst Jacques Lacan.

Pierre Bourdieu's critique of Lévi-Strauss and other structuralists on the ground that the notion of cultural 'rules' implicit in their work is too mechanical pointed in the same direction. As an alternative, he proposed the more flexible concept 'habitus', derived from Aristotle (via St Thomas Aquinas and the art historian Erwin Panofsky). 'Habitus' is defined as a set of 'schemes enabling agents to generate an infinity of practices adapted to endlessly changing situations' (Bourdieu 1972: 16, 78–87). The core of the concept is a kind of 'regulated improvisation', a phrase reminiscent of the formulae and themes of the oral poets studied above (p. 109).

Like Foucault (and the philosopher Maurice Merleau-Ponty), Bourdieu undermined the classic distinction between mind and body associated with Descartes and parodied as the doctrine of the 'ghost in the machine'. The practices he wrote about are not easy to classify as 'mental' or 'physical'. For example, the honour of the Kabyle of Algeria, among whom Bourdieu did his fieldwork, is expressed as much in their upright manner of walking as in anything they say. The 'tortoise-like deliberation' developed in conscious or unconscious resistance to the authorities by Hungarian farm workers such as Uncle Róka (described above, p. 91) provides another vivid illustration of what Bourdieu means by 'habitus'.

In the fields of literature and philosophy, or the space between them, a similar assumption of cultural creativity underlies the 'deconstruction' practised by the French philosopher Jacques Derrida and his followers, in other words their distinctive approach to texts – unravelling their contradictions, directing attention to their ambiguities or play of meanings, and reading them against themselves and their authors. If an interest in binary oppositions was the hallmark of the structuralist, the poststructuralist may be recognized by a concern to undermine these categories – hence Derrida's interest in the idea of the 'supplement', which at once adds to something and supplants it (1967: 141–64; 1972; cf. Norris 1982; Culler 1983).

How have historians reacted to these developments? If we define deconstruction, poststructuralism and related developments in a precise way, examples of their influence remain relatively few. Although the word 'deconstruction' (in the sense of 'taking to pieces') is increasingly fashionable, only a few historians, mainly North

Americans, reveal the inspiration of Derrida in their substantive work.

Joan Scott, for instance, has analysed the relationship between women's history and history in general in terms of the 'logic of the supplement'. Harry Harootunian has offered a new and controversial way of reading the discourse of 'nativism' (in other words, the sense of identity) in Tokugawa Japan, using the notion of 'conceptual schemes as forms of play' as an antidote to the traditional view of ideology as the reflection of society. Stuart Clark's study of the idea of witchcraft places unusual emphasis on language and on the instability of meanings. Inspired by Derrida, Clark notes that 'Even as educated Europeans combined to make the sixteenth and seventeenth centuries the great age of the anti-demonic, their belief systems depended necessarily on what they sought to exclude' (J. W. Scott 1991: 49–50; Harootunian 1988: esp. 1–22; S. Clark 1997: 143).

Again, Timothy Mitchell's study of nineteenth-century Egypt builds on Derrida's concept of difference – 'not a pattern of distinctions or intervals between things, but an always unstable deferring or differing within' – in order to rethink accepted views of the colonial city. Mitchell sustains the paradox that 'To represent itself as modern, the city is dependent upon maintaining the barrier that keeps the other out. This dependence makes the outside, the Oriental . . . an integral part of the modern city' (1988: 145, 149).

With a few exceptions such as these, the historical profession is still somewhat suspicious of postmodernism, as it was in 1991, when Lawrence Stone wrote a letter to the well-known journal *Past and Present* about the threat to history from people who claim that 'there is nothing besides the text' or that 'the real is as imagined as the imaginary'. Two replies to this letter were published in a later issue of the journal. It is significant that both were written by members of a younger generation of historians, and likely that the majority of even that generation, in Britain at least, remain closer to Stone's position (Stone 1991; Joyce 1991; C. Kelly 1991).

If, on the other hand, we turn from postmodernism to postmodernity, as it was described above, this vaguer term does seem appropriate for describing certain new features of historical practice. For instance, there has been a shift away from the 'social history of culture' of the kind practised by Arnold Hauser, towards what the French historian Roger Chartier (1997) has described as the 'cultural history of society'. Historians increasingly recognize the power of the 'imagined', as in the study by Georges Duby (1978) on the idea of the 'three orders' of society (above, p. 61), or in recent work on images of France and India (Nora 1984–93; Inden 1990). Again, recent studies on the social history of language have been concerned not only with the influence of society on language but also with the reverse – for instance, with the importance of opposed terms such as 'middle classes' and 'working classes' in the constitution of social groups (Burke and Porter 1987; Corfield 1991).

Forms of social organization such as 'tribe' or 'caste', once assumed to be 'social facts', are now viewed as collective representations. For example, according to the French anthropologist Jean-Luc Amselle, tribes or ethnic groups such as the Bambara or the Fulani in West Africa were effectively invented by colonial administrators and anthropologists, though these terms were appropriated later by the Africans themselves (some historians take a similar view of caste in India). Amselle (1990) himself treats terms such as 'Bambara' as descriptions not of entities – a view he criticizes as essentialist or 'substantialist' – but of systems of cultural transformation. His point is a double one, about both space and time. Spatially speaking, there are no clear boundaries between groups, while over time it is possible to observe a process of 'incessant reclassification' (on caste, see Dirks: 2001).

Even the city of bricks and mortar, a physical entity if ever there was one, is no longer regarded as a social entity. It has been dissolved by urban theorists such as Manuel Castells, who note the dispersal of social relations and the importance of flows – flows of people, flows of commodities, flows of information. In the world system of today, 'The city is everywhere and in everything', forcing geographers, sociologists and historians to reimagine the urban. Widening out from the city, Castells has argued that in the age of the Internet, 'Networks constitute the new social morphology of our society'. If he is right, then the network analysis described above is among other things a symptom of postmodernity, and possibly a projection of modern arrangements – we can no longer call them 'structures' – on to the past (Castells 1968, 1996: 469; cf. Abrams 1978; Amin and Thrift 2002).

For a rich historical account of the process of cultural construction, we may return to Schama's study of the Dutch in the seventeenth century. Schama was particularly concerned with the ways in which the Dutch, a new nation in this period, forged an identity for themselves. He discusses a wide variety of topics, from cleanliness to smoking and from the cult of the ancient Batavians to the myth of the Dutch Republic as the new Israel, viewing these topics in terms of the construction of identity. For example, following the interpretation of Jewish dietary laws by the anthropologist Mary Douglas, Schama suggests that 'to be clean, militantly, was an affirmation of separateness'. We are not far from Freud's idea of the narcissism of minor differences (Schama 1987: 375–96; Douglas 1966).

This shift in the study of culture has been immensely illuminating, but it also raises problems. It would be difficult to deny the reductionism implicit in some traditional approaches to culture, Durkheimian as well as Marxist, but the reaction in the opposite direction may well have gone too far. The current emphasis on cultural creativity and on culture as an active force in history needs to be accompanied by some sense of the constraints within which that creativity operates. Rather than simply replacing the social history of culture by the cultural history of society, we need to work with the two ideas together and simultaneously, however difficult this may be. In other words, it is most useful to see the relationship between culture and society in dialectical terms, with both partners at once active and passive, determining and determined (cf. Samuel 1991).

In any case, cultural construction should be regarded as a problem rather than an assumption, a problem deserving analysis in more detail. How does one construct a new conception of class (say) or gender? And who is 'one'? How can we account for the acceptance of the innovation? Or, to turn the problem round, is it possible to explain why traditional conceptions cease to convince certain groups at certain times?

Decentring

Parallel to the concern with destabilization, we find its spatial equivalent, displacement or 'decentring'. It is therefore no wonder that geographers have been making an important contribution to the study of postmodernity (Soja 1989; Harvey 1990; Amin and Thrift 2002). However, decentring is not confined to geography. It affects attitudes, for example. Scholars used to write from a single point of view, but now they are making an effort to view the subjects they study from multiple viewpoints. Here, as elsewhere, Norbert Elias was a pioneer, arguing a generation ago that 'sociology must take account of both the first- and third-person perspectives', in other words the perspective of the people written about as well as the person writing (1970: 127). The philosopher Hans-Georg Gadamer made a similar point in the context of the interpretation of texts. He suggested a dialogical approach starting from awareness of the necessary disagreement between the original writer and the later interpreter. Gadamer (1960) suggested that the text should be allowed to question the views of the interpreter as well as the other way round.

There is a sense in which this approach draws on a tradition. Historians have long attempted to reconstruct the attitudes characteristic of the particular period they study, and anthropologists since Malinowski have been concerned with what he called 'the native's point of view'. These attitudes used to be treated as part of the data, utilized but also overridden by the author, just as in the classic nineteenth-century novel the voices of the characters were subordinate to that of the omniscient narrator.

What is new is the decentring of this scholarly viewpoint in the sense of presenting it as simply one viewpoint among others. The people written about, living or dead, are treated less as raw material and more as partners, so that the historian or anthropologist moves backwards and forwards between past and present, the culture being studied and the culture of the student, comparing and contrasting their theories and interpretations and ours. Scholars are more aware than they used to be of the point made by Karl Mannheim in the 1920s, and again more recently, that knowledge – including their own – is socially situated (1952: 134–90; Haraway 1988). Hence the current appeal across the disciplines of the ideas on dialogue put forward by Bakhtin (1981; cf. Morson and Emerson 1990: 231–68).

In any case, the dual perspective advocated by Elias and Gadamer has been replaced by a multiple one. The people in the culture being studied never speak with one voice. The movement to write history 'from below', to reconstruct the 'vision of the vanquished' or the point of view of the 'subaltern classes', made this point very clear (above, pp. 89, 164). The rise of women's history added to the variety of perspectives, involving as it did attempts to write history from female points of view.

The attempt to combine these different perspectives has led some historians and others to experiment with new forms of narrative. Once rejected by scholars who wished to be 'analytic', narrative has regained prestige as a mode of understanding the world (Stone 1979; Ricoeur 1983–5; Burke 1991). For example, the anthropologist Richard Price (1990) has adapted the device of the multiple viewpoint, used to great effect in novels and films such as William Faulkner's *The Sound and the Fury* (1929) and Akira Kurosawa's *Rashomon* (1950), to an account of eighteenth-century Surinam. Instead of juxtaposing individual accounts, he presents the situation as it was seen through the eyes of three collective agents – the black slaves, the Dutch officials and the Moravian missionaries. The author links and comments on these three perspectives, but presents his commentary as simply another view, a fourth voice, that of an 'ethnographic historian' (cf. Berkhofer 1995: 170–201). In other words, he exemplifies the 'multivocal' or 'polyphonic' narrative that was both described and recommended by Bakhtin.

As a result of the scholarly discoveries of the people, women and the colonized, the last generation has seen the collapse of the so-called Grand Narrative (*le grand récit*) of the human past, essentially the story of human emancipation told in the Enlightenment. Doubts about the plausibility of this story are part of the postmodern condition, as the French philosopher Jean-François Lyotard described it. 'The Grand Narrative has lost its credibility.' The context in which Lyotard made this remark was a discussion of the legitimation of knowledge, but the term he coined, and its alternative formulations 'Great Story', 'Master Narrative' and 'Metanarrative', have been taken up, and the central proposition debated ever since. (Megill (1995) distinguishes between the 'master narrative' of a segment of the past, the 'grand narrative' of the whole past, and the 'metanarrative' that justifies the grand narrative.) There is an obvious fit between Lyotard's theory and the work of micro-historians such as Le Roy Ladurie, which also goes back to the 1970s (Lyotard 1979: 37; cf. Berkhofer 1995; Cox and Stromquist 1998).

The idea of a grand narrative is often associated with the rise of 'Western Civilization', the name for what used to be a compulsory course in some leading North American universities. The Renaissance, the Reformation, the European discovery of and expansion into other continents, the Scientific Revolution, the Enlightenment and the French Revolution were traditionally presented as so many chapters in a story of triumph, and the history of India, for example, was either incorporated into the story or (if it did not fit the model) 'disqualified' from serious attention (Cox and Stromquist 1998: 95–180). As Wolf sums up the story in deliberate caricature, 'ancient Greece begat Rome, Rome begat Christian Europe, Christian Europe begat the Renaissance, the Renaissance the Enlightenment, the Enlightenment political democracy and the Industrial Revolution' (1982: 5).

Today, however, all these stories within the Great Story have been decentred by some scholars. For example, awareness of the contribution of other cultures, especially the Muslim world, to the Renaissance has resulted in the 'reframing' of our image of that movement (Farago 1995; Burke 2004a). The story of the Scientific Revolution of the seventeenth century has been rewritten in similar fashion.

Ironically enough, the rise of the term 'Scientific Revolution' owed a great deal to Herbert Butterfield, the scholar most famous for his critique of the 'Whig' or present-minded interpretation of history (above, p. 113). All the same, Butterfield told a present-minded story of the 'origins of modern science' as a revolution associated with the rise of objectivity and freedom of thought. Even Joseph Needham, the great historian of Chinese science, believed that 'modern science was born in Europe and only in Europe', and wrote his history of science and civilization in China in order to explain why, as well as to draw attention to many Chinese achievements.

By contrast, Thomas Kuhn, as we have seen, used the term 'revolution' in the plural and stressed the regular replacement of paradigms. Today, some historians are telling a still more pluralist story, arguing that science is simply one way of knowing among others, a style of thought that has sometimes achieved an intellectual hegemony, but only in certain places and certain times (Butterfield 1949; J. Needham 1963; Cunningham and Williams 1993).

Beyond Eurocentrism?

One of the grandest of grand narratives that historians have told is the story of the 'rise of the West'. The challenge is to explain not only how (and when) the Europeans drew ahead of their economic and military competitors, but also what consequences for the rest of the world followed from the establishment of European hegemony. Needless to say, in the age of postcolonialism (above, p. 104) this story has become an increasingly controversial one.

In the last 100 years there has been a succession of attempts by Western scholars to break free of Eurocentrism and adopt a comparative perspective, only to be criticized in their turn for the very fault they were trying to avoid: for dating the rise of the West too early, for assuming the superiority of Western culture, for viewing the rest of the world through crude stereotypes (of the kind analysed by Edward Said), or for treating the history of the West as the norm from which other cultures diverge and asking why, for example, China had no scientific or industrial revolution.

Max Weber, for example, was surely one of the least Eurocentric scholars of his time. He spent much of his working life in the attempt to define the distinctive characteristics of Western civilization (notably what he called its institutionalized 'rationality'), by means of systematic comparisons between Europe and Asia in the economic, political and religious spheres and even in that of music. He paid particular attention to the rise of Protestantism, capitalism and bureaucracy in the West, arguing that the three phenomena were at once similar and connected, and contrasting them with phenomena elsewhere.

This has not prevented Weber from being accused of Eurocentrism. After all, he accepted the traditional Western theory of 'Oriental despotism'. He believed in a hierarchy of races with Caucasians at the top. He assumed the superiority of Western culture. In these respects Weber's views resembled those of the majority of Western intellectuals of his day. What was unusual in Weber was his systematic and unrelenting attempt to explain the Western lead in terms of rational (rule-observing) forms of organization such as law, bureaucracy and capitalism. His famous essay on the Protestant ethic and the spirit of capitalism was a contribution to this grander enterprise (Blaut 2000: 19–30).

One of the few historians to be as widely read in world history was Arnold Toynbee, whose *Study of History* has already been discussed. Whatever its faults – and critics have pointed to many – this massive work was a major attempt to decentre history. Again, like Weber and Toynbee (whose biography he has written), William McNeill is one of the least Eurocentric scholars of his generation, a crusader for world history and the author of one of the most successful books on the subject, *The Rise of the West* (1963).

In this book McNeill argued that for 2,000 years (500 BCE–1500 CE) there was a 'balance' of four major civilizations in Eurasia: the Chinese, the Indian, the Middle Eastern and the Western. 'Westerners are so much accustomed to putting their own history in the foreground', he wrote, 'that it is perhaps well to underlie the marginal character of Roman and European history between the fourth and second centuries B.C.' It was only around 1500 that Western Europe began to draw ahead of its competitors, for a mixture of reasons ranging from naval technology and relative immunity to disease to willingness to learn from other cultures, and only around 1850 that the collapse of the Chinese, Mughal and Ottoman empires ended the cultural balance in Eurasia.

In his turn, McNeill (1963) has been criticized as Eurocentric, for giving very little space to the history of Africa south of the Sahara or to the Americas before Columbus, and for operating with a binary opposition between 'barbarism' and 'civilization' that scholars today would wish to qualify, if not to avoid altogether (it is now half a century since McNeill began writing his book). Even his concern with the increasing intensity of cultural interaction over the millennia has been criticized. In an age of decentring, any attempt to write the history of the world with a clear story-line is bound to be criticized (cf. Feierman 1995: 41–2).

McNeill's world history contrasts cultural centres with what he calls 'fringes', or 'margins'. The economic history of the world written by Marxian world-system theorists such as Wallerstein makes even greater use of the concepts of 'core' and 'periphery'. These theorists too have a clear story-line, the rise of Western capitalism, imperialism and 'a European world economy' based on an international division of labour that led to the peripheralization and the underdevelopment of the rest of the world (Frank 1967; Wallerstein 1974; Frank and Gills 1993). For this and other reasons, they too have been criticized as Eurocentric.

Within this tradition, the most decentred story is surely that told by Janet Abu-Lughod about the world system between 1250 and 1350, with the Middle East as 'heartland' and Europe as a 'subsystem'. Abu-Lughod points out that there was an economic 'vacuum' in the Indian Ocean after the withdrawal of China in the fifteenth century, which the Europeans were able to fill. In that sense 'The fall of the East precedes the rise of the West' (1989: 361).

The rise of capitalism and a world market, and the consequences of this rise for the rest of the world is the central theme of another world history of Marxian inspiration, Eric Wolf's *Europe and the Peoples without History*. Wolf was an anthropologist by training, and his book has much more to say about cultural and social change than that of any of the world-system theorists, more concerned, as he says, 'to understand how the core subjugated the periphery' than to study how the peoples of the periphery were drawn into the system and how they reacted to this process. This series of reactions is the main theme of Wolf's study – but it has not prevented him from being criticized in his turn for attempting to construct a single master narrative, as well as praised for offering an alternative (1982: 22; cf. Robertson 1992: 30–1; Feierman 1995: 48–9).

Wolf and the world-system theorists concentrate on the consequences for the world of the rise of Western capitalism. By contrast, the economic historian Eric Jones and the sociologist John Hall have returned to Weber's problem but given it different answers. They offer opposed explanations of the rise of capitalism in the West. Although he discusses politics in some detail, borrowing from the theory of the firm to point out the 'economies of scale' enjoyed by large states, in *The European Miracle* (1981) Jones is essentially concerned with economic change in Europe over the very long term. Comparing and contrasting Europe with China and India, he argues that industrialization was 'a growth deeply rooted in the past'. He notes that Europeans did more than other peoples to hold down population growth, but his main explanation for the 'miracle' is an ecological one. His emphasis falls on Europe's 'geological, climatic and topographical variety', which produced a 'dispersed portfolio of resources' and a lower vulnerability to natural disasters. His book has recently been criticized for 'stating most of the Eurocentric positions as flat and undisputed facts', although it stresses Europe's good fortune, its ecological assets, rather than European achievements (E. L. Jones 1981; a critique in Blaut 2000: 78–112).

In his *Powers and Liberties* (1985) Hall, who describes himself as a latter-day 'philosophical historian' like Ernest Gellner and Michael Mann, places the emphasis on politics. He suggests that capitalism was unable to develop in what he calls 'capstone' states like the Chinese Empire, in which the government presided over a set of separate societies and viewed links between them, including economic links, as a threat to its power. In China, there was too much state, while in the Islamic world there was too little – governments were too weak or too short-lived to provide the services a commercial society needed.

If Adam Smith was right (as Hall believes) to suggest that the political conditions needed for 'the highest degree of opulence' are simply 'peace, easy taxes and a tolerable administration of justice', then Europe was an example of the golden mean. In Europe, the Church and the Empire neutralized one another, thus allowing a 'multipolar system' of competing states to emerge in which services were provided to merchants without too much interference with their trade. This state system removed the main blocks to the rise of capitalism and explains the 'unique dynamism' of the West. This approach too has been criticized as Eurocentric. Gellner's response to this critique (1988) was to say that the view that Europeans 'constitute the model which explains all else' has been abandoned, replaced by the idea that 'We are an aberration which can only be understood by investigating the other, more typical social forms' (J. A. Hall 1985, 1988; Smith quoted in J. A. Hall 1986: 154. The critique in Blaut 2000: 128–48).

As an old civilization in which a succession of technological innovations took place, from gunpowder to the printing-press, China raises particular problems for anyone trying to account for the rise of the West. One leading sinologist, Mark Elvin, came up with an ingenious solution a generation ago, arguing that the Chinese did not break through to an industrial revolution because they were caught in a 'high-level equilibrium trap' that allowed 'quantitative growth' but encouraged 'qualitative standstill' (1973: 285–316), the local equivalent of Le Roy Ladurie's 'immobile history'. A recent challenge to this interpretation comes from Kenneth Pomeranz (2000), who argues that the 'great divergence' between China and the West did not take place around 1500, as so many historians have argued, but 300 years later, and that it was essentially the result of European control of the resources of the Americas (Goody 2004).

The implications of this argument for the writing of world history are serious ones. If the rise of Western economies began as recently as 1800, there are even stronger reasons than before for decentring histories of the world. To decentre successfully, thus 'provincializing Europe', it will be necessary for scholars from different continents to write books in partnership, not only in large teams like the UNESCO *History of Humanity* but also in groups of three or four people, allowing for intense dialogue and perhaps what Gadamer called a 'fusion of horizons' (Chakrabarty 2000). Even so, a serious problem remains: how to show readers the 'big picture' without returning to a Eurocentric 'Grand Narrative'.

Globalization

Histories of the world are becoming more and more frequent. In English, McNeill's *Rise of the West* enjoyed a virtual monopoly for decades, at least in the academic field, but it now has various competitors. Three important essays on world history were published between 1997 and 2000: Jared Diamond's *Guns, Germs and Steel*, *The Wealth and Poverty of Nations* by David Landes, and Philip Curtin's *The World and the West*, all of them at more or less the same time as a new multi-volume *History of Humanity* supported by UNESCO.

Both the urge to write books of this kind and the urge to criticize them as Eurocentric may be viewed as signs of the 'globalization' of our time, in the sense of a greater consciousness of the world as a whole resulting from the increasing intensity of intercontinental communication. This cultural trend extends to history (even if many works of history are still written from a national perspective) and also to social theory. Freyre's dream of the tropicalization of social theory is gradually coming true, with postcolonial studies an outstanding example of the trend.

Like postmodernism, with which it is connected, the idea of globalization has become a subject of debate, and once again a debate in which historians have – at least until recently – played a relatively small part, even though 'globalization' describes a trend over time (A. G. Hopkins 2002: 1–10). The history of globalization is just beginning to be written, taking up McNeill's theme of a long-term trend towards increasingly intense interactions between different parts of the world, but liberating it from the loaded question of the rise of the West. This history is a possible arena for increasingly intense interactions between history and theory – economic, social, political or cultural. Geographers have been analysing the 'compression' of the world and the 'placelessness' resulting from the rise of new forms of communication; economists have been studying the rise of trans-national corporations; and specialists in politics have been debating the decline of the nation-state and the possible rise of cosmopolitan democracy. Sociologists have asked whether world culture is becoming more homogeneous or more complex. Anthropologists, whose traditional objects of concern are disappearing, are turning their attention to the interaction between the local and the global, or to what Arjun Appadurai calls 'diasporic public spheres' and 'mass-mediated sodalities', imagined communities spread over the globe but held together by television and the Internet (Hannerz 1992, 1996; Robertson 1992; Massey 1994; Archibugi and Held 1995; Appadurai 1996; Steger 2003, a tiny selection from an ever-expanding literature).

What historians can contribute to this multidisciplinary conversation is a more acute sense of process, making the relationship between the present and the past more visible. The term 'globalization' was used in the 1980s and taken up – globally – in the 1990s, but the process it describes is much older. If we define globalization in terms of increasingly close relations between people in different parts of the globe, then it is clear that the process has been going on for thousands of years, however much it may have accelerated in the last two or three decades. Some analysts, such as the historian Christopher Bayly, divide the process into stages such as 'archaic globalization', followed by the 'proto-globalization' of the seventeenth and eighteenth centuries (when the Dutch and British East India Companies were already trans-national corporations), 'modern' globalization from 1800 to 1950, and 'postcolonial' globalization since then. A number of historians have stressed the importance of the later nineteenth century as a turning point, not only in the history of a world market but also in that of global communications, thanks to the telegraph and the telephone (Robertson 1992: 57–60; A. G. Hopkins 2002; Bayly 2004).

If one contribution of historians to the global debate is to remind participants how long the process of interaction has been going on, another is to point out the limits to globalization in the present, especially where global identity is concerned. As Braudel liked to emphasize, different kinds of change take place at different speeds.

Technology now moves so fast as to leave most of us dizzy. Institutions lag behind, despite the need to adapt them to the changing world. Still slower are changes in mentalities: necessarily so, given the importance of the first two or three years for the future development of each individual.

In the nineteenth century, for example, nations were constructed much more quickly than national identities. As one political leader remarked, having made Italy, it was now necessary to make Italians. In similar fashion, attempts to create a European identity lag behind the institutions of the European Union – and before the problem of creating a European identity has been solved, it has been overtaken by events, or more exactly by a trend, the trend towards globalization.

Let us hope that a more global approach to history and social theory will become more common in the not too distant future, not only studying the process of cultural hybridization but exemplifying it as well.

To Conclude

This essay has been a deliberate attempt to occupy the middle ground between what David Hume used to call 'enthusiasm' and 'superstition' – in this case the uncritical zeal for new approaches and the blind devotion to traditional practice. I hope that it will persuade historians to take social theory more seriously than many currently do, and social theorists to take a greater interest in history.

It will be clear by now, if it was not obvious from the start, that empiricists and theorists are not two close-knit groups, but two ends of a spectrum. Conceptual borrowing tends to take place from neighbouring disciplines on the theoretical side. Thus historians borrow from anthropologists, who borrow from linguists, who borrow from mathematicians.

In return, historians, like ethnographers, offer reminders of the complexity and variety of human experience and institutions which theories inevitably simplify. This variety does not imply that theorists are wrong to simplify. As I tried to argue above (p. 32), simplification is their function, their contribution to the division of labour between approaches and disciplines. What this variety does suggest, however, is that theory can never be simply 'applied' to the past.

What theory can do, on the other hand, is to suggest new questions for historians to ask about 'their' period, or new answers to familiar questions. Theories too come in an almost infinite variety, which poses problems for would-be users. In the first place, there is the problem of choosing between rival theories, generally on the grounds of the more or less close fit between the general theory and the specific question the historian has in mind. There is also the problem of reconciling the theory and its implications with the whole conceptual apparatus of the borrower. This essay may well appear to some of its more philosophical readers to have been an apologia for eclecticism, a charge often levelled (sometimes with justice) against historians who appropriate concepts and theories for use in their own work. So far as this essay is concerned, however, I deny the charge, at least if eclecticism is defined as the attempt to hold inconsistent propositions simultaneously. If, on the other hand, the term means no more than finding ideas in different places, then I am happy to confess to being an eclectic. To be open to new ideas, wherever they come from, and to be capable of adapting them to one's own purposes and of finding ways to test their validity might be said to be the mark of a good historian and a good theorist alike.

To sum up the value of theory in a single sentence, one might say that, like comparison, it enlarges the imagination of historians by making them more aware of alternatives to their habitual assumptions and explanations.

Bibliography

Two useful recent works of reference are G. Delanty and E. F. Isin (eds), *Handbook of Historical Sociology* (London, 2003), and P. N. Stearns (ed.), *Encyclopaedia of European Social History*, 6 vols. (New York, 2001). The list of books and articles that follows is confined to works cited in the text.

Abbott, H. P. (2002) *The Cambridge Introduction to Narrative*, Cambridge.
Abercrombie, N., Hill, S. and Turner, B. S. (1980) *The Dominant Ideology Thesis*, London.
Abrams, P. (1978) 'Towns and Economic Growth: Some Theories and Problems', in P. Abrams and E. A. Wrigley (eds), *Towns in Society*, Cambridge, 9–33.
Abrams, P. (1982) *Historical Sociology*, Shepton Mallett.
Abu-Lughod, J. L. (1989) *Before European Hegemony: the World System A. D. 1250–1350*, New York.
Agnew, J. A. and Duncan, J. S. (eds) (1989) *The Power of Place*, Boston.
Agulhon, M. (1970) *The Republic in the Village*; English trans. Cambridge, 1982.
Ahearne, J. (1995) *Michel de Certeau*, Cambridge.
Allport, G. and Postman, L. (1947) *The Psychology of Rumor*, New York.
Almond, G. A. and Verba, S. (1963) *The Civic Culture*, Princeton, NJ.
Althusser, L. (1970) *Lenin and Philosophy*; English trans. London, 1971.
Amin, A. and Thrift, N. (2002) *Cities: Re-Imagining the Urban*, Cambridge.
Amselle, J.-L. (1990) *Mestizo Logics: Anthropology of Identity in Africa and Elsewhere*; English trans. Stanford, Calif., 1998.
Anderson, B. (1983) *Imagined Communities*; rev. edn London, 1991.
Anderson, B. (1990) *Language and Power*, Ithaca, NY.
Anderson, P. (1974) *Lineages of the Absolutist State*, London.

Anderson, P. (1976–7) 'The Antinomies of Antonio Gramsci', *New Left Review*, 100, 5–36.

Anderson, P. (1998) *The Origins of Postmodernity*, London.

Ankarloo, B. and Henningsen, G. (eds) (1990) *Early Modern European Witchcraft*, Oxford.

Appadurai, A. (1996) *Modernity at Large*, Minneapolis.

Archibugi, D. and Held, D. (eds) (1995) *Cosmopolitan Democracy*, Cambridge.

Ardener, E. (1975) 'Belief and the Problem of Women', in S. Ardener (ed.), *Perceiving Women*, London, 1–27.

Ariès, P. (1960) *Centuries of Childhood*; English trans. New York, 1962.

Aron, R. (1965) *Main Currents in Sociological Thought*; 2nd edn, Harmondsworth, 1968.

Assmann, J. (1992) *Das kulturelle Gedächtnis: Schrift, Erinnerung und Politisches Identität in frühen Hochkulturen*, Munich.

Assmann, J. (1995) 'Collective Memory and Cultural Identity', *New German Critique*, 65, 125–33.

Atkinson, P. (1990) *The Ethnographic Imagination: Textual Constructions of Reality*, London.

Atsma, H. and Burguière, A. (eds) (1990) *Marc Bloch aujourd'hui*, Paris.

Avineri, S. (1968) *Karl Marx on Colonialism*, New York.

Aya, R. (1990) *Rethinking Revolution and Collective Violence*, Amsterdam.

Bachrach, P. and Baratz, M. S. (1962) 'The Two Faces of Power', *American Political Science Review*, 56, 947–52.

Baechler, J., Hall, J. and Mann, M. (eds) (1988) *Europe and the Rise of Capitalism*, Oxford.

Bailey, F. G. (1993) *The Kingdom of Individuals*, Ithaca, NY.

Bailey, P. (1978) 'Will the Real Bill Banks Please Stand Up? Towards a Role Analysis of Mid-Victorian Working-Class Respectability', *Journal of Social History*, 12, 336–53.

Baker, K. M. (ed.) (1987) *The Political Culture of the Old Regime*, Oxford.

Bakhtin, M. (1952–3) 'The Problem of Speech Genres'; repr. in C. Emerson and M. Holquist (eds), *Speech Genres and Other Late Essays*, Austin, Tex. 1986, 60–102.

Bakhtin, M. (1965) *Rabelais and his World*; English trans. Cambridge, Mass., 1968.

Bakhtin, M. (1981) *The Dialogic Imagination*, Manchester.

Barth, F. (1959) *Political Leadership among the Swat Pathans*, London.

Bartlett, F. (1986) *Trial by Fire and Water*, Oxford.

Bascom, W. R. and Herskovits, M. J. (eds) (1959) *Continuity and Change in African Cultures*, Chicago.

Bauman, Z. (2000) *Liquid Modernity*, Cambridge.

Baumann, G. (1996) *Contesting Culture: Discourses of Identity in Multi-Ethnic London*, Cambridge.

Bayly, C. A. (2004) *The Birth of the Modern World, 1780–1914*, Oxford.

Beck, U. (2000) *Conversations*; English trans. Cambridge, 2002.

Bellah, R. (1957) *Tokugawa Religion*, Glencoe, Ill.

Bellah, R. (1959) 'Durkheim and History'; repr. in R. A. Nisbet (ed.) *Emile Durkheim*, Englewood Cliffs, NJ, 1965, 153–76.

Bendix, R. (1967) 'The Comparative Study of Social Change'; repr. in R. Bendix and G. Roth (eds), *Scholarship and Partisanship*, Berkeley, 1971, 207–24.

Bercé, Y. (1974) *History of Peasant Revolts*; abbrev. trans. Cambridge, 1990.

Berger, P. and Luckmann, T. (1966) *The Social Construction of Reality*, New York.

Berkhofer, R. F., Jr. (1995) *Beyond the Great Story: History as Text and Discourse*, Cambridge, Mass.

Bestor, J. F. (1999) 'Marriage Transactions in Renaissance Italy and Mauss's *Essay on the Gift*', *Past and Present*, 164, 6–46.

Béteille, A. (1991) *Some Observations on the Comparative Method*, Amsterdam.

Bhabha, H. K. (1994) *The Location of Culture*, London.

Blaut, J. M. (2000) *Eight Eurocentric Historians*, New York.

Bloch, M. (1924) *The Royal Touch*; English trans. London, 1973.

Bloch, M. (1928) 'A Contribution Towards a Comparative History of European Societies'; repr. in his *Land and Work in Medieval Europe*, London, 1967, 44–76.

Bloch, M. (1939–40) *Feudal Society*; English trans. London 1961.

Blok, A. (2001) *Honour and Violence*, Cambridge.

Boas, F. (1966) *Kwakiutl Ethnography*, ed. H. Codere, Chicago and London.

Boer, P. den (1996) *History as a Profession: The Study of History in France, 1818–1914*; English trans. Princeton, NJ, 1998.

Bourdieu, P. (1972) *Outlines of a Theory of Practice*; English trans. Cambridge, 1977.

Bourdieu, P. (1979) *Distinction*; English trans. Cambridge, Mass., 1984.

Bourdieu, P. (1993) *The Field of Cultural Production*, Cambridge.

Bourdieu, P. and Passeron, J.-C. (1970) *Reproduction in Education Society and Culture*, London and Beverly Hills, Calif.

Braudel, F. (1949) *The Mediterranean and the Mediterranean World in the Age of Philip II*; 2nd edn 1966; English trans. 2 vols, London, 1972–3.

Braudel, F. (1958) 'History and Sociology'; English trans. in his *On History*, Chicago, 1980, 64–82.

Braudel, F. (1979) *Civilization and Capitalism*; English trans. 3 vols, London, 1981–3.

Brewer, J. and Porter, R. (eds) (1993) *Consumption and the World of Goods*, London.

Bridenthal, R. and Koonz, C. (eds) (1977) *Becoming Visible: Women in European History*, Boston.

Brigden, S. (1982) 'Youth and the English Reformation', *Past and Present*, 95, 37–67.

Briggs, A. (1960) 'The Language of Class'; repr. in his *Collected Essays*, 2 vols, Brighton, 1985, vol. 1, 3–33.

Briggs, A. and Burke, P. (2002) *A Social History of the Media from Gutenberg to the Internet*, Cambridge.

Brown, P. (1971) *The World of Late Antiquity*, London.

Brown, P. (1975) 'Society and the Supernatural', *Daedalus*, 104, 133–47.

Brucker, G. (1999) 'Civic Traditions in Premodern Italy', *Journal of Interdisciplinary History*, 29, 357–77.

Bryant, C. G. A. and Jary, D. (1991) *Giddens' Theory of Structuration: A Critical Appreciation*, London and New York.

Bryson, A. (1998) *From Courtesy to Civility: Changing Codes of Conduct in Early Modern England*, Oxford.

Buisseret, D. and Reinhardt, S. G. (eds) (2000) *Creolization in the Americas*, Arlington, Va.

Bulhof, I. N. (1975) 'Johan Huizinga, Ethnographer of the Past', *Clio*, 4, 201–24.

Burke, P. (1972) *Culture and Society in Renaissance Italy*; 4th edn *The Italian Renaissance: Culture and Society in Italy*, Cambridge, 1999.

Burke, P. (1974) *Venice and Amsterdam: A Study of Seventeenth-Century Elites*; 2nd edn Cambridge, 1994.

Burke, P. (1978) *Popular Culture in Early Modern Europe*; 2nd edn, Aldershot, 1994.

Burke, P. (1986) 'City-States', in J. A. Hall (1986), 137–53.

Burke, P. (1987) *Historical Anthropology of Early Modern Italy*, Cambridge.

Burke, P. (1988) 'Ranke the Reactionary', *Syracuse Scholar*, 9, 25–30.

Burke, P. (1990) *The French Historical Revolution: The Annales School 1929–89*, Cambridge; 2nd edn Cambridge, 2005.

Burke, P. (1991) 'The History of Events and the Revival of Narrative', in P. Burke (ed.), *New Perspectives on Historical Writing*, 2nd edn Cambridge, 2001, 283–300.

Burke, P. (1992a) *The Fabrication of Louis XIV*, New Haven, Conn., and London.

Burke, P. (1992b) 'The Language of Orders', in Bush (1992), 1–12.

Burke, P. (1997) *Varieties of Cultural History*, Cambridge.

Burke, P. (2000) *A Social History of Knowledge from Gutenberg to Diderot*, Cambridge.

Burke, P. (2004a) 'Decentering the Renaissance', in S. Milner (ed.), *At the Margins: Minority Groups in Pre-Modern Italy*, Minneapolis.

Burke, P. (2004b) 'Is there a Cultural History of the Emotions?', in P. Gouk and H. Hills (eds), *Representing Emotions*, Aldershot.

Burke, P. (2004c) *What is Cultural History?* Cambridge.

Burke, P. (2005) 'Performing History', *Rethinking History*, 9, 35–52.

Burke, P. and Porter, R. (eds) (1987) *The Social History of Language*, Cambridge.

Burke, P. and Porter, R. (eds) (1991) *Language, Self and Society*, Cambridge.

Burrow, J. W. (1965) *Evolution and Society*, Cambridge.

Burrow, J. W. (1981) *A Liberal Descent*, Cambridge.

Bush, M. (ed.) (1992) *Social Orders and Social Classes*, Manchester.

Butler, J. (1990) *Gender Trouble*, London.

Butterfield, H. (1931) *The Whig Interpretation of History*, London.

Butterfield, H. (1949) *The Origins of Modern Science*, London.

Bynum, C. W. (1982) *Jesus as Mother*, Berkeley.

Cahill, J. (1982) *The Compelling Image: Nature and Style in Seventeenth-Century Chinese Painting*, Cambridge, Mass.

Calhoun, C. (ed.) (1992) *Habermas and the Public Sphere*, Cambridge, Mass.

Campbell, C. (1987) *The Romantic Ethic and the Spirit of Modern Consumerism*, Oxford.

Canclini, N. (1989) *Hybrid Cultures*; English trans. Minneapolis, 1995.

Cannadine, D. (1998) *Class in Britain*, New Haven, Conn.

Carneiro da Cunha, M. (1986) *Negros, estrangeiros*, São Paulo.

Carrithers, M., Collins, S. and Lukes, S. (eds) (1985) *The Category of the Person: Anthropology, Philosophy, History*, Cambridge.

Casey, J. (1989) *The History of the Family*, Oxford.

Castells, M. (1968) 'Is there an Urban Sociology?'; English trans. in C. G. Pickvance (ed.), *Urban Sociology: Critical Essays*, London, 1976, 33–59.

Castells, M. (1996) *The Rise of the Network Society*, Oxford.

Castelnuovo, E. and Ginzburg, C. (1979) 'Centre and Periphery'; English trans. in *History of Italian Art*, Cambridge, 1992.

Castoriadis, C. (1975) *The Imaginary Institution of Society*; English trans. Cambridge, 1987.

Castrén, A.-M., Lonkila, M. and Peltonen, M. (eds) (2004) *Between Sociology and History*, Helsinki.

Certeau, M. de (1980) *The Practice of Everyday Life*; English trans. Berkeley, 1984.

Certeau, M. de, Revel, J. and Julia, D. (1976) *Une Politique de la langue*, Paris.

Cerutti, S. (2004) 'Micro-History: Social Relations versus Cultural Models?', in Castrén, Lonkila and Peltonen (2004), 17–40.

Chabal, P. and Daloz, J.-P. (1999) *Africa Works: Disorder as Political Instrument*, London.

Chaffee, J. W. (1985) *The Thorny Gates of Learning in Sung China: A Social History of Examinations*, Cambridge.

Chakrabarty, D. (2000) *Provincializing Europe*, Princeton, NJ.

Chakrabarty, D. (2003) 'Subaltern Studies and Postcolonial Historiography', in G. Delanty and E. F. Isin (eds), *Handbook of Historical Sociology*, London, 191–204.

Charle, C. (1990) *Naissance des 'intellectuels' 1880–1900*, Paris.

Chartier, R. (1987) *The Cultural Uses of Print in Early Modern France*; English trans. Princeton, NJ, 1988.

Chartier, R. (1997) *On the Edge of the Cliff*, Baltimore, Md.

Chaturvedi, V. (ed.) (2000) *Mapping Subaltern Studies and the Postcolonial*, London.

Chayanov, A. V. (1925) *The Theory of the Peasant Economy*, ed. D. Thorner, B. Kerblay and R. E. F. Smith; repr. Manchester, 1986.

Chickering, R. (1993) *Karl Lamprecht*, NJ.

Clammer, J. (1997) *Contemporary Urban Japan: A Sociology of Consumption*, London.

Clark, P. (2000) *British Clubs and Societies 1580–1800*, Oxford.

Clark, S. (1997) *Thinking with Demons: The Idea of Witchcraft in Early Modern Europe*, Oxford.

Clifford, J. (1988) *The Predicament of Culture*, Cambridge, Mass.

Clifford, J. and Marcus, G. (eds) (1986) *Writing Culture*, Berkeley.

Codere, H. (1950) *Fighting with Property: A Study of Kwakiutl Potlatching and Warfare*, New York.

Cohen, A. P. (1985) *The Symbolic Construction of Community*, Chichester.

Cohen, G. (1978) *Karl Marx's Theory of History*, Oxford.

Cohen, S. (1972) *Folk Devils and Moral Panics: The Creation of the Mods and Rockers*, 2nd edn Oxford, 1980.

Cohn, B. (1962) 'An Anthropologist among the Historians'; repr. in his *An Anthropologist among the Historians*, Delhi, 1987, 1–17.

Cohn, N. (1975) *Europe's Inner Demons*, London.

Coleman, J. S. (1990) *Foundations of Social Theory*, Cambridge, Mass.

Confino, A. (1997) 'Collective Memory and Cultural History: Problems of Method', *American Historical Review*, 102, 1386–1403.

Connerton, P. (1989) *How Societies Remember*, Cambridge.

Corfield, P. (ed.) (1991) *Language, History and Class*, Oxford.

Coser, L. (1974) *Greedy Institutions*, New York.

Cox, J. and Stromquist, S. (eds) (1998) *Contesting the Master Narrative*, Iowa City.

Crosby, A. W. (1986) *Ecological Imperialism: The Biological Expansion of Europe 900–1900*, Cambridge.

Culler, J. (1980) *The Pursuit of Signs*, London.

Culler, J. (1983) *On Deconstruction*, London.

Cunningham, A. and Williams, P. (1993) 'De-centring the "big picture": The Origins of Modern Science and the Modern Origins of Science', *British Journal of the History of Science*, 26, 407–32.

Curtin, P. D. (2000) *The World and the West: The European Challenge and the Overseas Response in the Age of Empire*, Cambridge.

Dahl, R. A. (1958) 'A Critique of the Ruling Elite Model', *American Political Science Review*, 52, 463–9.

Dahrendorf, R. (1957) *Class and Class Conflict in Industrial Society*; English trans. London, 1959.

Darnton, R. (1991) 'History of Reading', in P. Burke (ed.), *New Perspectives on Historical Writing*, 2nd edn Cambridge, 2001, 157–86.

Darnton, R. (1995) *The Forbidden Best-Sellers of Pre-Revolutionary France*, New York.

Davis, J. (1992) *Exchange*, London.

Davis, N. Z. (1975) *Society and Culture in Early Modern France*, Stanford, Calif.

Davis, N. Z. (1983) *The Return of Martin Guerre*, Cambridge, Mass.

Davis, N. Z. (1987) *Fiction in the Archives*, Cambridge.

Davis, N. Z. (2000) *The Gift in Sixteenth-Century France*, Oxford.

Dekker, R. and van de Pol, L. (1989) *The Tradition of Female Transvestism in Early Modern Europe*, London.

Derrida, J. (1967) *Of Grammatology*; English trans. Baltimore, Md., 1977.

Derrida, J. (1972) *Disseminations*; English trans. Chicago, 1981.

Détienne, M. (1999) *Comparer l'incomparable*, Paris.

Diamond J. M. (1997) *Guns, Germs and Steel: A Short History of Everybody for the Last 13,000 years*, London.

Dias, M.-O. Leite da Silva (1983) *Daily Life and Power in São Paulo in the Nineteenth Century*; English trans. Cambridge, 1992.

Dibble, V. K. (1960–1) 'The Comparative Study of Social Mobility', *Comparative Studies in Society and History*, 3, 315–19.

Dirks, N. B. (2001) *Castes of Mind*, Princeton, NJ.

Ditz, T. L. (2004) 'The New Men's History', *Gender and History*, 16, 1–35.

Dodds, E. R. (1951) *The Greeks and the Irrational*, Berkeley.

Dollimore, J. (1991) *Sexual Dissidence*, Oxford.

Douglas, M. (1966) *Purity and Danger*, London.

Douglas, M. (1990) 'Foreword: No Free Gifts', in Mauss (1925), pp. vii–xviii.

Duby, G. (1973) *The Early Growth of the European Economy*; English trans. London, 1974.

Duby, G. (1978) *The Three Orders*; English trans. Chicago, 1980.

Duerr, H.-P. (1988–90) *Der Mythos von der Zivilisationsprozess*, 4 vols, Frankfurt.

Dumont, L. (1966) *Homo Hierarchicus*; English trans. London, 1972.

Dumont, L. (1977) *From Mandeville to Marx*, Chicago.

Dupront, A. (1965) 'De l'acculturation', 12th International Congress of Historical Sciences, *Rapports*, vol. 1, 7–36; revised and enlarged as *L'Acculturazione*, Turin, 1966.

Durkheim, E. (1893) *The Division of Labour in Society*; English trans. 1933; repr. Glencoe, Ill., 1964.

Durkheim, E. (1895) *Suicide*; English trans. London, 1968.

Durkheim, E. (1912) *Elementary Forms of the Religious Life*; English trans. 1915; repr. New York, 1961.

Edelman, M. (1971) *Politics as Symbolic Action*, Chicago.

Eisenstadt, S. N. (1973) *Tradition, Change and Modernity*, New York.

Eisenstein, E. (1979) *The Printing Press as an Agent of Change*, 2 vols, Cambridge.

Eisenstein, E. (1992) *Grub Street Abroad*, Oxford.

Ekman, P. and Davidson, R. J. (eds) (1994) *The Nature of Emotion*, New York.

Elias, N. (1939) *The Civilizing Process*; English trans., rev. edn Oxford, 2000.

Elias, N. (1969) *The Court Society*; English trans. Oxford, 1983.

Elias, N. (1970) *What is Sociology?*; English trans. London, 1978.

Elman, B. A. (2000) *A Cultural History of Civil Examinations in Late Imperial China*, Berkeley.

Elvin, M. (1973) *The Pattern of the Chinese Past*, London.

Erikson, E. (1958) *Young Man Luther*, New York.

Erikson, E. (1970) *Gandhi's Truth*, London.

Erikson, K. T. (1970) 'Sociology and the Historical Perspective', *The American Sociologist*, 5.

Evans-Pritchard, E. (1937) *Witchcraft, Oracles and Magic among the Azande*, Oxford.

Fairclough, N. (1995) *Critical Discourse Analysis*, London.

Farago, C. (ed.) (1995) *Reframing the Renaissance*, New Haven, Conn.

Farge, A. and Revel, J. (1988) *The Rules of Rebellion*; English trans. Cambridge, 1991.

Feierman, S. (1995) 'Africa in History: The End of Universal Narratives', in G. Prakash (ed.), *After Colonialism*, Princeton, 40–66.

Feldhay, R. (1999) 'The Cultural Field of Jesuit Science', in J. O'Malley et al. (eds), *The Jesuits: Cultures, Sciences and the Arts, 1540–1773*, Toronto, 107–30.

Feldman, D. (2002) 'Class', in P. Burke (ed.), *History and Historians in the Twentieth Century*, Oxford, 181–206.

Femia, J. V. (1981) *Gramsci's Political Thought*, Oxford.

Fentress, J. and Wickham, C. (1992) *Social Memory*, Oxford.

Field, J. (2003) *Social Capital*, London.

Fischer, D. H. (1976) 'The Braided Narrative: Substance and Form in Social History', in A. Fletcher (ed.), *The Literature of Fact*, New York, 109–34.

Foster, G. (1960) *Culture and Conquest*, Chicago.

Foucault, M. (1961) *Madness and Civilization*; abbrev. English trans. New York, 1965.

Foucault, M. (1966) *The Order of Things*; English trans. London, 1970.

Foucault, M. (1969) *The Archaeology of Knowledge*; English trans. London, 1972.

Foucault, M. (1971) *L'Ordre du discours*, Paris.

Foucault, M. (1975) *Discipline and Punish*; English trans. Harmondsworth, 1979.

Foucault, M. (1976–84) *History of Sexuality*; English trans. 3 vols, Harmondsworth, 1984–8.

Foucault, M. (1980) *Power/Knowledge*, ed. C. Gordon, London.

Fox, A. and Woolf, D. (eds) (2003) *The Spoken Word: Oral Culture in Britain, 1500–1850*, Manchester.

Fox-Genovese, E. (1988) *Within the Plantation Household*, Chapel Hill, NC.

Frank, A. G. (1967) *Capitalism and Underdevelopment in Latin America*, Harmondsworth.

Frank, A. G. and Gills, B. K. (1993) *The World System: 500 Years or 5000?*, London.

Freedberg, D. (1989) *The Power of Images*, Chicago.

Freyre, G. (1933) *The Masters and the Slaves*; English trans. Berkeley and Los Angeles, 1986.

Freyre, G. (1959) *Order and Progress*; English trans. Berkeley and Los Angeles, 1986.

Friedman, J. (1994) *Cultural Identity and Global Process*, London.

Fussell, P. (1975) *The Great War and Modern Memory*, Oxford.

Gadamer, H.-G. (1960) *Truth and Method*; English trans. London, 1975.

Gans, H. (1962) *The Urban Villagers: Group and Class in the Life of Italo-Americans*, New York.

Gay, P. (1985) *Freud for Historians*, New York.

Geertz, C. (1973) *The Interpretation of Cultures*, New York.

Geertz, C. (1980) *Negara*, Princeton, NJ.

Geertz, C. (1983) *Local Knowledge*, New York.

Geertz, H. (1975) 'An Anthropology of Religion and Magic', *Journal of Interdisciplinary History*, 6, 71–89.

Gellner, E. (1973) *Cause and Meaning in the Social Sciences*, London.

Gellner, E. (1974) *Legitimation of Belief*, Cambridge.

Gellner, E. (1981) *Muslim Society*, Cambridge.

Gellner, E. (1983) *Nations and Nationalism*, London.

Gellner, E. (1985) 'The Gaffe-Avoiding Animal', in *Relativism in the Social Sciences*, Cambridge, 68–82.

Gellner, E. (1988) *Plough, Sword and Book*, London.

Gellner, E. (1994) *Conditions of Liberty: Civil Society and its Rivals*; 2nd edn Harmondsworth, 1996.

Gellner, E. and Waterbury, J. (eds) (1977) *Patrons and Clients in Mediterranean Societies*, London.

Gershenkron, A. (1962) *Economic Backwardness in Historical Perspective*, Cambridge, Mass.

Geuss, R. (1981) *The Idea of a Critical Theory*, Cambridge.

Giddens, A. (1979) *Central Problems in Social Theory*, London.

Giddens, A. (1984) *The Constitution of Society*, Cambridge.

Giddens, A. (1985) *The Nation-State and Violence*, Cambridge.

Giddens, A. (1990) *The Consequences of Modernity*, Cambridge.

Giglioli, P. P. (ed.) (1972) *Language in Social Context*, Harmondsworth.

Gilroy, P. (1993) *The Black Atlantic: Modernity and Double Consciousness*, London.

Ginzburg, C. (1976) *Cheese and Worms*; English trans. London, 1980.

Glick, T. F. and Pi-Sunyer, O. (1969) 'Acculturation as an Explanatory

Concept in Spanish History', *Comparative Studies in Society and History*, 11, 136–54.

Gluckman, M. (1955) *Custom and Conflict in Africa*, Oxford.

Gluckman, M. (1963) 'Gossip and Scandal', *Current Anthropology*, 4, 307–15.

Godbout, J. T. (1992), *The World of the Gift*; English trans. Montreal, 1998.

Godelier, M. (1984) *The Mental and the Material*; English trans. London, 1986.

Goffman, E. (1958) *The Presentation of Self in Everyday Life*, New York.

Goldstone, J. A. (1991) *Revolution and Rebellion in the Early Modern World*, Berkeley.

Gombrich, E. H. (1960) *Art and Illusion*, London.

Gombrich, E. H. (1969) *In Search of Cultural History*, Oxford.

Goody, J. (1969) 'Economy and Feudalism in Africa', *Economic History Review*, 22, 393–405.

Goody, J. (1977) *The Domestication of the Savage Mind*, Cambridge.

Goody, J. (1983) *The Development of the Family and Marriage in Europe*, Cambridge.

Goody, J. (1987) *The Interface between the Written and the Oral*, Cambridge.

Goody, J. (2002) 'Elias and the Anthropological Tradition', *Anthropological Theory*, 2, 401–12.

Goody, J. (2004) *Capitalism and Modernity: The Great Debate*, Cambridge.

Gouk, P. and Hills, H. (eds) (2004) *Representing Emotions*, Aldershot.

Gray, R. Q. (1976) *The Labour Aristocracy in Victorian Edinburgh*, Oxford.

Greenblatt, S. (1988) *Shakespearian Negotiations*, Berkeley.

Greven, P. (1977) *The Protestant Temperament*, New York.

Greyerz, K. von (ed.), (1984) *Religion and Society in Early Modern Europe*, London.

Gribaudi, M. (2004) 'Biography, Academic Context and Models of Social Analysis', in Castrén, Lonkila and Peltonen (2004), 102–29.

Grillo, R. (1989) *Dominant Languages*, Cambridge.

Groebner, V. (2000) *Gefährliche Geschenke: Ritual, Politik und die Sprache der Korruption in der Eidgenossenschaft im späten Mittelalter und am Beginn der Neuzeit*, Konstanz.

Guha, R. (1983) *Elementary Aspects of Peasant Insurgency*, Delhi.

Guha, R. (1997) *Dominance without Hegemony: History and Power in Colonial India*, Cambridge, Mass.

Guha, R. and Spivak, G. C. (eds) (1988) *Selected Subaltern Studies*, New York.

Gurevich, A. Y. (1968) 'Wealth and Gift-Bestowal among the Ancient Scandinavians'; repr. in his *Historical Anthropology of the Middle Ages*, ed. J. Howlett, Cambridge, 1992, 177–89.

Habermas, J. (1962) *The Structural Transformation of the Public Sphere*; English trans. Cambridge, 1989.

Hacking, I. (1999) *The Social Construction of What?*, Cambridge, Mass.

Hajnal, J. (1965) 'European Marriage Patterns in Perspective', in D. V. Glass and D. C. E. Eversley (eds), *Population in History*, London, 101–43.

Halbwachs, M. (1925) *Les Cadres sociaux de la connaissance*, Paris.

Halbwachs, M. (1950) *Collective Memory*; English trans. New York 1980.

Hall, J. A. (1985) *Powers and Liberties*, Oxford.

Hall, J. A. (ed.) (1986) *States in History*, Oxford.

Hall, J. A. (1988) 'States and Societies: The Miracle in Comparative Perspective', in Baechler, Hall and Mann (1988), 20–38.

Handlin, O. (1941) *Boston's Immigrants, 1790–1865*, Cambridge, Mass.

Hannerz, U. (1986) 'Theory in Anthropology: Small is Beautiful', *Comparative Studies in Society and History*, 28, 362–7.

Hannerz, U. (1987) 'The World in Creolization', *Africa*, 57, 546–59.

Hannerz, U. (1992) *Cultural Complexity: Studies in the Social Organization of Meaning*, New York.

Hannerz, U. (1996) *Transnational Connections*, London.

Hansen, B. (1952) *Österlen*, Stockholm.

Haraway, D. (1988) 'Situated Knowledge', *Feminist Studies*, 14, 575–99.

Harding, R. (1981) 'Corruption and the Moral Boundaries of Patronage in the Renaissance', in G. F. Lytle and S. Orgel (eds), *Patronage in the Renaissance*, Princeton, NJ, 47–64.

Harootunian, H. D. (1988) *Things Seen and Unseen: Discourse and Ideology in Tokugawa Nativism*, Chicago.

Hartog, F. (1980) *The Mirror of Herodotus*; English trans. Berkeley, 1988.

Harvey, D. (1990) *The Condition of Postmodernity*, Oxford.

Hauser, A. (1951) *The Social History of Art*, 2 vols, London.

Hawthorn, G. (1976) *Enlightenment and Despair*; rev. edn Cambridge, 1987.

Heal, F. (1990) *Hospitality in Early Modern England*, Oxford.

Hebdige, M. (1979) *Sub-Culture: The Meaning of Style*, London.

Heckscher, E. (1931) *Mercantilism*; English trans. 2 vols, London, 1935.

Heers, J. (1974) *Family Clans in the Middle Ages*; English trans. Amsterdam, 1977.

Heesterman, J. C. (1985) *The Inner Conflict of Traditions*, Chicago.

Hexter, J. H. (1979) *On Historians*, Cambridge, Mass.

Hicks, J. (1969) *Theory of Economic History*, Oxford.

Higham, J., Krieger, L. and Gilbert, F. (eds) (1965) *History*, Englewood Cliffs, NJ.

Hilton, R. H. (ed.) (1976) *The Transition from Feudalism to Capitalism*, London.

Himmelfarb, G. (1987) *The New History and the Old*, Cambridge, Mass.

Hintze, O. (1975) *Historical Essays*, ed. F. Gilbert, New York.

Hirschman, A. (1970) *Exit, Voice and Loyalty*, Cambridge, Mass.

Hitchcock, T. and Cohen, M. (eds) (1999) *English Masculinities 1660–1800*, London.

Ho, P. T. (1958–9) 'Aspects of Social Mobility in China', *Comparative Studies in Society and History*, 1, 330–59.

Hobsbawm, E. (1959) *Primitive Rebels*; 3rd edn Manchester, 1971.

Hobsbawm, E. (1971) 'Class Consciousness in History', in I. Mészaros (ed.), *Aspects of History and Class Consciousness*, London, 5–19.

Hobsbawm, E. J. (1990) *Nations and Nationalism since 1980*, Cambridge.

Hobsbawm, E. and Ranger, T. (eds) (1983) *The Invention of Tradition*, Cambridge.

Hollis, M. and Lukes, S. (eds) (1982) *Rationality and Relativism*, Oxford.

Holquist, M. (1990) *Dialogism*, London.

Holub, R. C. (1984) *Reception Theory*, London.

Holy, L. and Stuchlik, M. (eds) (1981) *The Structure of Folk Models*, London.

Hopkins, A. G. (ed.) (2002) *Globalization in World History*, London.

Hopkins, K. (1978) *Conquerors and Slaves*, Cambridge.

Horton, R. (1967) 'African Traditional Thought and Western Science', *Africa*, 37, 50–71, 155–87.

Horton, R. (1982) 'Tradition and Modernity Revisited', in M. Hollis and S. Lukes (eds), *Rationality and Relativism*, Oxford, 201–60.

Huff, T. E. (1993) *The Rise of Early Modern Science*, Cambridge.

Hunt, L. (1984) *Politics, Culture and Class in the French Revolution*, Berkeley.

Ikegami, E. (1998) *The Taming of the Samurai*, Cambridge, Mass.

Illyés, G. (1967) *People of the Puszta*, Budapest.

Inalcik, H. (1973) *The Ottoman Empire: The Classical Age, 1300–1600*, London.

Inden, R. (1990) *Imagining India*, Oxford.

Jacob, C. (1992) *L'Empire des cartes*, Paris.

Jauss, H.-R. (1974) *Toward an Aesthetic of Reception*; English trans. Minneapolis, 1982.

Johns, A. (1998) *The Nature of the Book: Print and Knowledge in the Making*, Chicago.

Joll, J. (1977) *Gramsci*, London.

Jones, E. L. (1981) *The European Miracle: Environments, Economies and Geopolitics in the History of Europe and Asia*; 3rd edn Cambridge, 2003.

Jones, G. S. (1983) *Languages of Class*, Cambridge.

Jordanova, L. (2002) 'Gender', in P. Burke (ed.), *History and Historians in the Twentieth Century*, Oxford, 120–40.

Joyce, P. (1990) *Visions of the People: Industrial England and the Question of Class, 1848–1914*, Cambridge.

Joyce, P. (1991) 'History and Post-Modernism', *Past and Present*, 133, 204–9.

Kakar, S. (1990) 'Some Unconscious Aspects of Ethnic Violence in India', in V. Das (ed.), *Mirrors of Violence: Communities, Riots and Survivors in South Asia*, Delhi.

Kalman, J. (1999) *Writing on the Plaza: Mediated Literacy Practices in Mexico City*, Creskill, NJ.

Kane, J. (2001) *The Politics of Moral Capital*, Cambridge.

Kaye, H. J. and McClelland, K. (1990) *E. P. Thompson: Critical Perspectives*, Cambridge.

Kelly, C. (1991) 'History and Post-Modernism', *Past and Present*, 133, 209–13.

Kelly, J. (1984) *Women, History and Theory*, Chicago.

Kennedy, P. (1987) *The Rise and Fall of the Great Powers: Economic Change and Military Conflict from 1500 to 2000*, New York.

Kent, F. W. (1977) *Household and Lineage in Renaissance Florence*, Princeton, NJ.

Keohane, R. O. (1984) *After Hegemony: Cooperation and Discord in the World Political Economy*, Princeton, NJ.

Kerblay, B. (1971) 'Chayanov and the Theory of Peasantry as a Special Type of Economy', in Shanin (1971), 150–9.

Kershaw, I. (1989) *The Hitler Myth*, Oxford.

Kertzer, D. I. (1988) *Ritual, Politics and Power*, New Haven, Conn.

Kettering, S. (1986) *Patrons, Brokers and Clients in Seventeenth-Century France*, New York.

Kettering, S. (1988) 'The Historical Development of Political Clientelism', *Journal of Interdisciplinary History*, 18, 419–48.

Kindleberger, C. P. (1990) *Historical Economics: Art or Science?*, New York.

Klaniczay, G. (1990) 'Daily Life and Elites in the Later Middle Ages', in F. Glatz (ed.), *Environment and Society in Hungary*, Budapest, 75–90.

Knöbl, W. (2003) 'Theories that Won't Pass Away: The Never-Ending Story of Modernization Theory', in G. Delanty and E. I. Isin (eds), *Handbook of Historical Sociology*, London, 96–107.

Knudsen, J. (1988) *Justus Möser and the German Enlightenment*, Cambridge.

Kocka, J. (1973) *Klassengesellschaft im Krieg*, Berlin.

Kocka, J. (ed.) (1986) *Max Weber der Historiker*, Göttingen.

Köhler, W. (1929) *Gestalt Psychology*; English trans. New York, 1947.

Kołakowski, L. (1990) *Modernity on Endless Trial*, Chicago.

Koselleck, R. (1985) *Futures Past*, Cambridge, Mass.

Kosminsky, E. A. (1935) *Studies in the Agrarian History of England*; English trans. Oxford, 1956.

Kuhn, P. A. (1990) *Soulstealers*, Cambridge, Mass.

Kuhn, T. S. (1962) *The Structure of Scientific Revolutions*, Chicago.

Kuhn, T. S. (1974) *The Essential Tension: Selected Studies in Scientific Tradition and Change*, Chicago.

Kula, W. (1962) *Economic Theory of the Feudal System*; English trans. London, 1976.

Kuper, A. (1999) *Culture: The Anthropologist's Account*, Cambridge, Mass.

LaCapra, D. (1985) *History and Criticism*, Ithaca, NY.

La Fontaine, J. (1998) *Speak of the Devil*, London.

Lamb, C. (2002) *The Sewing Circles of Herat*, London.

Landes, D. L. (1998) *The Wealth and Poverty of Nations: Why Some are so Rich and Some so Poor*, London.

Landes, J. B. (1988) *Women and the Public Sphere in the Age of the French Revolution*, Ithaca, NY.

Langer, W. L. (1958) 'The Next Assignment', *American Historical Review*, 63, 283–304.

Larson, P. M. (1997) 'Intellectual Engagements and Subaltern Hegemony in the Early History of Malagasy Christianity', *American Historical Review*, 102, 969–1002.

Laslett, P. (ed.) (1972) *Household and Family in Past Time*, Cambridge.

Lasswell, H. (1936) *Politics: Who Gets What, When, How*; repr. New York, 1958.

Latour, B. (1993) *We Have Never Been Modern*, New York.

Latour, B. (1996) 'Ces réseaux que la raison ignore: laboratoires, bibliothèques, collections', in M. Baratin and C. Jacob (eds), *Le Pouvoir des bibliothèques*, Paris, 23–46.

Leach, E. (1965) 'Frazer and Malinowski'; repr. in Stephen Hugh-Jones and James Laidlaw (eds), *The Essential Edmund Leach*, 2 vols, New Haven, Conn., 2000, vol. 1, 25–44.

Lears, T. J. (1985) 'The Concept of Cultural Hegemony: Problems and Possibilities', *American Historical Review*, 90, 567–93.

Lee, J. J. (1973) *The Modernisation of Irish Society, 1848–1918*, Dublin.

Lefebvre, G. (1932) *The Great Fear of 1789*; English trans. London, 1973.

Le Goff, J. (1974) 'Mentalities'; English trans. in J. Le Goff and P. Nora (eds), *Constructing the Past*, Cambridge, 1985, 166–80.

León-Portilla, M. (1959) *Visión de los vencidos*, Mexico.

Lerner, D. (1958) *The Passing of Traditional Society: Modernizing the Middle East*, Glencoe, Ill.

Le Roy Ladurie, E. (1966) *The Peasants of Languedoc*; abbrev. English trans. Urbana, Ill., 1974.

Le Roy Ladurie, E. (1975) *Montaillou*; English trans. Harmondsworth, 1980.

Levack, B. P. (1987) *The Witch-Hunt in Early Modern Europe*, London.

Levi, G. (1985) *Inheriting Power*; English trans. Chicago, 1988.

Levi, G. (1991) 'Microhistory', in P. Burke (ed.), *New Perspectives on Historical Writing*, 2nd edn Cambridge, 2001, 97–119.

Levine, R. M. (1992) *Vale of Tears*, Berkeley.

Lisón-Tolosana, C. (1966) *Belmonte de los Caballeros*; repr. Princeton, NJ, 1983.

Litchfield, R. B. (1986) *Emergence of a Bureaucracy: The Florentine Patricians 1530–1790*, Princeton, NJ.

Lloyd, G. E. R. (1990) *Demystifying Mentalities*, Cambridge.

Lloyd, G. E. R. (2002) *The Ambitions of Curiosity: Understanding the World in Ancient Greece and China*, Cambridge.

Lloyd, P. C. (1968) 'Conflict Theory and Yoruba Kingdoms', in I. M. Lewis (ed.), *History and Social Anthropology*, London, 25–58.

Lord, A. B. (1960) *The Singer of Tales*, Cambridge, Mass.

Lotman, J. and Uspenskii, B. A. (1984) *The Semiotics of Russian Culture*, ed. A. Shukman, Ann Arbor, Mich.

Love, H. (1993) *Scribal Publication in Seventeenth-Century England*, Oxford.

Lucas, C. (ed.) (1988) *The Political Culture of the French Revolution*, Oxford.

Lukes, S. (1973) *Emile Durkheim*, London.

Lukes, S. (1974) *Power: a Radical View*, London.

Lyotard, Jean-François (1979) *The Postmodern Condition*; English trans. Minneapolis and Manchester, 1984.

Macfarlane, A. D. (1970) *Witchcraft in Tudor and Stuart England*, London.

Macfarlane, A. D. (1979) *Origins of English Individualism*, Oxford.

Macfarlane, A. D. (1986) *Marriage and Love in England 1300–1840*, Oxford.

Macfarlane, A. D. (1987) *The Culture of Capitalism*, Oxford.

McIntire, C. T. and Perry, M. (eds) (1989) *Toynbee: Reappraisals*, Toronto.

MacKenzie, J. M. (1995) *Orientalism: History, Theory and the Arts*, Manchester.

McKibbin, R. (1984) 'Why is there no Marxism in Great Britain?', *English Historical Review*, 99, 297–331.

McLuhan, M. (1962) *The Gutenberg Galaxy*, Toronto.

McNeill, W. H. (1963) *The Rise of the West*, Chicago.

McNeill, W. H. (1964) *Europe's Steppe Frontier*, Chicago.

McNeill, W. H. (1976) *Plagues and Peoples*, London.

McNeill, W. H. (1983) *The Great Frontier*, Princeton, NJ.

McNeill, W. H. (1986) *Mythistory*, Chicago.

McNeill, W. H. (1989) *Arnold J. Toynbee: A Life*, New York.

Maitland, F. W. (1897) *Domesday Book and Beyond*, London.

Malinowski, B. (1922) *Argonauts of the Western Pacific*, London.

Malinowski, B. (1926) 'Myth in Primitive Psychology'; repr. in his *Magic, Science and Religion*, New York, 1954, 93–148.

Malinowski, B. (1945) *The Dynamics of Culture Change*, New Haven, Conn.

Mann, M. (1986–93) *The Sources of Social Power*, 2 vols, Cambridge.

Mannheim, K. (1936) *Ideology and Utopia*, London.

Mannheim, K. (1952) *Essays in the Sociology of Knowledge*, London.

Marwick, A. (1965) *The Deluge: British Society and the First World War*, London.

Marx, K. and Engels, F. (1848) *The Communist Manifesto*; English trans. London, 1948.

Mason, T. (1981) 'Intention and Explanation: A Current Controversy about the Interpretation of National Socialism', in G. Hirschfeld and L. Kettenacker (eds), *Der Führer-Staat*, Stuttgart, 23–40.

Massey, D. (1994) *Space, Place and Gender*, Cambridge.

Matthews, F. H. (1977) *Quest for American Sociology: Robert Park and the Chicago School*, Montreal.

Mauss, M. (1925) *The Gift*; English trans. London, 1990.

Mauss, M. (1938) 'A Category of the Human Mind'; English trans. in Carrithers, Collins and Lukes (1985), 1–25.

Megill, A. (1995) 'Grand Narrative and the Discipline of History', in Frank Ankersmit and Hans Kellner (eds), *A New Philosophy of History*, Chicago, 151–73.

Melton, J. V. (2001) *Politics, Culture and the Public Sphere in Enlightenment Europe*, Cambridge.

Melucci, A. (1996) *Challenging Codes: Collective Action in the Information Age*, Cambridge.

Mennell, S. (1989) *Norbert Elias*, Oxford.

Mennell, S. (1990) 'Decivilizing Processes', *International Sociology*, 5, 205–23.

Merton, R. (1948) 'Manifest and Latent Functions'; repr. in his *Social Theory and Social Structure*, New York, 1968, 19–82.

Métayer, C. (2000) *Au tombeau des secrets: les écrivains publics du Paris populaire*, Paris.

Mignolo, W. (2000) *Local Histories/Global Designs: Coloniality, Subaltern Knowledges and Border Thinking*, Princeton, NJ.

Mill, J. S. (1843) *A System of Logic*; new edn. Toronto, 1973.

Miller, P. (2003) 'Gender and Patriarchy in Historical Sociology', in G. Delanty and E. F. Isin (eds), *Handbook of Historical Sociology*, London, 337–48.

Milo, D. S. (1990) 'Pour une histoire expérimentale, ou la gaie histoire', *Annales E. S. C.*, 717–34.

Mitchell, T. (1988) *Colonizing Egypt*, Cambridge.

Miyazaki, I. (1963) *China's Examination Hell*; English trans. New York and Tokyo, 1976.

Moi, T. (ed.) (1987), *French Feminist Thought*, Oxford.

Moore, B. (1966) *Social Origins of Dictatorship and Democracy*, Boston.

Moore-Gilbert, B. (1997) *Postcolonial Theory*, London.

Morris, C. (1975) 'Judicium Dei', in D. Baker (ed.), *Church, Society and Politics*, Oxford, 95–111.

Morson, G. S. and Emerson, C. (1990) *Mikhail Bakhtin: Creation of a Prosaics*, Stanford, Calif.

Mosse, G. (1996) *The Image of Man: The Creation of Modern Masculinity*, Oxford.

Mousnier, R. (1967) *Peasant Uprisings*; English trans. London, 1971.

Muchembled, R. (1978) *Elite Culture and Popular Culture in Early Modern France*; English trans. Baton Rouge, La., 1985.

Muir, E. (1981) *Civic Ritual in Renaissance Venice*, Princeton, NJ.

Muir, E. (1999) 'The Sources of Civil Society in Italy', *Journal of Interdisciplinary History*, 29, 379–406.

Muir, E. and Ruggiero, G. (eds) (1991) *Microhistory and the Lost Peoples of Europe*, Baltimore, Md.

Mukhia, H. (1980–1) 'Was there Feudalism in Indian History?', *Journal of Peasant Studies*, 8, 273–93.

Nafisi, A. (2003) *Reading Lolita in Tehran*, New York.

Naphy, W. G. and Roberts, P. (eds) (1997) *Fear in Early Modern Society*, Manchester.

Neale, W. C. (1957) 'Reciprocity and Redistribution in the Indian Village', in K. Polanyi (ed.), *Trade and Markets in the Early Empires*, Princeton, 218–35.

Needham, J. (1963) 'Poverties and Triumphs of the Chinese Scientific Tradition'; repr. in *The Great Titration: Science and Society in East and West*, London, 1969, 14–54.

Needham, R. (1975) 'Polythetic Classification', *Man*, 10, 349–69.

Nelson, J. S., Megill, A. and McCloskey, D. N. (eds) (1987) *The Rhetoric of the Human Sciences*, Madison, Wis.

Nipperdey, T. (1976) *Gesellschaft, Kultur, Theorie*, Göttingen.

Nisbet, R. (1966) *The Sociological Tradition*, New York.

Nisbet, R. (1969) *Social Change and History*, New York.

Nora, P. (ed.) (1984–93) *Realms of Memory*; English trans. 3 vols, New York, 1996–8.

Norris, C. (1982) *Deconstruction: Theory and Practice*, London.

Nye, R. (1993) *Masculinity and Male Codes of Honor in Modern France*, New York.

Oberschall, A. (1993) *Social Movements*, New Brunswick, NJ.

Obeyesekere, G. (1992) *The Apotheosis of Captain Cook*, Princeton, NJ.

Ogilvie, S. (2004) 'How Does Social Capital Affect Women? Guilds and Communities in Early Modern Germany', *American Historical Review*, 109, 325–59.

O'Gorman, F. (1992) 'Campaign Rituals and Ceremonies: The Social Meaning of Elections in England 1780–1860', *Past and Present*, 135, 79–115.

Olson, D. R. (1994) *The World on Paper: The Conceptual and Cognitive Implications of Writing and Reading*, Cambridge.

O'Neill, J. (1986) 'The Disciplinary Society', *British Journal of Sociology*, 37, 42–60.

Ong, W. (1982) *Orality and Literacy*, London.

Ortiz, F. (1940) *Cuban Counterpoint*; English trans. New York, 1947.

Ortner, S. and Whitehead, H. (eds) (1981) *Sexual Meanings*, Cambridge.

Ossowski, S. (1957) *Class Structure in the Social Consciousness*; English trans. London, 1963.

Ozouf, M. (1976) *Festivals and the French Revolution*; English trans. Cambridge, Mass., 1988.

Paine, R. (1967) 'What is Gossip About?', *Man*, 2, 278–85.

Pálsson, G. (ed.) (1993) *Beyond Boundaries: Understanding, Translation and Anthropological Discourse*, Oxford.

Pandey, G. (1995) 'Voices from the Edge: The Struggle to Write Subaltern Histories'; repr. in Chaturvedi (2000), 281–99.

Pareto, V. (1916) *The Mind and Society*; English trans. London, 1935.

Park, R. E. (1916) 'The City'; repr. in his *Human Communications*, Glencoe, Ill., 1952, 13–51.

Parker, N. (1999) *Revolutions and History*, Cambridge.

Parkin, F. (1971) *Class Inequality and Political Order*, London.

Parry, V. J. (1969) 'Elite Elements in the Ottoman Empire', in R. Wilkinson (ed.), *Governing Elites*, New York, 59–73.

Peabody, N. (1996) 'Tod's Rajast'han and the Boundaries of Imperial Rule in 19th-Century India', *Modern Asian Studies*, 30, 185–220.

Peck, L. (1990) *Court Patronage and Corruption in Early Stuart England*, Boston.

Peel, J. D. Y. (1971) *Herbert Spencer: The Evolution of a Sociologist*, London.

Peltonen, U.-M. (1999) 'The Return of the Narrator', in A. Ollila (ed.), *Historical Perspectives on Memory*, Helsinki, 115–38.

Perkin, H. (1953–4) 'What is Social History?', *Bulletin of the John Rylands Library*, 36, 56–74.

Peyre, H. (1948) *Les Générations littéraires*, Paris.

Phillips, A. (1958) 'The Cultural Cringe', in his *The Australian Tradition*, 2nd edn Melbourne, 1966, 112–17.

Pillorget, R. (1975) *Les Mouvements insurrectionels de Provence entre 1596 et 1715*, Paris.

Pinder, W. (1926) *Das Problem der Generation in der Kunstgeschichte Europas*, Berlin.

Pintner, W. M. and Rowney, D. K. (eds) (1980) *Russian Officialdom*, Chapel Hill, NC.

Platt, L. J. (1996) *A History of Sociological Research Methods in America, 1920–1960*, Cambridge.

Pocock, J. G. A. (1981) 'Gibbon and the Shepherds', *History of European Ideas*, 2, 193–202.

Polanyi, K. (1944) *The Great Transformation*; rev. edn Boston, 1957.

Pomeranz, K. (2000) *The Great Divergence: China, Europe and the Making of the Modern World Economy*, Princeton, NJ.

Popkin, S. (1979) *The Rational Peasant*, Berkeley.

Porshnev, B. (1948) *Les Soulèvements populaires en France 1623–48*; French trans. Paris, 1963.

Portes, A. (1998) 'Social Capital', *Annual Review of Sociology*, 24, 1–24.

Price, R. (1990) *Alabi's World*, Baltimore, Md.

Propp, V. (1928) *Morphology of the Folktale*; English trans. 2nd edn Austin, Tex., 1968.

Putnam, R. D. (1992) *Making Democracy Work: Civic Traditions in Modern Italy*, Princeton, NJ.

Putnam, R. D. (2000) *Bowling Alone: The Collapse and Revival of American Community*, New York.

Pye, M. (1993) *Syncretism versus Synthesis*, Cardiff.

Ramsden, H. (1974) *The 1898 Movement in Spain*, Manchester.

Ranum, O. (1963) *Richelieu and the Councillors of Louis XIII*, Oxford.

Reddy, W. R. (2003) *The Navigation of Feeling: A Framework for a History of Emotions*, Cambridge.

Revel, J. (ed.) (1996) *Jeux d'échelle: la microanalyse à l'expérience*, Paris.

Rhodes, R. C. (1978) 'Emile Durkheim and the Historical Thought of Marc Bloch', *Theory and Society*, 5, 45–73.

Ricoeur, P. (1983–5) *Time and Narrative*; English trans. 3 vols, New York, 1984–8.

Rigby, S. H. (1987) *Marxism and History*, Manchester.

Robertson, R. (1992) *Globalization: Social Theory and Global Culture*, London.

Röhl, J. C. G. (1982) 'Introduction', to J. C. G. Röhl and N. Sombart (eds), *Kaiser Wilhelm II*, Cambridge.

Rogers, S. (1975) 'The Myth of Male Dominance', *American Ethnologist*, 2, 727–57.

Romein, J. (1937) *Het onvoltooid verleden*, Amsterdam.

Rorty, R. (1980) *Philosophy and the Mirror of Nature*, Princeton, NJ.

Rosaldo, R. (1986) 'From the Door of his Tent', in Clifford and Marcus (1986), 77–97.

Rosenthal, J. (1967) 'The King's Wicked Advisers', *Political Science Quarterly*, 82, 595–618.

Rosenwein, B. H. (ed.) (1998) *Anger's Past: The Social Uses of an Emotion in the Middle Ages*, London.

Rostow, W. W. (1958) *The Stages of Economic Growth*, Cambridge.

Roth, G. (1976) 'History and Sociology in the Work of Max Weber', *British Journal of Sociology*, 27, 306–16.

Rudolph, L. I. (1967) *The Modernity of Tradition: Political Development in India*, Chicago.

Rudolph, L. I. and Rudolph, S. H. (1966) 'The Political Modernization of an Indian Feudal Order', *Journal of Social Issues*, 4, 93–126.

Runciman, W. G. (1983–9) *A Treatise on Social Theory*, 2 vols, Cambridge.

Sack, R. D. (1986) *Human Territoriality: Its Theory and History*, Cambridge.

Sahlins, M. (1981) *Historical Metaphors and Mythical Realities*, Ann Arbor, Mich.

Sahlins, M. (1985) *Islands of History*, Chicago.
Sahlins, M. (1988) 'Cosmologies of Capitalism', *Proceedings of the British Academy*, 74, 1–52.
Sahlins, P. (1989) *Boundaries: The Making of France and Spain in the Pyrenees*, Berkeley.
Said, E. (1978) *Orientalism*; repr. with new afterword, London, 1995.
Samuel, R. (1991) 'Reading the Signs', *History Workshop Journal*, 32, 88–101.
Samuel, R. and Thompson, P. (eds) (1990) *The Myths We Live By*, London.
Sanderson, S. K. (1990) *Social Evolutionism: A Critical History*, Oxford.
Schama, S. (1987) *The Embarrassment of Riches*, London.
Schochet, G. (1975) *Patriarchalism in Political Thought*, Oxford.
Schwarz, R. (1992) *Misplaced Ideas: Essays on Brazilian Culture*, London.
Scott, J. (ed.) (1994) *Power: Critical Concepts*, Oxford.
Scott, J. C. (1969) 'The Analysis of Corruption in Developing Nations', *Comparative Studies in Society and History*, 11, 315–41.
Scott, J. C. (1976) *The Moral Economy of the Peasant*, New Haven, Conn.
Scott, J. C. (1990) *Domination and the Arts of Resistance*, New Haven, Conn.
Scott, J. C. (1998) *Seeing Like a State*, New Haven, Conn.
Scott, J. W. (1988) *Gender and the Politics of History*, New York, 1988.
Scott, J. W. (1991) 'Women's History', in P. Burke (ed.), *New Perspectives on Historical Writing*, 2nd edn Cambridge, 2001, 43–70.
Scribner, R. W. (1987) *Popular Culture and Popular Movements in Reformation Germany*, London.
Segalen, M. (1980) *Love and Power in the Peasant Family*; English trans. Cambridge, 1983.
Sen, A. (1977) 'Rational Fools: A Critique of the Behavioural Foundations of Economic Theory'; repr. *Choice, Welfare and Measurement*, Oxford, 1982, 84–106.
Sereni, E. (1947) *Il capitalismo nelle campagne, 1860–1900*; 2nd edn Turin, 1968.
Sewell, W. H. (1967) 'Marc Bloch and the Logic of Comparative History', *History and Theory*, 6, 208–18.
Sewell, W. H. (1992) 'A Theory of Structure', *American Journal of Sociology*, 98, 1–29.
Sewell, W. H. (1996) 'Historical Events as Transformations of Structures', *Theory and Society*, 25, 841–81.
Sewell, W. H. (1999) 'The Concept(s) of Culture', in V. E. Bonnell and L. Hunt (eds), *Beyond the Cultural Turn*, Berkeley, 35–61.
Shanin, T. (ed.) (1971) *Peasants and Peasant Societies*, Harmondsworth.
Shields, D. (1997) *Civil Tongues and Polite Letters in British America*, Chapel Hill, NC.
Shils, E. (1975) *Center and Periphery*, Chicago.
Sider, G. (1986) *Culture and Class in Anthropology and History*, Cambridge.

Siebenschuh, W. R. (1983) *Fictional Techniques and Factual Works*, Athens, Ga.

Simiand, F. (1903) 'Historical Method and Social Science'; English trans. in *Review*, 9 (1985–6), 163–213.

Simmel, G. (1903) 'The Metropolis and Mental Life'; trans. in P. K. Hatt and A. J. Reiss (eds), *Cities and Society*, Glencoe, Ill., 1957, 635–46.

Simmel, G. (1908) *Conflict*; English trans. New York, 1955.

Simon, H. A. (1957) *Models of Man*, New York.

Sinha, M. (1995) *Colonial Masculinity*, Manchester.

Skocpol, T. (1979) *States and Revolutions*, Cambridge.

Skocpol, T. (ed.) (1984) *Vision and Method in Historical Sociology*, Cambridge.

Smith, B. (1960) *European Vision and the South Pacific*, 2nd edn New Haven, 1985.

Smith, B. G. (1998) *The Gender of History*, Cambridge, Mass.

Smith, B. G. (2001) 'Gender Theory', in P. N. Stearns (ed.), *Encyclopaedia of European Social History*, 6 vols, New York, 2001, vol. 1, 95–104.

Smith, D. (1991) *The Rise of Historical Sociology*, Cambridge.

Smith, D. (2001) *Norbert Elias and Modern Social Theory*, London.

Soja, E. (1989) *Postmodern Geographies*, Berkeley.

Sombart, W. (1906) *Warum gibt es in den Vereinigten Staaten keinen Sozialismus?*, Tübingen.

Sombart, W. (1929) 'Economic Theory and Economic History', *Economic History Review*, 1, 1–19.

Spicer, E. (1968) 'Acculturation', in *Encyclopaedia of the Social Sciences*, New York, vol. 1, 21–7.

Spierenburg, P. (1984) *The Spectacle of Suffering*, Cambridge.

Srinivas, M. N. (1966) *Social Change in Modern India*, Berkeley.

Stallybrass, P. and White, A. (1986) *The Politics and Poetics of Transgression*, London.

Stearns, P. N. and Stearns, C. Z. (1986) 'Emotionology', *American Historical Review*, 90, 813–36.

Steger, M. B. (2003) *Globalization: A Very Short Introduction*, Oxford.

Stevenson, J. (1985) 'The Moral Economy of the English Crowd: Myth and Reality', in A. Fletcher and J. Stevenson (eds), *Order and Disorder in Early Modern England*, Cambridge, 218–38.

Stewart, C. and Shaw, R. (eds) (1994) *Syncretism/anti-Syncretism*, London.

Stocking, G. (1983) 'The Ethnographer's Magic: Fieldwork in British Anthropology from Tylor to Malinowski', in *idem* (ed.), *Observers Observed*, Madison, Wis., 70–120.

Stone, L. (1965) *The Crisis of the English Aristocracy, 1558–1641*, Oxford.

Stone, L. (1977) *The Family, Sex and Marriage in England 1500–1800*, London.

Stone, L. (1979) 'The Revival of Narrative', *Past and Present*, 85, 1–24.

Stone, L. (1991) 'History and Post-Modernism', *Past and Present*, 131, 217–18.

Strathern, M. (1988) *The Gender of the Gift*, Berkeley.

Strauss, A. (1978) *Negotiations*, San Francisco.

Street, B. S. (1984) *Literacy in Theory and Practice*, Cambridge.

Street, B. S. (1993) 'The New Literacy Studies', in B.S. Street (ed.), *Cross-Cultural Approaches to Literacy*, Cambridge, 1–21.

Suttles, G. D. (1972) *The Social Construction of Communities*, Chicago.

Tarrow, S. (1994) *Power in Movement*, Cambridge.

Temin, P. (ed.) (1972) *The New Economic History*, Harmondsworth.

Thomas, K. V. (1971) *Religion and the Decline of Magic*, London.

Thompson, E. P. (1963) *The Making of the English Working Class*, London.

Thompson, E. P. (1978) *The Poverty of Theory*, London.

Thompson, E. P. (1991) *Customs in Common*, London.

Thompson, F. M. L. (1963) *English Landed Society in the Nineteenth Century*, London.

Thompson, J. B. (1990) *Ideology and Modern Culture*, Cambridge.

Thompson, P. (1975) *The Edwardians*, London.

Thorner, D. (1956) 'Feudalism in India', in R. Coulborn (ed.), *Feudalism in History*, Princeton, NJ, 133–50.

Tilly, C. (ed.) (1975) *The Formation of National States in Western Europe*, Princeton, NJ.

Tilly, C. (1978) *From Mobilization to Revolution*, Reading, Mass.

Tilly, C. (1990) *Coercion, Capital and European States 990–1990*, Oxford.

Tilly, C. (2004) *Social Movements 1768–2004*, Boulder, Colo.

Tilly, L. and Scott, J. W. (1978) *Women, Work and Family*, New York.

Tipps, D. C. (1973) 'Modernization Theory and the Comparative Study of Societies', *Comparative Studies in Society and History*, 15, 199–224.

Tóth, I. G. (1996) *Literacy and Written Culture in Early Modern Central Europe*; English trans. Budapest, 2000.

Touraine, A. (1984) *The Return of the Actor*; English trans. Minneapolis, 1988.

Toynbee, A. (1935–61) *A Study of History*, 13 vols, London.

Turner, F. J. (1893) 'The Significance of the Frontier in American History'; repr. in *The Frontier in American History*, Huntington, Va., 1976, 1–38.

Turner, V. (1969) *The Ritual Process*, London.

Turner, V. (1974) *Dramas, Fields and Metaphors*, Ithaca, NY.

Underdown, D. (1985) *Revel, Riot and Rebellion*, Oxford.

Vansina, J. (1961) *Oral Tradition*; English trans. London, 1965.

Vansina, J. (1985) *Oral Tradition as History*, Madison, Wis.

Veblen, T. (1899) *Theory of the Leisure Class*, New York.

Veblen, T. (1915) *Imperial Germany and the Industrial Revolution*; new edn London, 1939.

Vernant, J.-P. (1966) *Myth and Thought among the Greeks*; English trans. London, 1983.

Viala, A. (1985) *Naissance de l'écrivain: sociologie de la littérature à l'âge classique*, Paris.

Vinogradoff, P. (1892) *Villeinage in England*, Oxford.

Volkov, V. (2000) 'Notes on the Stalinist Civilizing Process', in S. Fitzpatrick (ed.), *Stalinism*, London, 210–30.

Vovelle, M. (1973) *Piété baroque et déchristianisation en Provence*, Paris.

Vovelle, M. (1982) *Ideologies and Mentalities*; English trans. Cambridge, 1991.

Wachtel, N. (1971) *The Vision of the Vanquished*; English trans. Hassocks, 1977.

Waite, R. G. L. (1977) *The Psychopathic God: Adolf Hitler*, New York.

Wallerstein, I. (1974) *The Modern World-System*, vol. 1, New York.

Washbrook, D. (1999) 'Orients and Occidents: Colonial Discourse Theory and the Historiography of the British Empire', in R. Winks (ed.), *Oxford History of the British Empire*, Oxford, vol. 5, 596–611.

Weber, M. (1920) *Economy and Society*; English trans., reissue, 3 vols, Berkeley, 1978.

Weber, M. (1948) *From Max Weber*, ed. H. H. Gerth and C. W. Mills, London.

Weber, M. (1964) *The Religion of China*; English trans. London and New York, 1964.

Wehler, H.-U. (1987) *Deutsche Gesellschaftsgeschichte*, vol. 1, Munich.

Weissman, R. F. E. (1985) 'Reconstructing Renaissance Sociology: The Chicago School and the Study of Renaissance Society', in R. C. Trexler (ed.), *Persons in Groups*, Binghamton, NY, 39–46.

Wertheim, W. F. (1974) *Evolution and Revolution*, Harmondsworth.

White, H. V. (1973) *Metahistory*, Baltimore, Md.

White, H. V. (1978) *Tropics of Discourse*, Baltimore, Md.

White, L. T. (1962) *Medieval Technology and Social Change*, Oxford.

Wierzbicka, A. (1999) *Emotions across Languages and Cultures*, Cambridge.

Wiesner, M. E. (1993) *Women and Gender in Early Modern Europe*; rev. edn Cambridge, 2000.

Wiesner-Hanks, M. E. (2001) *Gender and History*, Cambridge, Mass.

Wilkinson, R. G. (1973) *Poverty and Progress: An Ecological Model of Economic Development*, London.

Williams, R. (1962) *Communications*, Harmondsworth.

Wilson, B. R. (ed.) (1979) *Rationality*, Oxford.

Winkler, J. J. (1990) *The Constraints of Desire: The Anthropology of Sex and Gender in Ancient Greece*, London.

Winter, J. and Sivan, E. (eds) (1999) *War and Remembrance in the 20th Century*, Cambridge.

Wolf, E. (1956) 'Aspects of Group Relations in a Complex Society'; repr. in Shanin (1971), 50–66.

Wolf, E. (1969) *Peasant Wars of the Twentieth Century*, London.

Wolf, E. (1982) *Europe and the People without History*, Berkeley.

Wouters, C. (1977) 'Informalization and the Civilizing Process', in P. Gleichmann, J. Goudsblom and H. Korte (eds), *Materialen zu Norbert Elias' Zivilisationstheorie*, Frankfurt, 437–53.

Wrigley, E. A. (1972–3) 'The Process of Modernization and the Industrial Revolution in England', *Journal of Interdisciplinary History*, 3, 225–59.

Wyatt-Brown, B. (1982) *Southern Honor*, New York.

Yeo, E. and Yeo, S. (eds) (1981) *Popular Culture and Class Conflict 1590–1914*, Brighton.

Young, R. (2001) *Postcolonialism: An Historical Introduction*, Oxford.

Zaret, D. (2000) *Origins of Democratic Culture: Printing, Petitions and the Public Sphere in Early-Modern England*, Princeton, NJ.

Index

Radcliffe-Brown, Alfred R. (1881–1955), British anthropologist, 11–12
Ranke, Leopold von (1795–1886), German historian, 3, 5, 14, 125, 146–7
rationality, 89, 96, 116–19, 138, 143, 182
Ratzel, Friedrich (1844–1904), German geographer, 8, 13–15
reading, 103
reception, 103–4
reciprocity, 68–9, 74
Reddy, William M., American historian, 140
re-employment, 94, 103
re-enactment, 121, 168
refeudalization, 151
regression, 146
relative deprivation, 29
relativism, 116–19
religion, 10, 37–8, 59, 72, 88, 90–5, 106
repertoire, 50, 94, 100–1, 121–2, 140
reproduction, cultural, 71, 169–70
resistance, 89–92
retarding lead, 148
revolts, 61–2, 92–4, 120–1
revolutions, 23, 29, 111, 151–3, 156, 160–1, 168, 182
Ricoeur, Paul (1913–), French philosopher, 103
rituals, 50, 57–8, 78, 80, 94, 132, 154, 169
Robertson, William (1721–93), British historian, 96
Robinson, James Harvey (1863–1936), American historian, 14
Rokkan, Stein (1921–79), Norwegian political scientist, 84
Romein, Jan (1893–1962), Dutch historian, 148

Rostow, Walt W. (1916–2003), American economist, 147
routinization, 95
rumour, 109, 122
Runciman, W. G. (1934–), British sociologist, 144

Sahlins, Marshall D. (1930–), American anthropologist, 17, 71, 169–70, 173
Said, Edward (1935–2003), Palestinian-American critic. 100, 103, 108, 153
scenario, 50
Schama, Simon (1945–), British historian, 122–3, 178
Schemata, 100, 109–10, 112, 125, 160
Schmoller, Gustav (1838–1917), German economic historian, 7, 11
Schumpeter, Joseph Alois (1883–1950), Austrian economist, 10, 16
Schwarz, Roberto (1938–), Brazilian critic, 105
Scott, James C., American anthropologist, 30, 91
Scott, Joan W., American historian, 51, 177
Scribner, Robert W. (1941–98), Australian historian, 92
script, cultural, 50
semiotics, 134
Sen, Amartya (1933–), Indian economist, 119
Sereni, Emilio (1907–77), Italian historian, 153
shame cultures, 138
Shields, David S., American literary historian, 80
Shils, Edward (1911–95), American sociologist, 86
Siegfried, André (1875–1959), French political geographer, 9, 16